SOME CHOSE TO STAY

society / religion
religion / society

Series Editor

ROGER S. GOTTLIEB

Published

WHY ALTHUSSER KILLED HIS WIFE
GERALDINE FINN

A FEMINIST COSMOLOGY
NANCY R. HOWELL

OLD DEAD WHITE MEN'S PHILOSOPHY
LAURA INGLIS & PETER STEINFELD

WAR, BATTERING, AND OTHER SPORTS
JAMES McBRIDE

SOME CHOSE TO STAY
ALAN C. MERMANN

MADE IN WHOSE IMAGE?
THOMAS A. SHANNON

DEEP ECONOMY
HANS D. van HOOGSTRATEN

DIRTY VIRTUES
LOUKE van WENSVEEN

TRIANGULATING POSITIONS
CAROL WAYNE WHITE

SOME
CHOSE
TO STAY

FAITH AND ETHICS IN A
TIME OF PLAGUE

ALAN C. MERMANN

HUMANITIES PRESS
NEW JERSEY

First published in 1997 by Humanities Press International, Inc.
165 First Avenue, Atlantic Highlands, New Jersey 07716

© 1997 by Alan C. Mermann

Library of Congress Cataloging-in-Publication Data
Mermann, Alan C., 1923–
    Some chose to stay : faith and ethics in a time of plague / Alan
C. Mermann.
        p.   cm. — (Society/religion/religion/society)
    Includes bibliographical references and index.
    ISBN 0–391–04028–6 (cloth). — ISBN 0–391–04029–4 (pbk.)
    1. Religious ethics. 2. Christian ethics.— 3. Social problems—
    Moral and ethical aspects. 4. Plague—Moral and ethical aspects.
    I. Title. II. Series.
    BJ1188.M47   1997
    241—dc21   96–52123
                            CIP

Chapter Illustrations by Cecily Reynolds Mermann

Printed in the United States of America

10 9 8 7 6 5 4 3 2 1

To Cecily

Whose affection, assurances, and insights confirm for me the words of H. D. Thoreau: "[I]f one advances confidently in the direction of his dreams, and endeavors to live the life which he has imagined, he will meet with a success unexpected in common hours. . . . Say what you have to say, not what you ought. Any truth is better than make-believe."

CONTENTS

INTRODUCTION

We must learn to reawaken and keep ourselves awake, not by mechanical aids, but by an infinite expectation of the dawn, which does not forsake us in our soundest sleep.

—Henry David Thoreau, *Walden*

THE ADVENT OF AIDS in the early 1980s reintroduced the word *plague* as a way of presenting and interpreting the impact of this disease on our lives as persons and as a society. At first, AIDS was the affliction of a specific group of persons—homosexual men—and public response was mixed. In subsequent years we learned about the worldwide incidence of this disease that affects all categories of human beings, the disturbing mutational possibilities of HIV and other viruses, and our current inability to cure or prevent AIDS. The reality of plague became present to us. We suffer other afflictions that are not bacterial or viral infections but nevertheless cause a level of devastation that make the label *plague* fully applicable. For those who have lived in this twentieth century, the evidence is impressive as we count the killed, survey the damage to the environment, and study the incalculable costs of our isms: race, sex, religion, culture, and politics, to name a few.

Our understanding of the plagues of our time; the ways in which we respond to them personally, professionally, and publicly; and the resources we call upon to do so are determined by our beliefs. I am convinced that faith, conviction, and commitment are central to understanding and acting in these days of turmoil, conflicting promises, terror, and struggle. We all confess a faith. The object of faith—and there are many options—will be studied in the process of developing this text. Be it a divinity, the self, money and fame, intellect, power over others, or one of many alternative options, there is an "other" that we worship and whose call we obey. Faith in that first cause is the source of our ethical responses to plague and the ultimate determinant of our actions. To define and study the bases for our responses to the manifold afflictions of our time—the sources of faith in our ethical lives—I use plague as a metaphor. I examine how various authors present issues as plagues, describe our actions in times of peril, reveal the complexity of the dilemmas introduced, and offer choices for decisions and the placing of our faith.

1

The Uses of Metaphor

How do we understand ourselves, our world and our universe, and the experiences that we have as individuals and as members of such varied communities? Who am I, and what is this all about? Are we alone in a hostile—or at least uncaring—universe? Any inquiry into the meaning of our human enterprise involves also a lifelong search for truth, for what is true for us in our time. The individuality of experience, the reading of life through lenses unique to each person, and the necessary highlighting of one interpretation of an event over another by personal choice preclude, for me, any claim for absolute truths.

Truth is relative. That is, my understanding of myself and my world is always partial, determined as it so often is by ignorance, prejudice, and error. A constant process of correction occurs that forces adjustment to freshly perceived realities, absorption of new facts, rejection of former—now untenable—beliefs. Important concepts for this process of self-knowledge and self-understanding are usually abstract and philosophical in nature, not concise and easily defined. Metaphors, therefore, provide a vehicle for imaginative concepts that lie outside ordinary experience. George Lakoff and Mark Johnson write that "Metaphor is one of our most important tools for trying to comprehend partially what cannot be comprehended totally; our feelings, aesthetic experiences, moral practices, and spiritual awareness."[1] With metaphoric language we attempt to understand one thing in terms of another, highlighting one part of a concept with an idea from another, usually material, encounter. A significant aspect of the use and value of metaphoric thinking and argument is repeated testing of the concepts, a process that leads to ongoing learning and teaching: what we know as imaginative reasoning. The final goal of this process is comprehending the self.

> Understanding of ourselves is not unlike other forms of understanding—it comes out of our constant interactions with our physical, cultural, and interpersonal environment. . . . Just as we seek out metaphors to highlight and make coherent what we have in common with someone else, so we seek out *personal* metaphors to highlight and make coherent our own pasts, our present activities, and our dreams, hopes, and goals as well.[2]

Metaphor—the statement that some experience, encounter, or feeling is like another well-known and understood reality—is used in literature to teach us. As with parable, myth, legend, and fable, we interpret and attend to a lesson obliquely offered to us. As we grasp the meaning, we say, "Ahaah!" In this manner I use plague as a metaphor for understanding some perennial catastrophes we experience as inevitable parts of human existence. I hope to define these devastations, describe our possible responses to them, and outline the role that faith plays in establishing an ethical basis to an examined life lived honestly in times of plague. Our experiences in the twentieth century provide ample evidence for the ubiquity of pestilence.

A Brief History of Plague

Plague is a powerful metaphor to describe disastrous events in our history and the responses we make to them. The plague that has, at various times, shattered the structure of family and society by killing vast numbers of persons is bubonic plague. It is an overwhelming infection with a bacterium, *Yersinia pestis*, transmitted from infected black rats to humans by the bites of fleas. Usually fatal in a few days, it is characterized by fever; swollen and darkened lymph nodes, called buboes; swollen spots on the skin caused by bleeding; and, in rapidly fatal cases, pneumonia or a bloodstream infection called sepsis. The terror associated with this disease was escalated in earlier times by complete ignorance of its epidemiology and the belief that the resultant widespread destruction of society was caused by the wrath of God, visited upon the world as punishment for our obvious sins. Although the disease took a higher toll among the poor, all levels of society were victims.

Plague confirms our worst fears: we are not in control of our lives, evil abounds in the world, and God either does not exist or is viciously vengeful. The anxiety associated with plague has repercussions in behavior. The time of plague is a time of moral and religious decline; relaxation of sexual mores; a search for a life of luxury, self-satisfaction, and leisure; and sharp loss of the cohesive power of family life. Plague years are described as a time of decay, emotional flatness, and failure of faith. These reactions to plague—social, personal, psychological, and religious—are the concerns addressed here.

Perhaps the best-known plagues in Western history are the ten catastrophes visited upon the Egyptians by the God of the Israelites and described in the Book of Exodus. John S. Marr and Curtis D. Malloy, in an elegant study, write, "Causes and interpretations of the Ten Plagues have fascinated theologians, historians, Egyptologists, musical composers, scientists, and physicians for centuries."[3] These authors integrate the work of their many predecessors and offer a unified approach to the crises of that fateful year. They place the meteorological, agricultural, entomological, bacterial, viral, and fungal devastations in the reign of Thutmose III in the fifteenth century B.C.E. The tenth plague, the deaths of firstborn humans and animals, is ascribed to a poison—a mycotoxin—produced by the fungus *Stachybotrys atra*, present in rotting stored grain and known as the cause of death of thousands of people and animals in recent history. The Hebrews, living in Goshen and eating their Passover meal, were spared destruction. Marr and Malloy conclude:

The long, Jewish tradition about the very first Passover began at the end
of the ninth plague. It is a celebration of the first meal to mark the Hebrews' escape from the many plagues, and from the tenth plague. This
Passover celebration consists of eating symbolic new-born, healthy lamb
shank, fresh herbs, and horseradish—all safe from mycotoxin exposure. It
also requires eating un-leavened bread made from fresh flour, which is,
by definition, free of any yeasty or other mycotoxin contamination.[4]

The earliest account of probable bubonic plague is found in the Bible.
According to the account in I Samuel 5 and 6, dating from the fourteenth
century B.C.E., the ark of the Lord, holy to Israel, was captured by the
Philistines, who were then afflicted with tumors that decimated them in their
several cities. The Philistines interpreted this as an act of the God of Israel
and returned the ark, along with a guilt offering of five golden tumors and
five golden mice—our clue to the diagnosis of the disease that ravaged their
land. Upon return of the ark to Israel, some of the men looked into it—a
forbidden act—and promptly died. Probably the rats carrying the plague
were in the ark, and their fleas found the men of Beth-she'mesh, who had
sinned by opening the ark. Later, in the seventh century B.C.E., the angel of
the Lord decimated the army of Sennach'erib, king of Assyria, which was
besieging Jerusalem, and forced its retreat. Hezekiah, king of Israel, also
became sick and was near death. In a later campaign in Egypt, the Assyrians
were defeated because their bowstrings and other leather equipment was
chewed up by an onslaught of field mice. It is possible that this, also, was
the plague carried by rats.

In the sixth century C.E., the first recorded pandemic of plague occurred,
spreading across northern Africa and Europe over a period of fifty years.
The disease appeared first in seaports, then moved inland, decimating the
area and laying waste the Roman Empire. Known as the Plague of Justinian,
it was described "by Procopius of Caesarea, a medical writer who lived
from 490 to 562 C.E. and therefore saw the plague victims himself: 'The
fever made its attack suddenly. Generally on the first or second day, but in
a few instances somewhat later, buboes appeared, not only in the groin, but
also in the armpits and below the ears.'"[5]

The line that divides the Middle Ages and the Renaissance is the time of
the Black Death, the great plague that swept through Europe from 1348 to
1350, killing, by contemporary estimates, approximately one-third of the
population from India to Ireland. The plague probably appeared first in central Asia and was carried to Sicily by Genoese ships arriving from the Cri-
mea, where Genoa maintained a trading post at Caffa. This city had been
under siege by a Tartar army for a year until the army was struck by plague
and forced to withdraw. The retreating attackers, however, catapulted the
dead into the city, successfully infecting the Genoese, who then sailed for

Messina with sailors dying of plague. Although small outbreaks of the disease continued for several decades, 1351 saw the end of the pandemic.

As a catastrophe whose origin was completely misunderstood, and for which no therapy was possible, the Medieval Plague tested to the limit our ability to survive when death is everywhere and possible at any moment. The social and economic upheavals were overwhelming, further undermining a faltering psychological and religious understanding of the meaning of life. Developing and sustaining a functional religious faith that was capable of undergirding altruistic service as an ethic of behavior were severe challenges—then as now. An added horror of the plague years that must always be remembered is the massive persecution of Jews, who were accused of poisoning wells and causing the plague. This response to the plague was a direct result of the efforts of a party of religious fanatics called the Flagellants, and it reached its peak in Germany. Jewish communities in Europe were wiped out in numbers not seen again until the twentieth century.

PLAGUES, BOOKS, AND A SPIRITUAL JOURNEY

My persistent quest is for an articulated faith that supports and informs my personal ethic of behavior: a convinced belief that makes coping with the varied plagues of my day possible, even rewarding. I am persuaded by Henry David Thoreau's central assertion that "Every man is tasked to make his life, even in its details, worthy of the contemplation of his most elevated and critical hour." I, too, "wished to live deliberately, to front only the essential facts of life, and see if I could not learn what it had to teach, and not, when I came to die, discover that I had not lived."[6] Two hopes underlie my continuing search for a faithful ethic: that I will recognize the appearance of plague when I see it, and that I will have the courage to act on my faith. As an example, let me cite two differing responses by physicians to the appearance of plague in their communities. In 1348 the plague swept through Avignon, the resident city of Pope Clement VI, who considered it his duty to remain in the city. His physician, Guy de Chauliac, chose to stay, although he "confessed that he performed his medical visits only because he dared not stay away for fear of infamy, but 'I was in continual fear.'"[7] Honest in self-assessment and in full knowledge of the risks, he continued to make his rounds through the disaster. Two centuries later, during the 1665 plague in London, we see a different response from a renowned physician often cited as the English Hippocrates—Thomas Sydenham. He was one of the prominent London doctors who fled the city with their wealthy patients. W. G. Bell writes, "Dr. Sydenham—a great name in seventeenth century medicine—afterwards wrote a short treatise on the Plague which he did not stay to see."[8] It is enlightening to read a learned paper on the plague by a famous doctor who abandoned his plague-ridden city. The moral questions raised by writing scientific papers with questionable data and secondhand experience have a noteworthy precedent in the profession.

In sorting through the guides and maps that I have relied on in my own search for a faithful ethic, I begin with two Sunday school teachers and their respective texts that instituted my journey of the spirit and continue to inform me: the Bible and *Walden*. Anna Ray Robinson, a physician and the wife of our Presbyterian pastor, was a faithful person, confident in biblical narrative and gospel message. She was my Sunday school teacher and gave me my first Bible at Christmas 1935, beginning a long and distinctive excursion of discovery into the profound experiences written there for us to ponder and interpret for our understanding. The Bible, the sourcebook for Jewish and Christian faiths, is a vast and diverse collection of stories, sayings, histories, warnings, and revelations that bear the weight of tradition and hope for believers. The array of authors, unknown to us as persons, presents an ongoing attempt to understand the world in terms of faith in a creative God who is present to us in varied ways but is characterized by the commandments for love and justice. Subject to centuries of criticism—scholarly, pious, faithful, or confused—the Bible continues to call Jew and Christian to attend to its stories of a God beyond our knowing who calls forth our gratitude, affirmation, and obedience.

At Christmas 1946, during my last year of medical school, my Sunday school teacher, Edwin Way Teale, gave me my first copy of *Walden*. It was a new edition with Teale's Introduction, commentary, and photographs of the pond, houses in Concord, the woods, and flowers. *Walden* became a polestar in my search for understanding myself, my world, and my work. Thoreau asks the utmost from us in honest assessment of the self, reverence for nature, and an intense commitment to virtue and integrity. His reiterated demand is that we awaken to the morning that is always present: that we wake up to life! In its style and content, *Walden* is an American scripture. Thoreau is explicit: we must understand that human encounters with the sacred and the profane are so varied through history, so determined by circumstance and chance, and so exquisitely personal and limited that we are required to find our own path through life. There are no prescriptions, only trail markings for the journey. But these guidelines form those foundations upon which we commit our lives, make our promises, confirm our allegiances.

PLAGUES WE WILL MEET

Throughout history, certain diseases sweep through the world, bringing death and wreaking havoc on the social structure. These pestilences are often devastating and can be of short duration or last for many years, even centuries.

Two diseases are of note in our considerations. The classic plague is bubonic plague. I look at this plague in two eras, the fourteenth and seventeenth centuries, using two novelists, Giovanni Boccaccio and Daniel Defoe, as sources. One of the latest pandemics, AIDS, is discussed through contemporary writings—play and essay—as a prediction of the possibility of new viral diseases spreading across our globe. Our difficulties in treating and containing these diseases are powerful contemporary concerns.

My introduction to the plague of fascism—in all its possible forms—was a short story, "Address Unknown," I read in 1938. This account of the new plague that would kill millions of us frightened me as a teenager and alerted me to events to come. As the century progressed, the magnitude of this plague and its persistence have been detailed for us. Using bubonic plague as his metaphor, Albert Camus described in *The Plague* the varied responses we make when pestilence suddenly appears. Another masterpiece of our times that restated and reopened the enduring question of faith in God in times of catastrophe is Elie Wiesel's *Night*. The power of the questions and the possible answers that this plague presents are discussed.

The ancient and persistent plague of subjugation of and discrimination against women could never be discussed briefly, simply, or easily. However, the poetry of Emily Dickinson provides an artistic and novel way of looking at the eternal relation between the sexes. Her configurative descriptions of men and women, of day and night, of creativity and faith clearly confirm her central place in American poetry. Few writers have so beautifully documented a lifelong struggle to know and believe in God despite the evidence of abandonment and suffering all around us.

All the hospital wards where we medical students trained were segregated by sex and race, with the exception of pediatrics. I was told that the children were too young to understand the importance of differences in color. My growing awareness of racism, begun in East Baltimore, was focused at once and clearly by reading *Cry, the Beloved Country* by Alan Paton. This 1948 novel set in South Africa laid out options that confronted me, as if with a call, and opened possibilities for my own reconstruction. The differing lives of the two brothers, the tragic events so tellingly presented, and the hopes for change altered my consciousness and set the stage for events that would occur in the United States a decade later. The political changes that would take place in South Africa forty-five years later were hardly a dream.

A growing sense of a call to a deeper and more clearly articulated faith came with active involvement in the civil rights and peace movements from the early 1960s to the end of the Vietnam War in 1975. The relationships between faith and behavior became increasingly obvious, crying out for expression in action. Occasional work in the South during those years—

looking, listening, and praying for insight, courage, and a faith that empowered action—led to my decision to begin studies at Yale Divinity School in 1972. Eventually, with the prodding of a few acute questions, I became aware of a call to the ministry that had been voiced for a long time but not heard.

Hunger was an unexpected finding in a 1967 study we did in Mississippi for the Field Foundation of possible ways to offer preschool education to rural black children in the South. To a New England pediatrician, this was startling, almost unbelievable. Our small group of doctors wrote a paper, "Hungry Children in Mississippi,"[9] and presented findings to a Senate committee in 1967 that sparked an ongoing federal program of aid. This plague of hunger affecting children has worsened in recent years both here and abroad, remaining a blight that does not disappear. It also sends a clear message of the value we place on our children.

The rider of the white horse of the Apocalypse brings the destruction of life and culture by war. Our century has seen a refinement in our capacity to destroy what could be imagined only in wildest fantasy. In his novel *Narcissus and Goldmund*, Hermann Hesse uses plague as a powerful metaphor for the destruction he witnessed in Europe during the World War of 1914–18. His characters, wonderfully crafted in the context of Jungian individuation, reveal the power of faith to create a structured and empowered life capable of surviving this plague. The close parallels in European history between the Medieval Plague and the Great War in the dissolution of social structure and ethical personal behavior recur in our literature.

In 1963, a lawyer from Appalachia, Harry M. Caudill, published a book, *Night Comes to the Cumberlands*, that awakened us to the destruction of land and people by the coal-mining industry. This plague—the seemingly intractable and irreplaceable loss of our resources—continues as mining, lumbering, and fishing deplete our environment, perhaps beyond recovery. That book and *Silent Spring* by Rachel Carson were landmark accomplishments that alerted us to yet other destroyers.

Progress is a word that characterizes changes in Western civilization that we consider, on the whole, to be good. Not all see this as true. The Industrial Revolution—the beginning of the Modern Age—is explicitly called a plague by Charles Dickens in *Little Dorrit*. The terrible price of greed, the human costs of bureaucracy, and exploitation of workers by corporations are issues raised by Dickens. One of the characters in *Little Dorrit*, with the un-Dickensian name of Physician, presents a saintly, albeit fanciful, image of the life and work of a doctor in Victorian England. Dickens's antipathy toward evangelism and his denial of Christian faith, while holding to the teachings of Jesus as a good man, placed him in a position where ethical behavior had as its basis goodwill toward the unfortunate.

The presence of evil—both natural and moral—in the world raises consistent and understandable doubts about the existence of a loving and powerful God. Certainly, our experiences with plague in our century support that doubt. The psychology of Carl Jung helps our attempts to become whole persons as we recognize that evil is an integral part of our personalities. In *An Answer to Job*, the book he considered his best, Jung names evil as inevitable, because it is integral to creation. Commentary on the Book of Job is essential to understanding the place of evil in religious thought in our time. Robertson Davies's novel *Fifth Business* is an account of a discovered life that understands and accepts the shadow part of us as necessary for an ethical, indeed a faithful, life. A learned and experienced faith that is present in hours of evil can carry us.

The increasing number of old persons has introduced a new and frightening plague among us—Alzheimer's disease. It epitomizes the horrors of inexorable loss, both of memory and of self-identity. Memory is crucial if we are not to lose our past and be forced to live over again the horrors of this century. In his 1992 novel *The Forgotten*, Elie Wiesel tells the story of a survivor of the Holocaust whose premature senility causes progressive loss of memory. In the face of this, how is he to ensure that we will not forget what has happened to us? Accurate and detailed remembering is essential if we are to counter a plague of our time—fascism—that will return, that lies waiting for us to forget.

Plague is an apt metaphor to describe much of the gratuitous evil in our world. Even minimal knowledge of contemporary events reveals a variety of plagues in our midst: economic, social, political, and psychological conditions destructive of our common and our personal lives. But this is not new to human experience. We have a long history of living in the presence of plague. How we cope with these plagues will determine our integrity and our worth and truly define who we are. I have chosen a number of stories central to my own discoveries that show various possible ethical responses to plagues we recognize. These stories have obviously been important to me. As Robert McAfee Brown notes:

> Stories have power to challenge us and engage us, and . . . they may lead us in directions we never intended to go. . . . The power of a story is a power over which we do not have ultimate control, since it can catch us off guard, tell us things about ourselves we would prefer not to know, and liberate us to move in directions we would never have imagined.[10]

In my own continuing search for an ethic of behavior founded in a faith that will not deceive or embarrass me, I use these gifted works to question and strengthen my actions. I place them in the context of an understanding of myself that is informed primarily by the texts of my early teachers: the

Bible and *Walden*. Confident that growth and metamorphosis are always possible, I continue to define this man by thought and action—the very heart of this book.

NOTES

1. George Lakoff and Mark Johnson, *Metaphors We Live By* (Chicago: University of Chicago Press, 1980), 195.
2. Ibid., 232–3.
3. John S. Marr and Curtis D. Malloy, "An Epidemiological Analysis of the Ten Plagues of Egypt," *Caduceus* 12, no. 1 (Spring 1996): 7.
4. Ibid., 22.
5. Geoffrey Marks, *The Medieval Plague* (Garden City, NY: Doubleday, 1971), 18.
6. Henry David Thoreau, *Walden*, ed. J. Lyndon Shanley (Princeton, NJ: Princeton University Press, 1971), 90.
7. Barbara W. Tuchman, *A Distant Mirror* (New York: Alfred A. Knopf, 1978), 100.
8. Walter George Bell, *The Great Plague in London in 1665* (London: Bodley Head, 1951), 62.
9. Joseph Brenner, Robert Coles, Alan Mermann, Milton J. E. Senn, Cyril Walwyn, and Raymond Wheeler, "Hungry Children in Mississippi." Special Report of Southern Regional Council (Atlanta, 1967).
10. Robert McAfee Brown, *Persuade Us to Rejoice* (Louisville, KY: Westminster/ John Knox Press, 1992), 28–9.

C h a p t e r 1

O n e

FINDING THE FOUNDATION

Our whole life is startlingly moral. There is never an instant's truce
between virtue and vice.

—Henry David Thoreau, *Walden*

WHEN ARCHAEOLOGISTS SEARCH FOR characteristics of civilizations
that preceded ours, photographs show them digging around in foundations,
searching for clues to help them understand the ways in which we lived
then. Foundations give us important hints about the plans of the builders
and the confidence they placed in materials and in the locations of their
cities. Of course, the vast majority of buildings constructed have long since
disappeared: some too fragile, others overwhelmed by forces none could
withstand. But foundations that have survived instruct us. Even the cities
that were leveled by invaders and destroyers by land or by air still contain
substructures laid by the builders that tell a tale. Our imagination senses the
expectations of the builders, and study suggests the experiences of others as
they built. The location of foundations in cities that go back to some of our
earliest recorded history provides another facet of our story: the city as the
locus, even the cause, of plague.

In like manner, the course of our lives is informed and supported by the
foundations we set. Our values and our commitments—our building blocks—

11

will bear the burden of our lives. If I would be the wise man who builds his house upon a rock, so that when the floodwaters rise and the hurricane winds blow the house stands, I must find that rock. Thoreau tells us, in one of his arresting metaphors, that we must

> settle ourselves, and work and wedge our feet downward through the mud and slush of opinion, and prejudice, and tradition, and delusion, and appearance, . . . through church and state, through poetry and philosophy and religion, till we come to a hard bottom and rocks in place, which we can call *reality*, and say, This is, and no mistake; and then begin, having a *point d'appui*, below freshet and frost and fire, a place where you might found a wall or a state, or set a lamp-post safely.[1]

The central purpose in designing and constructing a moral and ethical base for my life—in "founding" my life on a hard bottom—is to prepare as well as possible for times of self-defining decisions, ethical dilemmas, and binding commitments that lie ahead, correlates of "plagues" that beset me now and lie ahead. To assemble foresight, knowledge, and conviction into a workable pattern for response to the challenges that mere living entails, we call upon many resources. A major source for understanding the issues, weighing the possibilities, and understanding the responses that I make is found in the teachings and the writings of chosen mentors who preceded me in thought and in deed and detailed the characteristics of their ethical foundations.

The biological inheritance that is ours without choice is certainly an important determinant of our abilities and many of our opportunities. But there is a strong element of choice in what we make of our lives, and a significant measure of the influences we acknowledge comes from authorities—from models—we choose. My beliefs, my values, my structured thought and reflection, and my final foundation are all strongly flavored by the teachers I select. In a very real sense, we choose our moral ancestors. In his distinctive way, the psalmist says:

> The LORD is my chosen portion
> and my cup.
> You hold my lot.
> The boundary lines have fallen
> for me in pleasant places:
> I have a goodly heritage.[2]

There is a confidence in this song; the singer is satisfied with the moral and religious inheritance that was chosen.

Of course, we must be cautious in attending to the advice and the experiences of others. A quick study of history and of our behavior over these centuries advises hesitation in accepting counsel from those who have gone before. Thoreau, again, warns us:

No way of thinking or doing, however ancient, can be trusted without proof. What every body echoes or in silence passes by as true today may turn out to be falsehood tomorrow, mere smoke of opinion. . . . One may almost doubt if the wisest man has learned any thing of absolute value by living.[3]

My ongoing search for building stones and a mortar to cement them into a solid substratum still occupies my thought and study. My lifetime has been a time of plague for our world and all its species, probably no worse nor better than many other times in our brief human history, but terrifying in its scope. We live in a century when, for the first time, annihilation—the loss of all determinants of civilization—is possible. It is a time when situations arise unexpectedly that call for interpretation, for decision, and for action if one is to be a responsible person. How we make these decisions with candor and a willingness to be answerable for their consequences is a persistent concern. As persons, we present an infinite variety of finely shaded reactions to personal and social alarms, the acute and chronic plagues of our day. It is possible to classify, to place in a limited number of specific categories, the types of ethical responses we make to the offenses we witness in our world.

What determines my behavior, my thoughts, and my actions? What are the footings of my constructed life that sustain me when evil lies close by? This query is presented, in a sense, each moment in the news of this day and in the prospects for tomorrow. These questions are also part of the ongoing assessment of the past. Why did I do this rather than that? Most of us have been told, since earliest childhood, how we are expected to behave in various social situations. We should say "Thank you" and "Please, may I . . ." and hold the door open for our elders. But with daily experience and the trials and challenges we face, we find that there is more to behavior than manners. There are decisions and actions that truly broadcast who we are, that reveal our true selves to us and to others in ways that we may or may not wish to acknowledge. We are always in the process of self-creation. Each hour sees decisions, comments, proposals, and commitments that define, stroke by stroke, the portrait being created in the here and now. There are no inconsequential additions to the work in progress.

My high school Sunday school teacher in the late 1930s, Edwin Way Teale, used his experiences as a special writer for *Popular Science* to captivate his class. A close observer and reporter on the American scene, he drew on his interviews and adventures, rather than fiction or Bible stories, for models for his teaching. One of his stories about preparing for the future by expecting the unexpected continues to inform me as I sketch my own developing caricature: A transcontinental passenger train was traveling across the vast spaces of Montana at its usual high speed. As it came around a long curve, a freight train was derailing on an inner track, rolling across the track of the passenger train racing toward it. The engineer pulled the throttle to full speed, and his train sliced through the freight train with no loss or injury to his passengers.

When interviewed later and asked why he chose to increase the speed of the train rather than jam on the brakes, he said that he had, during all the uneventful years on that trip, tried to conceive of unanticipated events that could occur anywhere along those thousands of miles of rails. Rather than staring at the track, he had playacted and critiqued the decisions available to him for each imagined accident or untoward event so that if, and when, an accident appeared inevitable, he would not have to begin to think about what to do: he would act in the way that his skill, logic, and experience had chosen in advance from the responses now suddenly possible for him in this particular stretch of the railroad line. He had set his foundation as best he could.

As an example of a technique of foundation setting, our railroad engineer informs us. However, the crises he anticipated do not have the flavor of malevolence, wrongdoing, or ill will that characterizes so many of the plagues we know. I am more interested here in thinking through our personal responses to events, to accidents of nature, and to the distortions in our interpersonal relations that have been interpreted as evil or as proof of an absence of goodness in our world. Is it possible to prepare for the terrible consequences of plague: destruction of the innocent, disintegration of the social order, loss of moral sensibility, an exquisite focus on the self? In times of near-overwhelming stresses, what are the bases for exemplary behavior that are reliable and will not fail us? These questions are perennial and must be answered by each of us so that we will not be ashamed of ourselves. One way to begin to look at these issues is to consider the origins of the evils we know and the varied responses that are available.

Plague as metaphor provides a setting for studying the ways in which we align our senses, our intellect, our past promises, and our hopes for the future into a coherent pattern. The necessity for an active and fertile imagination becomes apparent when we confront the unknown and the unimaginable. Raymond Stephanson writes:

Responses to the plague form the spectrum of imaginative life itself: . . . Plague initially is a symbol of imaginative potential, a symbol whose unformed significance we create ourselves; but plague also becomes an unsymbolic fact that confronts us with our imaginative emptiness in the face of the permanence of time, matter, and the contingencies of human existence.[4]

THE QUESTION OF EVIL

What are the moral and ethical bases for our self-defining decisions when we confront evil? How do we explain the coexistence of evil and a God defined by Judaism and Christianity as loving, just, and merciful? How do we explain evil in a world believed in faith to be created by a God characterized as always present, all-powerful, and all-knowing and considered the ultimate expression of love? Within the Judeo-Christian tradition that is my particular heritage, philosophers and theologians debate, argue, and plead a variety of theories to explain the existence of evil, and have done so through 3,500 years of biblical history and criticism. A technical word, *theodicy*— the justice of God—is the label that theologians use to discuss the profound paradox of the existence of evil. The logical inconsistency of the existence of a God of love and justice and the ubiquitous presence of gratuitous evil has been discussed, defended, and refuted for centuries, with no resolution. Attempts are made to categorize evil. *Natural* evils are beyond our control: hurricanes, floods, earthquakes, and the Black Death of the fourteenth century. Some writers define a group of *metaphysical* evils: the wolf killing the lamb, the farmer killing the chicken. The category of *moral* evils is our concern here, the needless suffering and pain—the evil that we visit upon all life— that are completely at odds with any concept of a loving and just God. How we understand this issue, how our behavior mirrors our beliefs and convictions, and the foundation we have chosen to support them and our relations with one another are the questions at the core of this study. To do this, I look at works important to my understanding, written to confirm, question, illuminate, encourage, and deny faith as a reliable foundation for a moral life.

We all have an object of ultimate faith, and we should define it with confidence: will it be God, the self, the intellect, the passions, nature, or humankind? Our history is replete with the names of these objects, our ways of worship and obeisance, and the expectations we have of response from them. For many of us, a wide discrepancy appears when what we have professed to believe is challenged by obvious catastrophe—by a plague. We find that either the house has been built upon sand or we chose building blocks that could not withstand the pressures of the storm. My recurring concerns that are considered in this study are how do we accurately designate the object of our faith and then translate our fidelity to it—those foundational beliefs—into a lively and recognizably moral life that will sustain us. The range of these beliefs is wide. Are we like Job in our acceptance? "Naked I came from my mother's womb, and naked shall I return there; the LORD gave, and the LORD has taken away, blessed be the name of the LORD."[5] Or are we rather like Albert Camus, who found us alone in the universe and recognized the evil of this world to be a call to join the oppressed and the tortured in a revolt against the horrors and oppressions delivered freely—gratuitously—to them by fellow humans? Or is Emily Dickinson our mentor, a poet whose confirmed belief in God as punitive, inattentive, and the giver of the gift of endless death called forth a powerful and cryptic artistry that reveals her profound autonomy as a competitive creator?

PLAGUE IN THE CITY

Throughout our history, plague is identified with cities: Athens, London, Marseilles, Florence, Avignon, and Bombay are notable. Contemporary journals and letters attest to plague occurring in all communities, both urban and rural. The city, however, is the locus of the learned—clerical and academic— who document the personal, social, medical, religious, and political implications of plague. Also, the city is usually a circumscribed community with a hierarchy of power and influence and a strong commercial base, the center of a series of concentric circles analogous to the structure of our personal and communal lives. The city is a model for understanding the intimate devastations of plague, the responses that we make to it as a people, and the ways of attenuating its horrors. An intriguing view of the metaphoric use of plague can be found in writings that suggest that the city itself is a plague, and that the multiple signs and symptoms of the disease are caused by the objective reality we know as the city, the bright star of civilization.

I begin with the Great Plague that entered Europe through the port of Messina in Sicily in October 1347. The Black Death, as it was called, is now known to have been caused by a bacterium, *Yersinia pestis*, easily treated today by antibiotics. Then, however, it was viewed as a ruination, exquisitely obvious evidence of the wrath of God delivered as punishment for the sins of the people. For a concise and stark view of the response of Florence to the appearance of plague, I turn to one of the outstanding writers in Italian literature.

In his introduction to *The Decameron*, Giovanni Boccaccio describes some aspects of our response to pestilence that he observed when bubonic plague appeared in Florence in 1348. He begins with a note about contemporary understanding of the cause of plague and the lack of any effective treatment. He writes:

> Let me say, then, that thirteen hundred and forty-eight years had already passed after the fruitful Incarnation of the Son of God when into the distinguished city of Florence, more noble than any other Italian city, there came a deadly pestilence. Either because of the influence of heavenly bodies or because of God's just wrath as a punishment to mortals for our wicked deeds, the pestilence, originating some years earlier in the East, killed an infinite number of people as it spread relentlessly from

one place to another until finally it had stretched its miserable length all over the West. And against this pestilence no human wisdom or foresight was of avail. . . . Neither a doctor's advice nor the strength of medicine could do anything to cure this illness; on the contrary, either the nature of the illness was such that it afforded no cure, or else the doctors were so ignorant that they did not recognize its cause.[6]

Boccaccio continues with a discussion of the responses citizens made to plague in their midst. The disease killed quite indiscriminately, regardless of personal behavior. Neither riotous living nor abstention from pleasures determined who died. The wealthy could escape the city, but the poor, unable to leave, were decimated. An exquisite self-concern determined behavior toward others, even family members and close friends. A characteristic response to incipient catastrophe was a sharp focus of each person on the self and a disregard for the welfare of others. The fact was that one citizen avoided another, that

almost no one cared for his neighbor, and that relatives rarely or hardly ever visited each other—they stayed far apart. This disaster had struck such fear into the hearts of men and women that brother abandoned brother, uncle abandoned nephew, sister left brother, and very often wife abandoned husband, and—even worse, almost unbelievable—fathers and mothers neglected to tend and care for their children as if they were not their own.[7]

The prevailing opinion was that the wrath of a just God was being visited upon the entire inhabited earth. This interpretation confirms, of course, the conviction of each individual of personal and communal sin sufficient to justify the visitation. A close reading of the Sermon on the Mount in the Gospel of Matthew, for instance, leaves no believer free from being assessed as a sinner. If our innermost thoughts are known to God, all are guilty and will be judged accordingly. Anger directed toward a brother or sister is equated with murder in the sense of liability to judgment; to look at a woman with lust is the same as committing adultery in one's heart. We are commanded to love our enemies, turn the other cheek when struck, ignore the treasures of this earth, and, of all unimaginable orders, not to worry. The reality of universal sin, the impossibility of saving the self by action or thought, and the utter inexplicability of the spread of a disease that killed in three to five days made the wrath of God a plausible explanation. The concept of an angry God was fully acceptable, and the Great Mortality of the middle of the fourteenth century received amazingly little comment from historians of those years: it was taken as a given.

One result of the search for the cause of this mysterious and terrifying fatal plague was the mass persecution of the Jews, who were accused of poisoning the wells. Although strongly rejected by the church as the work of the Devil, the pogroms spread throughout Europe, a bitter inheritance of centuries of official and papal oppression, causing the massacre of Jews and the destruction of their religious and economic communities. A strange movement known as the Flagellants appeared in Germany and spread swiftly across Europe in 1348. Begun as an effort to appease an angry God by severe whipping and beating of one's own body, the Flagellants were soon joined by others whose powerful anti-Jewish and anticlerical feelings sought expression; the social and personal disintegration of those years was fearsome.

THE CITY STRICKEN

With Daniel Defoe's novel of 1722, *A Journal of the Plague Year*, we engage a powerful description—a fictionalized personal account—of the plague that swept through London in 1665. Through the device of the memory of his uncle, H. F., Defoe presents the choices, the decisions, and the responses that we make when confronted by overwhelming catastrophe. Defoe places the reader in the city of London as the first cases of plague appear, and we stay with the recorder until the end of it. All the experiences of that time are described in detail: the nature of the illness, the varied attempts to prevent its spread, efforts at cure, the disposition of the dead, and the utter disintegration of the city. There are several points to the narrative that dramatically illustrate the crushing effects of disaster on the assumed and accepted morals of the day. The effort to maintain a faithful and ethical posture toward others becomes extremely difficult, and Defoe is brilliant in his exegesis of popular responses to the scourge. The author is convinced that this deadly disease is a direct result of the wrath of God visited upon a sinful people. Perhaps in a defensive response to the rising star of Enlightenment, Defoe presents a city and a people desolated by a God who is providential to the last detail. Also, the *Journal* is more a tale of the city of London than of individuals within it. As Louis Landa points out:

> The real tragedy is corporate. It applies less to this or that person or family, more to the greater organism, the stricken city ravished by plague, its people either fled or dying, its marts closed, its vast energies replaced by silence and inaction.[8]

A central ethical question developed carefully by Defoe is flight from the city. Should a faithful person stay or leave until the plague abates? The narrator, H. F., presents Defoe's conviction that there is no place to hide from the wrath of a just God, and punishment or death will find one whether in the city or in the country. He opts to stay, but his elder brother elects to leave the city with his family. This view is also presented by Defoe with acceptance, as a sign of intelligent adherence to the advice of physicians: it is the way of faith to attempt to preserve life as a gift of God. However, for Defoe, there is a clear moral imperative to stay. Also elegantly developed by Defoe is a series of circumstances that bring to mind the warning of Jung: we must be alert to unexpected events and attend to our thoughts as signals from a deep source of information—the unconscious. H. F. decides to leave London with his servant, who, sensing his master's indecision, has already left without him. Defoe writes:

> So I was put off for that Time; and one way or other, I always found that to appoint to go away was always cross'd by some Accident or other, so as to disappoint and put it off again; . . . I mention this Story also as the best Method I can advise any person to take in such a Case, especially, if he be one that makes Conscience of his Duty, and would be directed what to do in it, namely, that he should keep his Eye upon the particular Providences which occur at that Time, and look upon them complexly, as they regard one another, . . . he may safely take them for Intimations from Heaven of what is his unquestion'd duty to do in such a Case.[9]

In 1660, the restoration of the monarchy also brought the restoration of the Church of England. The government attempted to suppress Dissenters—Independents and Presbyterians—by closing their meetings. With the arrival of plague, there was an exodus of Anglican priests to the country with their wealthy patrons and friends—a shameful betrayal of their flocks, and a comment upon personal religious conviction. The result was that, for the duration of the devastation, preachers of varied faiths led congregations gathered without regard for doctrine but called together by the desperate times to seek the mercy of their God, to declare their sinfulness, and to seek communion with other believers. But the end of the pestilence brought the end of these spontaneous communities of faith. Defoe writes:

> The People flockt without Distinction to hear them preach, not much inquiring who or what Opinion they were of: But after the Sickness was over, that Spirit of Charity abated, and every Church being again supply'd with their own ministers, or others presented, where the Minister was dead, Things return'd to their old Channel again.[10]

As a person of faith, Defoe was distressed by the immediate turning of the people to astrologers, magicians, wizards, oracles, and fortune-tellers for advice, explanations, and assistance. He considered these to be works of the Devil, attractive to the "working labouring poor" as a distraction. But he points out that the working classes, and especially servants, were most vulnerable to being abandoned in the city when their employers fled to country estates. Our narrator is clear that his decision to remain in the city is strongly influenced by his concern for his employees. Rage, despair, and wild hopes abounded in London as the year wore on. The plague wrote a clear line that determined personal behavior in this hour of calamity. Defoe records the praise and honor due those who chose to stay: magistrates, clergy, doctors, public employees who continued to serve the desperate needs of the people. He has only words of reproach for those who left. An important and expected observation was that, as the plague subsided, the feelings and expressions of charity subsided with it.

> It was not the least of our Misfortunes, that with our Infection, when it ceased, there did not cease the Spirit of Strife and Contention, Slander and Reproach, which was really the great Troubler of the Nation's Peace before: It was said to be the Remains of the old Animosities, which had so lately involv'd us all in Blood and Disorder.[11]

This observation of the "Unthankfulness and Return of all manner of Wickedness among us" closes this fictional account of the plague year of 1665.

THE CITY AS PLAGUE

Defoe was one of many eighteenth-century novelists and pamphleteers who portrayed the city as a place "infected" by greed and selfishness. Several generations before Dickens's powerful attacks on the effects of the Industrial Revolution, the relations between business and crime and the devastations this partnership wrought on the poor, on children, and on the working class were described in poignant and bitter detail by popular authors, Defoe among them. Instability of the economy—the "boom and bust" cycle of capitalism—reveals its effects in the scenes that fill the streets of London: homelessness, robbery, prostitution, and despair. These same pictures are presented in the *Journal* as results of the attack of plague. Newgate prison was a horrible place, known to Defoe in several incarcerations of his own; the symbolic significance of its location across from the Exchange was not lost to Defoe and others as they described the impact of economic insecurity on the city. In his presentation of London in the time of plague, we read a biting description of greed, of class distinctions, of hopelessness and despair, of abandonment and desolation that fits as well with a failed economic system as with a disease sent by God to punish a sinful people.

The plague also converts the city into a prison. Defoe uses city walls, houses locked to confine sick persons, widespread and profound distrust and animosity everywhere, and ever-present death to illustrate the prison character of city life. His description suggests that what we see in London in the year of the plague has always been there. Max Byrd writes, "The vision of London set down in the *Journal*, a vision bodied forth in its remorseless images of sickness, prison, and grave, haunts every modern reader: no later artist of catastrophe has surpassed Defoe's creative truthfulness here." Byrd goes on to ask a central question for me. "But as we turn over in our minds the effects of the *Journal*—the anecdotes of terror and loneliness, the vignettes of a collapsing city—it becomes possible to think of Defoe's vision in another way: is this not only London as it is in plague, but also London as it always is?"[12]

The rapid growth of London as the commercial center of England brought into being a middle class defined by wealth and the acquisition of goods, usually at the expense of the working class. The massive assault of commercialism upon the people produced a large class of urban poor utterly dependent on the grace of powerful industrial and banking forces centered in the city. Any decline in demand for goods and services caused unemployment and suffering; a result of this well-known economic cycle was conversion of the unemployed into thieves of varied and enterprising sorts. The increasingly technical and mechanical aspects of manufacturing (in which persons seem to be part of the machinery), linked with the impersonal nature of aggressive free enterprise, greatly intensified the suffering seen in London, further linking the city and plague.

Defoe, writing within the Puritan tradition, sees the plague as an act of God to punish a wicked city. An ardent believer in a God who has determined all events from the beginning of time, he has H. F. tell us that staying or fleeing London would have no effect on his personal existence: God's will would be done. He does not see the plague as punishment of individual persons for specific sins. He understands it, rather, as punishment of the *city*. The city is the archetypal symbol for the worship of man-made gods: power, wealth, prestige, control. The city is the home of wicked enterprises that reverse the command to love God and neighbor. Failure to do so brings punishment. As Byrd writes:

> Sickness only makes visible on the external body the inner moral disease of London; the plague rages like a fever or a great fire, deliberately, furiously, as if to castigate: . . . In the angry, unforgiving plague is the fullest possible expression of the theme of London corruption.[13]

We, in these days, are more inclined to see political, social, and psychological pathology as causes of the disintegration of our cities: classic signs and symptoms of plague are certainly apparent everywhere. Crime, deterioration of many classic structures—family, economy, work, education, and housing—and a pervasive loss of hope for the future characterize life in the inner city. The behavior of city dwellers today mirrors that of London under siege: loneliness, fear of others different from and unknown to us, superstition, false dealing and false pretenses, corruption of those in civil authority, and abandonment of the afflicted to impersonal agencies for help. But this is not new in our experience, is it? Biblical accounts of the desperate nature of life in the city go back to the story of Cain and Abel. In a remarkable book, *The Meaning of the City*, Jacques Ellul develops the thesis that the city is an accursed place, the site of our futile attempt to create our own structures for life without God. The very loss of an ethical base for our common life, the absence of bonds among us that can sustain us in the hours of trial, the destruction of the environment, the cynicism and hopelessness we experience—these are the results of our creating the city as a symbol of our power. The city is also the tempter, the magnet that draws us to seek prizes that are ephemeral and lead to our separation from the love of God and from the needs of one another. The biblical accounts of Babel—Babylon—detail the confounding of our unity in language by God to thwart our attempt to wall ourselves off, to build our own tower to heaven, to make a center for the waging of war.

An important qualification in our account of the city as evil, as plague, as a reality opposed to the ultimate welfare of the created order, is the distinction between the city and the persons who live there. Ellul, commenting upon Jesus' chastisement of the three cities in the Gospel of Matthew, writes:

> The city is a specific being, independent of its inhabitants. Jesus speaks to the city itself and threatens it with punishment, against the collectivity of its inhabitants, of course, but even more certainly against the city as an independent being. He speaks of judgements against the city, and so magnifies what Scripture has already taught us. For it is not a question of the inhabitants, but of the city itself.[14]

The city represents our efforts to live outside the realm of a creative spirit. Byrd, commenting on Ellul's thesis, writes:

> Built first by Cain in defiance of God's order, [the city's] original intention was to exclude God from its boundaries; and in the Old Testament, Babylon, Jerusalem, and all secular cities are archetypal seats of corruption, endlessly subject to catastrophe.[15]

From the beginning, when Cain became a wanderer and built the first city, we have used our skills and strengths to make our world secure in walls and gates, civil authority and the supremacy of the state, the university, and the cathedral. These institutions that we honor in the city are potential agents of confusion and deception.

I think that the university is a compelling topic for reflection on the city as a plague. Over many centuries, we have honored scholarship and learning and their roles in improving health and the common welfare, dispelling superstition, building justice, preserving the arts and letters of the past, and presenting new challenges to the inventive mind. But there is a walled-in and fearful component to college life that isolates the work from the obvious and expressed needs of our citizens infected by the plague of the city. The university is a plagued city within a city, a ghetto of its own making. Concerns of faculty and students revolve around promotion, tenure, fame and reputation in academic societies, and other common human aspirations. Studies are usually published in esoteric journals whose readership is limited in numbers and in personal concern for public issues. Four graduate schools common to large universities—law, medicine, divinity, and business—deftly illustrate the unwillingness or perhaps the inability of "higher" education to confront the issues of our time in either city or country. Crime is rampant in our cities; the legal system is severely and proudly adversarial, with mediation a rare occurrence. Medical centers are confronted with the diseases of society: accidents, homicides, sociopathic interpersonal disasters, catastrophes caused by bad diet, unwitting or self-chosen exposure to carcinogens, and self-destructive lifestyles. Vast funds are spent on highly specialized care for persons in the final days of life. The current socioeconomic status of our citizenry is a wilted laureate to the accomplishments of MBAs in the struggle for economic stability, full employment, and justice in the distribution of goods. Finally, what public evidence do we have for the influence of departments of religious studies and seminaries? Where can one find evidence of the resurgence of spiritual power, personal sacrifice for the good of the displaced and suffering, and hope for an enriched world community held in the bonds of love and joy? We are indeed beset by plagues.

A song from World War I asked how it was possible to keep a young man down on the farm after he had seen Paris. The attraction of the city has always been magnetic, drawing the young and the ambitious from rural life to the excitements and the expected luxuries of urbanity. In a pattern consonant with the warnings of our earliest religious traditions, to leave the country for the city was to go against the will of God; to seek the gifts of humankind considered to be of dubious, even sinful, value; and to become a wanderer in a hostile world. The American tradition has followed all others. The Puritans' hope to establish a city set upon a hill that would be a model for all was shattered in a few years by bitter theological argument and narrow ethnic decision. As colonial America became an independent nation an ocean away from the rigidly structured and faulted economy of Europe, the wide-open lands of the West offered the opportunity for the realization of a moral and healthy society. Thomas Jefferson was a strong advocate of an economic policy that would leave manufacturing in the workshops of Europe, keeping America an agricultural nation. In his *Notes on the State of Virginia* (1785) he writes:

Those who labour in the earth are the chosen people of God, if ever he had a chosen people, whose breasts he has made his peculiar deposit for substantial and genuine virtue. It is the focus in which he keeps alive that sacred fire, which other wise might escape from the face of the earth. Corruption of morals in the mass of cultivators is a phenomenon of which no age nor nation has furnished an example. It is the mark set on those, who not looking up to heaven, to their own soil and industry, as does the husbandman, for their subsistence, depend for it on the casualties and caprice of customers.

Any loss of easy access to manufactured goods would be easily compensated by a stable economy, a gracious government, and inner peace generated in an agrarian life. "The mobs of great cities add just so much to the support of pure government, as sores do to the strength of the human body."[16] An enigma in the lives of civilized and educated persons committed to the public welfare is the profound lapse we see between values professed and lives lived. Jefferson, perhaps as starkly as any of us, demonstrates this baffling paradox. He was a founder of a persisting democracy whose writings ring with the call for freedom and self-determination, and an agrarian whose vision of the future was a nation of farmers each owning an equal parcel of land, yet Monticello was a plantation of 5,000 acres maintained by some 125 slaves. This dichotomy is obvious in many of the responses to plague that I have presented: the bases for exemplary behavior can vanish when we are confronted with the possibility of loss of life or loss of property.

WHAT SHALL BE THE FOUNDATION?

Toward the close of the *Journal*, Defoe describes the retreat of the court to Oxford and its minimal concern for London, the reproach of physicians and clergy who abandoned their charges, and the rapid resurgence of old animosities and strife. But he also adds a caution for those who would condemn:

> For all Men have not the same Faith, and the same Courage, and the Scripture commands us to judge the most favourably, and according to Charity. A Plague is a formidable enemy, and is armed with Terrors that every Man is not sufficiently fortified to resist, or prepar'd to stand the Shock against.

Defoe cautions his readers not to brand others as cowards, but with due reflection to see

> that it is not an ordinary Strength that cou'd support it; it was not like appearing in the Head of an Army, or charging a Body of Horse in the Field; but it was charging Death itself on his pale Horse; to stay was indeed to die.[17]

The fourth horseman of the Apocalypse on his pale green horse is a most formidable opponent and one not easily ignored in our attempts to define a personal ethic that will maintain us if we stay in the city. Defoe presents a specific and clear case for us to consider. His narrator, H. F., believes that God has determined the life of each of us; we shall perish or live for the moment based on the providence of our creator. We can stay or flee, based on our own desires and plans, but our fate is already sealed—whatever it will be. Defoe's foundation of faith is firmly set upon a reformed tradition that eliminates personal choice. I am reminded of W. Somerset Maugham's story of the servant who flees to Samarra on his master's horse after a terrifying encounter with Death in the marketplace in Baghdad. Death, in relating the story to the master later that day, expresses her surprise at seeing the servant in Baghdad that morning: they have an appointment in Samarra that very night.[18]

Certainly, the faith of Defoe is one that frees the individual for moral decision and action based on the needs of others and the command to serve. Unfortunately for the faithful, there is a long history of self-righteousness associated with the tradition that finds vivid expression in many sects, denominations, and major faiths today. Orthodox Judaism, Christian fundamentalism, Roman and Greek Catholicism, and Islam have protagonists who proclaim possession of a saving and exclusive faith. Difficult as it may be for others, this type of faith can engender deeds of caring and sacrifice in the name of a deity or holy other that are remarkable and praiseworthy. The issue remains the one that Thoreau presents: find a foundation upon which one can, with utter reliance, base the decisions and the expressions of a dutiful, truthful, and faithful life.

I have presented two outstanding literary works on the plague and responses to it. Boccaccio, in his introduction to *The Decameron*, records his own observations of civil and personal disintegration in Florence with the appearance of bubonic plague in 1348. Defoe, in a fictional journal, recounts the horror of the Great Plague in London in 1665, possibly recording experiences recounted by his uncle, H. F., who survived. With consummate skill, Defoe tells a story in which plague may well be a metaphor for the city, an institution that has been interpreted since early times as a cursed place. Representative of our attempt to erect a barrier against God, a place where we can express our own creative acts, the city is—to this day—the home of wealth and crime, of power and destitution, of isolation and death, of despair and deception. The plague—bubonic or civic—tests our faith and the ethic we claim to derive from it. We flee or we become health workers; we resist those who do evil or we connive for a position of power; we maintain an exquisite self-centeredness or we open our arms and hearts to those who suffer. Whatever is truly the foundation of our faith will be evident to all, even to us.

A significant work that presents plague as a metaphor appeared in English in 1948: *The Plague* by Albert Camus. In the next chapter I look at this novel, which describes with power the impact of plague on the city of Oran in the 1940s, and the responses that are possible. I analyze the moral foundations of a strong ethic with an illustrious history going back twenty-five centuries that survives and empowers during the plague that visited Europe in the fourth and fifth decades of the twentieth century.

NOTES

1. Henry David Thoreau, *Walden*, ed. J. Lyndon Shanley (Princeton, NJ: Princeton University Press, 1971), 97–8.
2. Psalms 16:5–6, New Revised Standard Version (NRSV).
3. Thoreau, *Walden*, 8–9.
4. Raymond Stephanson, "The Plague Narratives of Defoe and Camus: Illness as Metaphor," *Modern Language Quarterly* 48, no. 3 (1987): 224.
5. Job 1:21, NRSV.
6. Giovanni Boccaccio, *The Decameron*, trans. M. Musta and Peter Bondanella (New York: W. W. Norton, 1982), 6.
7. Ibid., 9.
8. Daniel Defoe, *A Journal of the Plague Year*, ed. Louis Landa (London: Oxford University Press, 1969), xvi.
9. Ibid., 10.
10. Ibid., 26.
11. Ibid., 234–5.
12. Max Byrd, *London Transformed* (New Haven, CT: Yale University Press, 1978), 35.
13. Ibid., 39
14. Jacques Ellul, *The Meaning of the City* (Grand Rapids, MI: William B. Eerdmans, 1970), 114.
15. Byrd, *London Transformed*, 39.
16. Thomas Jefferson, "Query XVIII, Manners," in *Notes on the State of Virginia*, ed. W. Peden (Chapel Hill: University of North Carolina Press, 1955), 162–3
17. Defoe, *Journal*, 236.
18. W. Somerset Maugham, *Sheppey, A Play in Three Acts* (London: William Heinemann LTD, 1933), 112.

Chapter 2
Two

ALONE TOGETHER

We had to fashion for ourselves an art of living
in times of catastrophe in order to be reborn
before fighting openly against the death instinct
at work in our history.

—Albert Camus, Nobel Prize Address, 1957

THE DEVASTATION WROUGHT IN our twentieth century surpasses that of the plague years of the fourteenth. The frightening difference between these eras is that our century's deaths, tortures, and massive destruction are caused by us and not by a bacterium or an act of God. Albert Camus, in a stunning example of metaphoric writing, offers a novel that describes an outbreak of plague in the Algerian city of Oran. This fiction documents the effects of plague and our varied personal and social responses to it. *The Plague*, published in France in 1947, became available in English in the United States in 1957. It was an immediate success, widely acclaimed wherever it was read. According to critical studies on Camus, this novel lies near the middle of his philosophical and political development as an author deeply concerned about our common life. David Sprintzen writes:

In a world without transcendent significance, in which we are all condemned to death, what, he asks, are the possibilities for an honest and

27

clear-sighted coming to terms with our condition. . . . Focusing upon the central drama of the West—its root metaphors or metaphysic, its agony and its future, its exile and its kingdom—his work speaks to us at a level below that of conscious awareness. . . . It subtly confronts us with a mirror and seeks to mark out a tortuous and risky path toward our natural salvation.[1]

There is both a close association and a clear distinction between *A Journal of the Plague Year* and *The Plague*. Both authors use bubonic plague as a metaphor to present the human condition, especially the life we live in the city, the place where the basic conflicts, mortal sins, and flowers of civilization flourish. The deterioration of the political and social structures that we assume function in our behalf, the exposure of our raw and self-centered concerns for survival, and the appearance of virtue and sacrifice are present in both novels. Another similarity in the novels is the concept of the city as a prison. Both authors observe the finitude of our lives, the restraints we know in time and space and freedom, and the sure knowledge that death closes our story. I return to this theme in my discussion of *The Plague*. A major difference in the stories lies in the etiology of the epidemic. Defoe, a confirmed Puritan, places the first cause of the plague in the hands of a God who is angry with us because of our failure to be concerned about the common good and the meaning of community as a people of God. Camus, in contrast, finds the causes of plague to be inherent in the perennial human quest for power and control, simple answers to enigmatic questions, and casual resolution of dilemmas epitomized in our time by the catastrophic plague of Nazism.

The development of Camus's political and personal philosophy has been carefully traced by many critics. His story begins with early poverty, a silent mother, and the death of a father he never knew. Central to most analyses of his thought is his great love of his native country, Algeria; the pleasures of the Mediterranean Sea; and his preference for Greek philosophy over Christian—particularly Roman Catholic—religion. Early in his life, he recognized the "discovery" by Friedrich Nietzsche that God was dead in the thoughts and the lives of contemporary Western Christians. A belief that was central to 3,500 years of civilization, a source of values, and the core of what it means to be a person in an ordered universe was nowhere to be found operative by Nietzsche. Camus, rather than acceding to the nihilism that that discovery offered or joining the growing group of existentialists among whom Jean-Paul Sartre was a major force, chose another path, one that presents a powerful and rigorous alternative to traditional Christian faith.

A working philosophy for an ethical life that is then lived out in the time of plague is a type of faith that must be considered seriously. But it is not only the plague itself that is so threatening to us; the isolation, the exile that it enforces, is just as formidable a foe. Camus, inserting quotations from Nietzsche, writes:

> From the moment that man believes neither in God nor in immortal life, he becomes "responsible for everything alive, for everything that, born of suffering, is condemned to suffer from life." . . . Then the time of exile begins, the endless search for justification, the aimless nostalgia, "the most painful, the most heartbreaking question, that of the heart which asks itself: where can I feel at home?"[2]

The philosophical route Camus chose for his life provides a remarkably strong ethic for personal and communal behavior, one that tests to the limits of thought and action any religious faith. And that is what draws me to this influential writer as I continue to define and enlarge my own faith and ethical perspectives.

To view the world in a realistic way in the first third of this century is, for Camus and many others, to witness loss of meaning for life. The world, as it was known for so long, is transformed. The natural laws that govern motion in stellar and subatomic worlds function without regard for human need or wish. Death is the only event we can expect with complete confidence. If there is no transcendent source of morality and a good conscience, and if no ultimate purpose or event is known by us, then we are free to do whatever we please. Anything and everything is permissible. For Camus, our longing for coherence, meaning, and order in our lives and our world is confronted by the indifference and unresponsiveness of that world, with death as the ultimate defeat and confirmation of our insignificance. This experience of awakening to meaninglessness and the sure knowledge of defeat opens two pathways of thought and behavior for us. Nihilism, finding its ultimate expression in our time in Nazism, permits all behavior: whatever we can get for ourselves is allowable, in the absence of a common morality. Camus rejected this response to the death of God in our time and developed his acceptance of the absurdity of life into a highly moral and deeply personal commitment to revolt in the cause of sufferers from the plague. In *The Rebel* he writes:

> In absurdist experience, suffering is individual. But from the moment when a movement of rebellion begins, suffering is seen as a collective experience. Therefore the first progressive step for a mind overwhelmed by the strangeness of things is to realize that this feeling of strangeness is shared with all men and that human reality, in its entirety, suffers from the distance which separates it from the rest of the universe. The malady experienced by a single man becomes a mass plague.[3]

Our responses—both as persons and as communities in history with cultures—to the reality of the absurd in our lives are varied. Outrage, anger, despair, anomie, acceptance, and revolt are all possibilities. It is that last—revolt—that Camus chooses as his mode. His repeated call is that we not only assist the victims of the plagues of our day but also join forces to free all persons from their status of victims. His argument for revolt is presented in one of his most important works, *The Rebel*. But my aim here is not to present a review of his developed philosophy; rather, it is to examine his popular novel, *The Plague*, as a concise and skilled discussion of the responses we make to devastation.

Camus lived for twelve years after publication of *The Plague* and was actively engaged in political and philosophical arguments, particularly about the Algerian war for independence from France. Later developments in his thinking, though necessary for following his evolving thought, lie outside this study of the bases we choose for an ethic of behavior in the time of pestilence. Certainly his concerns about torture and human rights, capital punishment, and the threat of nuclear annihilation and his ambiguity over Algeria are important facets of his impressive development. I focus on his thoughts about our behavior toward victims, our need for collective security, and the rejection of totalitarian answers to the threats we all sense as being so pervasive. His call for collective unity to oppose totality as the way of dealing with plague, so persistent in his work, is a foundation for our own studied and developing responses to it.

The Plague

The epigraph to Camus's novel (italicized below) is from Robinson Crusoe's preface to part III of Defoe's classic *Serious Reflections During the Life and Surprising Adventures of Robinson Crusoe*. It states clearly the intentional use of metaphor by both authors to teach us from their experiences:

> All these reflections are just history of a state of forced confinement, which in my real history is represented by a confined retreat in an island; and *it is as reasonable to represent one kind of imprisonment by another, as it is to represent anything that really exists by that which exists not.*[4]

Note also the reference, again, to imprisonment as a condition of the cities in which we live: London in 1665, Oran in the 1940s—the setting for Camus's novel.

Critics assign numerous allegorical symbols to the plague in this novel, and rightly so, confirming the power of metaphor to reveal and instruct. For my purposes, I prefer to stay with the stated comments of the author. Camus, in a 1955 letter to Roland Barthes, writes:

> *The Plague*, which I wanted to be read on a number of levels, nevertheless has as its obvious content the struggle of the European resistance

movements against Nazism. The proof is that although this enemy is no-where named, everyone in every European country recognized him. . . . *The Plague* does represent, beyond any possible discussion, the move-ment from an attitude of solitary revolt to the recognition of a community whose struggles must be shared.[5]

Camus goes on to note three other themes: the pain of isolation and separa-tion when survival is threatened by an enemy, the requirement that we be willing to sacrifice private relationships for the good of the community, and the certainty of the return of pestilence and its associated struggles in the future. In other words, the plague and its ravages are the setting forth of "facts" that recount both our suffering and our need to express our revolt inspired by it.

THE STORY

The plot is easily told. In 194–, bubonic plague suddenly appears in the Algerian city of Oran. The concerns of the city are for business, diversion and leisure, the rules and regulations that govern daily living, and relation-ships that shun deeper human needs and hopes. The populace is disbeliev-ing at first, and people retreat even further into their own concerns. Their responses to the onset of the epidemic are expected: apathy, self-concern, the search for brief pleasures, and disregard for the serious community cri-sis. A mixture of disbelief and denial pervades the city as dead rats are seen in the streets and the disease makes it appearance in people. A variety of responses by the general population to the plague and the enforced quaran-tine of the city is sketched by Camus. We watch the count of the dead rise, the inept efforts of the bureaucracy to reassure the people, the efforts of sanitary squads to halt the spread, and the eventual production of a serum to counter the bacillus. The plague subsides, and the city returns to its former life.

THE CHARACTERS

Camus presents the actors in this novel in an allegorical style fitting his philosophical development at the time, and offering diverse understandings of how we respond to pestilence. We learn at the end of the novel that the narrator is the physician, Dr. Rieux, whose behavior is admirable and self-effacing in the time of plague. We return to him later when we attend to the voice of the author as our instructor; Camus was very clear about the role of the artist—regardless of the discipline—to speak for those of us without a voice. First, let us see ourselves in the other characters. The challenge of these creations lies in their expression of conflicting values and ambivalent feelings, making us mindful of our own hearts and minds.

Rambert. This young man, trapped in quarantined Oran away from the woman he loves, expresses the existential position of pure chance, the accidental occurrence that puts me in a situation over which I have limited or no control. The reasons for being in this city rather than that city at this particular time are insignificant, yet they seem to be altering my life in large measure. The problem at hand, the pestilence that is present, is not a part of my doing or my responsibility, and yet I find myself in this place, at this moment, with the need to make a decision: do I stay or do I leave? My real life is with the persons I love, those who enrich my life, making happiness a reality. This city, with its plague, is just a fact of a forsaken world, and I have no part to play in its resolution. To be happy in my love and its full expression with another person is to realize what it means to be human. The delights and the gifts we give and receive in the fullness of romantic love are so definitive of what we truly are that we must hold firmly to them.

After making plans to escape the quarantine, Rambert changes his mind and decides to stay and work with Rieux. The ache of separation that he feels, that deep longing to be with his beloved, is soothed by his awareness that the crisis of plague has transcended his own needs. In caring for the many nameless, in working beside others who have left their loves to be with the sufferers, Rambert acknowledges a broader value needing consideration. There may even be a sharpening of his love for the lovely woman waiting for him in Paris. Although Rambert begins with the announcement that he does not belong in Oran, he stays to work. He stays not just because he is needed; his vacated position on the sanitary squad has already been filled. Perhaps he senses that he is witnessing a deeper love in the time of plague, a perception that there is a profound human need for a community that shares its joys and sorrows and sacrifices for others.

Rambert is a central figure for me as I think through my responses to the plagues of my lifetime. He is "converted" to action by watching another person persist in working to overcome the effects of pestilence. His initial refusal to participate in the work of the sanitary squads centers on his unwillingness to risk death for an idea—the vague idealization of man. He speaks of his disbelief in heroism and his commitment to love as the central force in his life. He finds, unfortunately, that we have lost our capacity for a love powerful enough to drive us to work for others. The idea of love has faded as much as the idea of heroism as a response to our common needs in times of dire stress. Rieux counters that argument with his conviction that common decency—not heroism, but merely doing one's job in the hour of need—is reason enough for the risk involved. This theme recurs in the novel, restating that those who rebel against the suffering and the injustices in our world simply need to do what they can to help the victims. There is no overriding sanction or command to do so; we are, each one alone, presented with the situations of our time and must decide for or against joining the revolt.

The Rambert-Rieux conversation offers a sharply focused point for decision. Is the suffering of others a sufficient cause, in itself, to justify the sacrifice that I know is called for? Is the stark reality of the horrors of our life on this earth an acceptable reason for giving myself over to the endless struggle to free us from them? There is an unnerving freedom offered to me to define myself by my actions without regard for a code of ethics, a religious doctrine, or even the expectation of some sign of appreciation from the recipients of any service I might offer. In the decision of Rambert to stay and work, I find the unavoidable realization of self-creation by my own actions, an existentialist view of my unending definition of who I am to be.

Tarrou. One of the rewards in reading this book is the discovery—not always pleasant—of myself in each of the main characters. Tarrou is one who holds my attention as I follow his dogged search for saintliness. Introspective and fully engaged in a deadly serious critique of his life, he tells us that he "had plague already, long before I came to this town and encountered it here. Which is tantamount to saying I'm like everybody else."[6] With his sharp study of himself and how he reacted during years of exposure to political tyrannies, he comes to the conclusion that we are all infected. For him, murder, legal or otherwise, is the sure sign, the bubo, the purple spot of *la peste* that we all carry. He found that, even when doing good by opposing evil, we still bring death to others, and this makes involvement in the affairs of the world impossible. While we think we are fighting plague, we are the infected and the infecting ones. There is no escape from it. Whatever we do, we can, and probably will, bring destruction to others. Tarrou withdraws from the struggle between ideologies, leaving others to make history, as he puts it.

Tarrou is close to being paralyzed by his experiences with the conflicting social and political dogmas of our time. He says:

> I have realized that we all have plague, and I have lost my peace. And today I am still trying to find it; still trying to understand all those others and not to be the mortal enemy of anyone. I only know that one must do what one can to cease being plague-stricken, and that's the only way in which we can hope for some peace, or failing that, a decent death. This, and only this, can bring relief to men and, if not save them, at least do them the least harm possible and even, sometimes, a little good.[7]

The quest of Tarrou is to become a saint without the felt presence of God. On his good behavior as one who cares for the victims, he hopes for an inner peace and rest from a life of witnessed horror. I find his vision and his search poignant and compelling. As I watch my world and my life, I am not certain which side, if any, is the right one for me to elect. My complicity in the sins and errors of these years is obvious, and I, too, long for peace and inner security based on a sure foundation. But where is that foundation, and how shall I find it in these complex and destructive days? Tarrou is one of my teachers in that search.

Paneloux. In the character of this priest, Camus presents his case against Christian faith. In two sermons that he preaches, Paneloux states what Camus considers to be central tenets of Christian faith in the time of plague. The first sermon, a carefully reasoned construct, depicts the plague as punishment from God and reminds us immediately of our need to examine our lives, repent of our sins, and hope that God will look kindly upon us. Natural evil is seen not as a characteristic of God but as evidence of wrath directed toward a sinful people. The plague is what we deserve for our faithlessness and our evil acts. His second sermon, preached after witnessing the horrifying death of a child, offers only blind acceptance of suffering as our lot. There are no reasons, no justifications for suffering.

Camus, distressed by intellectual religious inventions that explain our suffering, sharply declines acceptance of any kind of truth, either given by God or invented by man. The first of these constructs accepts submission to evil as a given; the second justifies totalitarian answers to evil and the death of innocents. If this hard love of God is our lot, Camus declines it. Paneloux offers the existentialist option that Rambert chooses, only here it is God who puts us in the position where we must choose what we are to do; our faith in God will determine that choice. The plague is a test of that faith. Sprintzen writes:

> However active Paneloux's practice, it is ultimately constrained and probably vitiated by its metaphysical resignation. Here, in Camus's view, is the root moral failure of Christianity. It is built upon the acceptance of the death of innocence and is thus the ultimate negation of revolt.[8]

Grand. This minor municipal clerk is an important figure in the novel. Somewhat shadowy, he represents for Camus the heroism of the many who fought oppression, who served the victims, who refused to surrender to the power and the blind destruction of the plague. Doing their work every day, maintaining the structure of society as best they can, while struggling to find some happiness in their lives with others—these are the women and men who quietly sustain our world as we resist forces that destroy us. The teller of our story writes:

> Yes, if it is a fact that people like to have examples given them, men of the type they call heroic, and if it is absolutely necessary that this narra-

tive should include a "hero," the narrator commends to his readers, with, to his thinking, perfect justice, this insignificant and obscure hero who had to his credit only a little goodness of heart and a seemingly absurd ideal. This will render to the truth its due, . . . and to heroism the secondary place that rightly falls to it, just after, never before, the noble claim of happiness.[9]

Rieux. In the struggle that Tarrou lives out—the quest for sainthood without God—we see the possibility of another role that lies between that of executioner and that of victim. Camus offers Rieux as the personification of the true healer. As the narrator of the story, physician to the victims of the plague, and exegete of the text, Rieux is the person that I, as a physician, see as Camus's model for me at this point in his development as a social philosopher. Certainly, I can find a part of myself in each of the main characters; that is a given in good writing. But the doctor is central to the story. For Rieux, it is seeing someone die that sparks his revolt, his determination to become a caring physician, one who will stay with the victims until death—the symbol of absurdity—makes its claim. The observance of suffering points the way to the meaning of our work: the struggle against evil. We are to attend to, not save, our patients. Death is the final victor, and the physician can only stave it off for a time, offering care and expert medical attention during the journey.

Rieux presents an honored and sensitive position in the unequal struggle to conquer the plague. Without expression of grandeur, he extends himself, faithful to his commitment to the work he is called to do. Camus also presents, in conversations between Rieux and Rambert, the dilemma he sees between happiness and duty to combat the plague. Rieux encourages Rambert to leave, to join his love and enjoy the happy state he remembers from the rapidly disappearing past.

The poignancy of the dilemma is heightened by our knowledge that Rieux left a wife dying of tuberculosis in a sanatorium. Why did he turn away from the happiness that he encourages others to pursue? His answer is vague, yet fitting with his inner moral stance toward plague: we must fight pestilence and stay with the victims. Rieux says, "For nothing in the world is it worth turning one's back on what one loves. Yet that is what I am doing, though why I do not know."[10] There is, in Rieux's words and actions, a moral foundation that transcends the obvious public morality he favors. In conversations between the two men, we see a developing understanding of public behavior. Although reassured by Rieux that he should not be ashamed to prefer happiness, Rambert's observation of life in a city with plague leads him to his final conviction to stay. It may be shameful to be happy by oneself when misery is all around one.

The realization that the plague has become everyone's concern awakens in us the extent of our exile, our separation from all that we love and cherish. The intensity of engagement needed to join the suffering is eloquently expressed in the moment of the death of a boy. Rieux almost physically attempts to will the survival of the child. This scene also provides Camus with the opportunity to present one of the most powerful arguments against the existence of a God that could be seen, in any sense, as loving and supporting. Rieux uses the same argument so powerfully expressed by Ivan Karamazov in that astounding chapter "Rebellion," which immediately precedes "Grand Inquisitor" in *The Brothers Karamazov*. Nothing can justify the suffering of children, not even the achievement of peace and happiness for all. Ivan says to his brother, "I don't want more suffering. And if the sufferings of children go to swell the sum of sufferings which was necessary to pay for truth, then I protest that the truth is not worth such a price."[11]

I think that Albert Maquet states Camus's position in *The Plague* very well:

> Yes, the individual is the captive of an incomprehensible universe, against which his desire for coherence and his passion for justice miserably collide. Yes, his abandonment is irremediable, definitive, and the evil of which he is the prey is a pure absurdity. His sense of dignity commands him to reject this misfortune, which he shares with his fellow men; hence his revolt, but a revolt that postulates the greatest solidarity with his fellow men.[12]

We are to live in hope, sure only of the community of all the other victims in a life that leads only to death, and a death without a purpose. But we can, and we must, strive at all times and with our best efforts to reduce the suffering that we see all about us. That work will create the person I will become as I respond to my calling to be with and for others. For Camus, the task seems to be a barren one. At the very time that the plague begins to subside, Tarrou loses "the match" and dies. Rieux asks, what has he himself won?

> No more than the experience of having known plague and remembering it, of having known friendship and remembering it, of knowing affection and being destined one day to remember it. So all a man could win in the conflict between plague and life was knowledge and memories.[13]

PERSONAL REFLECTIONS

The Plague has been a significant part of my life, both personal and professional, since it was published in this country. I attend to it, both in my understanding of what it means to be a doctor and in my ongoing struggles to define myself as a worthy person. After so many decades of being a pediatrician, it is difficult to see myself as a person other than a doctor. My work since 1982 as chaplain of the Yale University School of Medicine is enlightening as I observe physicians, students, instructors, and their telltale interactions with one another and with patients. Unsure of what my new profession would entail, I spent my early months listening to students talk about their experiences as their four years of graduate study evolved from scientific preclinical work through the patient-oriented years in the hospital and the clinics. While making full allowance for the likelihood of overstatement in student applications that declare a commitment to becoming a compassionate and caring physician, I found that these are usually honestly presented reasons for coming to medical school. What became an annoying and troubling source of distress to the students in their third year was the observation that many physicians had obvious difficulties communicating with patients about the personal aspects of disease, the impact that serious illness has upon the varied facets of our lives. The real anxiety behind the students' concerns was their expressed fear that they might become as dissociated as their instructors from feelings about, and for, their future patients. Compassion, empathy, even sympathy were rarely expressed by the attending physicians or residents. Certainly, personal concerns such as sexual function, diminishment of work capacity and the ability to carry out duties as a family member, the reality of pain, the possibility of death, and the stresses associated with therapy are issues that many doctors find too difficult to discuss.

I thought that it was important to take advantage of the interest that entering students expressed in providing sympathetic care for the sick. In my own years in the practice of medicine, I learned that patients and families have a lot to say about the care they have received and witnessed in others. It seemed appropriate to combine these observations and have patients teach the students the essentials of humane care. To this end, I have supervised a seminar for first-year medical students in which each student has a patient-teacher for the semester. I interview patients—usually those with leukemia, various cancers, or AIDS—and find an appropriate one for each student. Patients are assured that the students have just started medical school and know little about medicine; they will be of no help. But they—the patients— have the opportunity to instruct students in the personal and professional characteristics of a good doctor. For most of the patients, this is an offer that cannot be refused. After the initial anxiety is overcome, and schedules are adjusted, the students begin to learn what medical care is about.

Students refer to the seminar as a "course on death and dying." Much to their surprise, most patients are not interested in talking about these acknowledged facts of being human. Their interest is focused on living until they die. They, as we, know that death is inevitable for all. There are questions about how to live until that event, how to continue with personal activities that have enriched them in the past and form strong ties to others. There are many facets to the interaction between patient and physician, features that test our capacity to understand, our willingness to listen to astounding revelations and observations about this human venture, and our ability to be with and for the victims. It is this last point that patients emphasize: their need for a doctor who will stay with them, hear them, and comfort and care for them with compassion. Dr. Rieux, narrator of *The Plague*, is that physician, a valued model for a student.

A number of reasons are offered for the distance that many doctors maintain from their dying patients. Some see death as the "enemy" and retreat before this implacable foe. Others, fearful of death themselves, cannot talk about it except as an abstraction. Others, without training or experience in talking with seriously ill patients, simply avoid the issue, leaving that work to nurses, social workers, and family. If, as I believe to be true, we would like to be compassionate and caring physicians for our fellow travelers ending their lives, then we must learn how to find a deep and satisfying professional relationship with our patients. There is a rich and fulfilling middle position between becoming intimately involved with patients and separating ourselves completely from their personal concerns. The line is not easily drawn between these positions and, like most important parts of our experiences, requires ongoing personal supervision and study.

One analogy I use with students is that of developing love between two persons. As we begin to build a relationship, we find that there are strength and enlightenment in it. It seems that the more we give, the more we receive. Difficulties overcome and confusions settled confirm the seriousness of our relationship and our willingness to make some sacrifices so that it may prosper. As an old parable would put it, bread cast upon the waters will be returned fivefold. The personal sustenance we receive from others builds our own resolve, urges us to learn and perfect techniques and skills that will further our ability to serve. But the important aspect is the inner, personal one of self-knowledge, the certainty that those we care for are a serious responsibility and a form of mirror in which we see ourselves in the future following a similar course. To be with and for others—the message of our text, *The Plague*—is to achieve unity with the rest of the victims of the plagues we all know. This solidarity of both understanding and commitment to the good of others is a gift that we are offered each day in our work and our communities.

FAITH AND ETHICS IN THE TIME OF PLAGUE

This novel by Camus is a superb example of the use of metaphor to describe the human condition. In a sense, we are allowed to choose the plague that besets us in our lives. In the eyes of Camus, there is a certain desolation in finding oneself in the absurd position of being in a situation over which one has no control (genetic and environmental predeterminants). The destruction that we witness in this, the most devastating century in our history, is cause for joining with the victims, seeking unity among all who suffer from loss and pain and death. The multiple social and political diseases that we interpret as plague are sufficient reason to band together for comfort, for mutual support, and perhaps even for a bit of happiness. Camus is very careful to tell us, at the close of the book:

> What we learn in the time of pestilence [is] that there are more things to admire in men than to despise.
> Nonetheless, he [Rieux] knew that the tale he had to tell could not be one of a final victory. It could only be the record of what had had to be done, and what assuredly would have to be done again in the never ending fight against terror and its relentless onslaughts, despite their personal afflictions, by all who, while unable to be saints but refusing to bow down to pestilences, strive their utmost to be healers.[14]

Camus offers a powerful challenge—as does Ivan Karamazov—to any theology that would suggest a loving and creating God who sustains and nourishes the world that we know. Camus calls on us to pay attention to what we see: evil, needless suffering induced by us on others, and a life that ends in death, the ultimate absurdity. There is only one satisfactory response open to us: revolt against the perpetrators of the evil. In this revolt, we shall discover our selves, the core of our being in relation to all others who are victims of the plague.

The Plague has been a reliable foil against which I test my own faith and the ethics of behavior that stem from it. At first viewing, the world, particularly as seen by Rieux and Tarrou, seems desolate and devoid of much that would offer us happiness. The protagonists struggle admirably to stem the plague, often being able to offer no more than their presence when death conquers. This is certainly true of most experience, regardless of the nature of faith that would support action. But the basis of their common efforts is the absurdity of their existence, the nonsensical nature of chance, prejudice, and luck. As I drive the pilings for the building of the self that I am becoming, I need a foundation more supportive in human experience, with a sense of the transcendent, a common root that extends below my idiosyncratic existence to unite me with the source of my being. Certainly the courage, the stamina, and the willingness for sacrifice of the workers against the plague are examples we must all admire, real as they have been in my lifetime. There is, for me, a looking back to others who have been faithful to God despite the plagues of their time. I do not look for reassurance or for easy explanations, but for the driving force of faith that can hold me to an ethic that is sane, supportive, and graced with power. The decision to become a physician was the beginning of a journey toward knowing myself and finding the reasons and the strength to make that journey. Again, a book made its mark.

NOTES

1. David Sprintzen, *Camus: A Critical Examination* (Philadelphia: Temple University Press, 1988), xiv.
2. Albert Camus, *The Rebel* (New York: Vintage Books, 1956), 70.
3. Ibid., 22.
4. Daniel Defoe, "Robinson Crusoe's Preface," in *Serious Reflections During the Life and Surprising Adventures of Robinson Crusoe*, part III (Boston: David Nickerson Company, 1903), xiii (emphasis added).
5. Albert Camus, "Letter to Roland Barthes on *The Plague*," in *Selected Essays and Notebooks*, ed. Philip Thody (New York: Penguin Books, 1970), 220.
6. Albert Camus, *The Plague*, trans. Stuart Gilbert (New York: Vintage Books, 1972), 228.
7. Ibid., 235.
8. Sprintzen, *Camus*, 97.
9. Camus, *The Plague*, 130.
10. Ibid., 195.
11. Fyodor Dostoyevsky, *The Brothers Karamazov*, trans. C. Garnett (New York: Random House, 1933), 254.
12. Albert Maquet, *Albert Camus: The Invincible Summer*, trans. H. Briffault (New York: George Braziller, 1958), 107.
13. Camus, *The Plague*, 270–1.
14. Ibid., 287.

A CALLING

Each Life Converges to some Centre—
Expressed—or still—
Exists in every Human Nature
A Goal

—Emily Dickinson

IT IS WITH SOME hesitancy that I write about a palpable sense that I have been called, at various times, to listen to some word being spoken to me from the depths of my being. I am quite aware of our outrageous history of persecution, crusade, and torture inflicted by those with a similar conviction. No one with any knowledge of the histories of religions, of our search for sociopolitical answers to the sickness in our souls, or of racial and ethnic concepts of purity and superiority can fail to be wary of the words of anyone who speaks of a calling. And yet, I would speak of three episodes in my life when I knew that I was addressed and must pay attention. A gift, a request, a command, a plea: it is hard to say. All I know is that there came to my consciousness a clear feeling of purpose, of commitment, and of relief at knowing, at least for that hour, what direction I was to take. It is easy to use the word *calling* in a superficial way to denote an inclination, or to legitimate what in reality is merely a wish. I use *calling* here as a driving force that tells me that I must be alert to what is happening at this moment in my life.

The *Oxford English Dictionary* lists, as one of the definitions of *calling*, "summons, invitation, or impulse of God to salvation or to his service; the inward feeling or conviction of a divine call; the strong impulse to any course of action as the right thing to do."[1] In my limited experience, I sense the call to be a response to a question confronting me. There is a discontent within me, a restlessness without obvious cause, a feeling that some central change is needed, but I do not know what that change should be. I find the questions to be closely related to my understanding of myself in this world, on this journey that is my life. I am pressed for thought and decision about the very nature of my person, of who I am and shall become. These questions will not let me go; they enter my mind and interrupt my thoughts, demanding answers that I do not seem to have. My reply to these questions is determined, finally, by a period of introspection, prayer, and argument with myself over the evidence I have for the need to act. I use the word *prayer* with some hesitancy. I am not skilled in this work and am distracted by the fall of a pine needle, the slightest sound from the street, a remembered line of a song. But I do try to open my heart to that numinous presence I call God, certain that, in a way I shall recognize, a suggestion, a hint, a shove will occur that will change my life if I allow it. It is confidence in a response that permits the presumption to continue to pray. Of course, the response is often quite unexpected and contrary to what I consider to be to my personal advantage. Fortunately, the sense of credibility, the conviction that change must occur, and the certainty of the direction that it will take build when the heart is open to the profound depths of the eternal, to the transcendent creative being that calls us and engages us. It has been these experiences that have confirmed for me the honest nature of a calling. As I noted earlier, I am aware that this can be an excuse for the most heinous crimes against humanity. However, I am grateful for the moments that I have been given in which insight, purpose, and courage have graced me in these years. There is a strange and immanent power sensed when possibility becomes actuality, and a new chapter of life begins.

Three times of calling that were crucial for me are associated with books. Whether I read them purely by chance at just the right moment, or whether there was some part of my unconscious self that directed me to that type of reading, I will never know. In each instance, these texts offered a new way that I might live what we commonly call life. Freedom and the courage to be and to act were explicit in two; the third revealed the underpinning for my inner life, the hard bottom I sought. These books represent, for me, a progression in my inner life. I could, perhaps more wisely, call the path a descent into my deeper person, a searching for that foundation that would carry the weight of my life. The first book, a popular and romantic-style novel, bolstered my courage to redirect my studies and my professional career. The second, a profound call to a revised and understood life, started me on the search for foundation stones. The third, a searching religious work in the form of a diary, confirmed the source of the stones I needed to support this life and to move into the struggles of the day. My interpretation of these books is not to be understood as necessary for any other person. Instead, they point to an essential process: informed reflection in those hours of redefinition of my self.

THE VALOROUS YEARS

In December 1940 I came home at the end of my first semester at Lehigh University, where I had enrolled as an engineering student. My grade point average was below 2.0, as I recall, and I was despondent. I had no one to talk to about my distress. I, like Camus, had a silent mother who spoke only of practical household matters and the necessity that I achieve success in the world out there. A profoundly withdrawn woman, she would, today, be treated for clinical depression. She was remarkably unresponsive to her only child: I cannot recall her ever kissing me. I had few friends and spent most of my time with my dog or reading, studying, and listening to music. When I returned to my hometown fifty years later for a high school reunion, I left long before the end of the evening. I was terribly saddened by the loneliness, social ineptness, and self-doubts that were recalled by listening to my classmates recount the many hilarious and exciting times they had enjoyed, almost none of which I remember attending. It is no surprise that these feelings haunt me still.

I was a good student in high school and entered college, just having turned seventeen, with advanced placement in three courses. Neither of my parents had attended college, and the counsel I was given was that anyone good in math and science should be an engineer. This proved to be a disaster; I was overwhelmed by advanced physics and chemistry, to say nothing of studying Goethe's *Faust* in German with a scholar. My grades were poor, I was dejected by my limited vision of the work that engineers do, and I was sad for myself. As I think about that childhood, I can remember a time in my early teens when I wanted to be a doctor. Why, I do not know, since I rarely went to see a physician except for injuries or a required examination for camp or sports. I had no working knowledge of medicine or the biological sciences, as do so many students today. I recall the clear conviction of my parents that they could not afford physicians' fees. My mother, carrying her burden of Scottish Presbyterianism, considered illness to be weakness, a penalty for wrongdoing, an errant feeling to be rejected.

During that winter break between semesters, I found a stack of *Good Housekeeping* magazines in the house. In them was A. J. Cronin's novel *The Valorous Years*, serialized from September 1940 through February 1941. Although touted on the cover as even better than *The Citadel*, I believe that it was not published in book form. But no matter; the story of the young man absolutely captured me as I recognized so much of what I thought was me in the hero. When I returned to Lehigh for the spring term, I changed my major to premed. My parents were sharply opposed to my decision and assured me that they could not afford medical school tuition. That term was very difficult for me. I took the chemistry and physics courses I had signed up for and survived, but barely. There were no easier alternatives for those who were not going to be engineers, no "chemistry for poets" courses.

I learned one of the most important lessons of my life that spring of 1941. I was in deep trouble in a physics course on electricity and "borrowed" a term paper from the file that my fraternity maintained for its members who needed help. A few days after turning it in, I had a call from the instructor, who had no difficulty recognizing that it was not my work. In our conversation, he kindly pointed out that that type of behavior was not suited for one who hoped to be a doctor. Dishonesty, even in times of panic, is not acceptable. I then wrote my own paper, was given a B as my final grade for the course, and have never forgotten the lesson. I have also never forgotten the generosity of an instructor who, realizing my feeling of hopelessness, supported me in my despair over my faithlessness and defined and clarified the vital significance of ethical behavior for a frightened boy.

But let me return to the serialized novel I read between those first two difficult semesters. I sat alone in the house and read the six installments of *The Valorous Years*. It is a romantic piece. A poor young Scot, Duncan Stirling, angrily rejects the possibility of a minor job as clerk of the town council, is disowned by his mother, and goes to a university city, where he wins a full scholarship to medical school. By dint of hard work and the support of a skilled surgeon, he becomes renowned as a pathologist and is about to be appointed principal of a major medical research institute. A small-town practitioner who befriended him earlier is seriously injured in an accident and is saved by the devoted care of our hero. Turning down the prestigious academic appointment, the young doctor assumes the country practice, realizing that the care of patients is his real calling; it was pride and the need to prove his skills to the world that drew him to the other work. He marries the country doctor's daughter, whom he discovers he has always loved, and is reconciled with his mother.

The reason I know the story so well is that I reread it recently in bound volumes of *Good Housekeeping* that I found in the New Haven Free Public

Library. I was curious about the power and the significance of this minor novelette for me during those painful months over half a century ago. What the story did for me was press home the need to do what I wanted to do, what I felt "called" to do, although I doubt that I would have thought in those terms then. For probably the first time in my life, I decided to do something that my mother opposed, a major change that my parents told me firmly would not be supported. I returned to college and that difficult semester described earlier, and I became fully engaged in the premedical program in my sophomore year. I was told, as was the young man in the story, not to dream, but to do the practical thing. I do not recall any suggestion that I should—even could—stretch myself to achieve in any area other than schoolwork. The choice of the young man to follow his inclination without regard for support or encouragement was a clear signal to me. I remember the excitement I felt realizing that *I* had made a choice that would, in some way not clear at the time, define who I would be. I certainly had no concept of the varied work that doctors do, nor of the training that they endured. But the idea of helping others who were ill and in need was a sufficient motive for me. I was aware that I was now on a path of my own choice for which I alone would be responsible.

My parents would not have understood the personal experience that I know as a calling. With all those years of Sunday school and Bible study behind me, I did know, and I also knew the source of that call. Many years later I would learn of the work of Carl G. Jung and the role of the unconscious in guiding the self to reach its goals. As a young man, as a persistent seeker within the Christian tradition, I prayed to God for direction in many of the paths I sought. Through many times of doubt, confusion, and arid unbelief, I have continued to do so with a quiet confidence that it will be made known to me what I am to do. The sense of relief and inward confidence that is received from prayer—whatever the individual practice—is an affirming gift that strengthens purpose.

I smile in my rereading of this short novel; there are some parallels in our stories that are surprising and revealing to me. As a poor student, Duncan Stirling worked as a houseboy for the dean of the medical school to support his room and board. I was a V-12 student during World War II, with my tuition and expenses paid by the U.S. Navy. I had been a corpsman at a naval hospital between graduation from Lehigh and starting medical school at Johns Hopkins, so the navy continued to pay my tuition and a small stipend. Since my parents still would not support me, I worked Sundays for the hospital, operating the autoclaves that sterilized surgical equipment and intravenous fluids. My pay was free meals in the employees' cafeteria. The experience was actually a good one in that it gave me confidence in myself while affirming a part of me that I am comfortable with—my working-class background. Like the fictional student, I also had several mentors at Hopkins who were clear examples of the type of physician I hoped to become. Even now, after so many years, I remember them well and recall the depth of their experience, counsel, and kindness.

Another parallel in the two stories of the fictional and the real doctors is the choice of private practice in a small town over an academic career. Duncan Stirling realized, in his attendance upon the injured country doctor, that he would stay there and decline an appointment at the institute. I made a rapid decision to do the same, but for a different reason. My final year of pediatric training was as the first full-time resident in the children's unit at Memorial Hospital in New York during 1950–51. This was followed by two years in the navy, during which time I decided to go back to Memorial Hospital–Sloane-Kettering Institute and applied for a fellowship in pediatric oncology. It was work that I enjoyed, and the field was suddenly producing remarkable results. My expectations were for a career in research and hospital patient care. One morning during my first year, we were on rounds with the chief, who asked our opinions on specific clinical questions. As he went around the room, he addressed all the other fellows by their first names, but me by my last. I had a sudden revelation about myself. I was distressed that he did not know my first name; even worse, I thought that this might be the portent of an unsuccessful career. I had a vision of myself being anxious because I had not been invited to a party or had received some other perceived slight that would make promotion questionable. To advance my career, I might well find myself saying or doing something or being a person that I would find repellent in order to move up the academic ladder. These concerns now seem infantile and foolish, as they were. Yet the mere fact that I had gone through this brief and startling encounter with psychic anxiety, which any other person would have smiled at, was a warning about my own self and its unique need for fulfillment. I decided to go into practice in a small New England town, a decision that was made quickly and wisely. Three decades of practice were challenging, humbling, and affirmation of a special call to serve.

I accept my reading of A. J. Cronin's novella as a call to a different future, a shifting of my focal point of hope and joy to a new image. It was a summons to the work that I would do for many years, work that would define me to myself, to my community, and to all who knew me. If, as I believe, I am determined by the loves and the work that point to my faith in this brief lifetime, then I count my reading of *The Valorous Years* as a calling to a way of life.

WALDEN

Walden is a book to which I have granted the status of scripture. Similar to the Bible, *Walden* is a treatise that I turn to, again and again, in the ongoing search for understanding who I am, where I am going, what I am to do. My experiences with this book are a reflection, like an image in a mirror, of the changes I have made in my life.

My use of the word *scripture* is quite intentional. I read the Bible as a record of a people's profound encounter with God over many generations. The amazing variety in the writing, the exquisite record of personal and communal experiences with an eternal and present creator, and the confidence I know hearing the story confirm my acceptance of the Bible as scripture for my life. A delight in my study of the Bible is the encounter with scholarly criticism and commentary that challenge me with new interpretations of ancient texts. Historical research, linguistic analysis, and archaeological findings keep us awake to the meanings of scripture for understanding the self and the world, just as reading medical journals is essential if one is to remain a competent physician.

My education at Yale Divinity School stressed the need for a developed study of scripture, and I remain grateful for that training, which is an integral part of my professional and personal lives. It holds as well for my study of *Walden* as scripture. Thoreau means every word that he writes. Any reader of his works must always be alert to this fact. One of the major challenges to reading Thoreau is the realization that every word has been chosen with care. Words such as *almost, appear, seem, likely, wish, might*— these are to be evaluated precisely. The hesitancy they suggest is accurate. He expresses in words what he expressed with his life—a search for a faith and the hope that a legitimate self can be brought into being by conscious thought and honest action. In six revisions over ten years, he produced a book that must be studied with diligence for the carefully constructed models and images he uses for our instruction. Because his construct is so deliberate and significant, Thoreau is one of the most critiqued authors in U.S. literature. It is his insistence that I pay attention to his every word that impels my ongoing encounters with this book. I find, as I do with other works that aid in my self-definition, that I must do what the author tells me to do: look to my life and its meaning, and fully assume the responsibility for *my* life.

Walden is a call to regain, to realign, even to begin again. We know well whom the great prophets of Israel address: both the nation and the individual are called to account. The clarion calls are for justice and mercy, for attention to the needy in our midst, for the abandonment of our persistent love of idols and a return to the Lord. We are to know that our hope for salvation lies in understanding reality and in rejecting false gods and inadequate and immature constructs of our created worlds: the one called into being by God; the other our poorly built and transient selves. Using the metaphor of building a house in the woods, Thoreau proclaims two prophetic calls: (1) the desperate need to reclaim the American land for a new settlement, to build a new nation, even a new literature; and (2) the equally serious need for the individual to find the foundation for a reflective, valued, and rich personal life in full accord with nature. Our call to confront the ecological crisis—a frightening and spreading plague—is loud and clear. I discuss this environmental pestilence in a later chapter.

"God himself culminates in the present moment, and will never be more divine in the lapse of all the ages."[2] These urgent words—"the present moment"—interrupt my plans for the future, my long-term goals, with the importance of the immediate act or thought. It is this present moment that is, as Thoreau puts it, "the meeting of two eternities, the past and future."[3] For me, this is the beginning of a calling: who am I now, what am I doing, how are my loves demonstrated this hour? This moment is when I act out the ethical bases of my profession, my relationships, my humanity. I am always amazed at how this conviction informs my life. When Jesus called his early disciples, they dropped what they were doing and followed. I sense a similar calling in *Walden*, that insistence on this moment for decision, for faithful scrutiny of what I am doing and why.

In his repeated use of metaphor and allegory, Thoreau calls me to awaken. There is a new person within me that can be freed to be, truly, a new self. Transformation is a theme that he employs well. The fantastic metamorphosis I see from egg to larva to butterfly is but a model for what is possible for me if I permit my spirit to stretch itself to its limits, whatever they may be. But to do this, I must explore myself, find the hidden sources of what creativity I have, search through the heart and mind for impulses that will be acted out in a faithful ethic. I must examine myself, reflecting steadily on who I am at this moment. Part of this process is the painful rejection of all those prejudices I nurture: the authority of the past, success in the eyes of the world, the role that goods and honors play in living a good life, and the impact of my life on our world. Repeated examination of myself in this natural world will keep me on track as I follow that calling to know who I am. Thoreau makes it clear to me that my ideas of self and others inform and alter the circumstances of my life, not the other way around. I set the pattern for who I will be now and in the future.

To do all this, I must awaken to the dawn of this day. Again, all in metaphor, Thoreau pushes me to examine who I am, what options and hopes are possible—many more than I know—and when I am going to accept the responsibility to become a new man. I sometimes wonder at the phrase *growing old*. It seems to me that one of the gravest risks in the aging process is a shrinking, not a growing. It is a constant struggle to keep awake to this day, to seek the opportunities to serve and to love, and to be a model for what I say I cherish and take delight in. I am but a sojourner, a traveler on this road of life, stopping off now and then for rest, refreshment, and encouragement. For me, these have come in full measure from my encounter with *Walden*.

Several themes developed in *Walden* summarize its function as a calling to me all these years:

1. What I am to, and with, others must be an accurate reflection of my inner life. There should be a certain and available knowledge of who I am when I look in that mirror. If I am to be true to my self, I must know my self as truly as I can. I am called to lead a faithful life.

2. I must steadily search for the point of origin of my being, that moral foundation of my life. Thoreau writes:

> I love to weigh, to settle, to gravitate toward that which most strongly and rightfully attracts me; . . . to travel the only path I can, and that which no power can resist me. It affords me no satisfaction to commence to spring an arch before I have got a solid foundation. . . . There is solid bottom every where.[4]

His search for that base is informed by his conviction that we can find the supports for our life. We will, in this search, "meet with a success unexpected in common hours. [We] will put some things behind, will pass an invisible boundary." Thoreau advises us, "If you have built castles in the air, your work need not be lost; that is where they should be. Now put the foundations under them."[5]

3. With the self-exploration that all this calls forth, I am assured of success, although perhaps not as the world sees success. If I am confident in pursuing my dreams to realize my self, if I am honest in my evaluations of that self and of society, if I live the life I imagine to be possible, I will not be disappointed. Each day will be bring a renewal of the self, a call to witness in life to the faith that supports that life. An ethic of honesty and service can be forged through this call.

Walden is a heroic book that calls me to live a redeemed and rigorously faithful life. Through the intensity of its revelation of who I am, it has deepened my knowledge of myself and who I can become. The call to the spiritual journey inherent in this U.S. scripture is the call to be a sojourner, living each day in confidence and in seasoned hope for union and fulfillment in the grand scheme of nature—our created order. One of his most often quoted lines summarizes the heart of his call to me to attend to my life:

I went to the woods because I wished to live deliberately, to front only the essential facts of life, and see if I could not learn what it had to teach, and not, when I came to die, discover that I had not lived. I did not wish to live what was not life, living is so dear.[6]

THE DIARY OF A COUNTRY PRIEST

A number of years ago, at a wedding reception I attended, the music was provided by a pianist and a vocalist, both blind. They are talented performers of popular music; he is a strong interpreter of classic ragtime music, a particular favorite of mine. As I wandered rather aimlessly around the room, they began playing a song popular at that time, "You Light Up My Life." As I watched and listened, I realized that no one else had caught the amazing paradox: two blind musicians telling us that love can light up a life. What a delightful scene: sightless persons telling us that love enlightens. I try to remember this as I work each day; it is so easy to forget to recall what informs me. I find that it is often the simplest of events that triggers a response. I try to hold to my confidence that, in the mundane events of my life, I am constantly challenged by spiritual questions and urgings of the deepest significance. These challenges are always present to me. It is my unawareness, ignorance, insensitivity, and egotism that cause my blindness. So often I find that I *finally* see what is happening and hear the demand to be and to act. I awaken, as Thoreau might say, to the quiet and insistent call to be alert to the day.

I have presented two experiences of my life that I interpret as callings— callings to alter and focus my life in a different way. Both are intimately associated with reading a text that opened up possibilities for a new way of seeing myself in this world. The third calling that I describe unfolded during a decade, the 1960s. The civil rights movement began during the 1950s and grew slowly as leadership and local organizations appeared. Although I followed and supported the movement, it was the "Mississippi Summer of 1964" that awakened many of us. One of the persons who worked with the students who went South that summer is Robert Coles, a child psychiatrist who has written about his experiences. One article in particular, in the *Saturday Review of Literature*, showed, in children's drawings, the dehumanizing impact of racism on self-image. To a pediatrician, this was important. When I went to Boston in early 1965 for a continuing medical education course at Harvard Medical School, I called Coles. He graciously invited me to come to his home to talk. Joseph Brenner, another psychiatrist from the Massachusetts Institute of Technology, was there, and they told me about their work and their personal experiences with student-activists that previous summer.

In the course of our conversation, Coles suggested that I might want to read a book that is very important to him. He wrote later, "No book has meant more to me than Georges Bernanos's *The Diary of a Country Priest*. I have read it and reread it, and I keep it in front of me on my desk."[7] I, too, have read and reread it; for nearly thirty years, *The Diary* has clarified and redefined my quiet but persistent calling to ministry. This intimate account of the last few months in the life of a young priest serving a poor rural village presents in depth the personal challenges, ambiguities, and self-knowledge I faced in that decade of 1965–75. Limited but determining involvement in both the civil rights and the peace movements led me—literally—to attend divinity school and, finally, to ordination as a minister in the United Church of Christ. In *The Diary*, we hear the older priest in a neighboring village give one explanation of a calling:

> I've thought a lot about the question of vocation. We're all called to the priesthood, I agree, but not always in the same way. So to get things straight, I start off by taking each one of us back where he belongs in Holy Writ. . . . I tell myself that long before we were born—from a "human" point of view—Jesus met us somewhere, in Bethlehem, or perhaps Nazareth, or along the road to Galilee—anywhere. And one day among all the other days, His eyes happened to rest upon you and me and so we were called, each in his own particular way, according to the time, place and circumstance.[8]

To this day, I carry the image of a young man forever coming toward me down a dusty road. There is a certain poignancy in his smile, a distinct question in his eyes: will you follow me? His mission for me is to feed the hungry and heal the sick, knowing full well that the task will not be accomplished in this world, and certainly not by me. But these are the tasks that are so clearly laid before all of us by him. A question that the priest asks himself is mine also: "Am I where Our Lord would have me?"[9]

But I need to go back and look at steps along the way, the several themes in *The Diary* that recount the depth and the intention of this third calling. It is the calling that reveals the faith, and the faith that frames an ethic of living in this world.

Youth. Not to experience youth is a sad loss. To enter so early the world of competition, with its need to excel, and the adult world, having neither the opportunity nor the stimulus to develop an imagination, is a crippling event for a developed life. Friendships, bonds of shared hopes and dreams, and an opportunity to talk endlessly about the terrors of adolescence are experiences I did not know. As the priest writes in his diary:

> My youth had passed me by, as many strangers pass so closely who might have become brothers, yet disappear for ever. I was never young because

I never dared be young. Around me, no doubt, life went on and my companions knew and tasted that wondrous bitter spring, whilst I tried not to
think of it and drugged myself with work.[10]

I look back with sadness to a loss I did not—could not—recognize at the
time. So much time spent alone took their toll—all those hours and years
spent with my dog walking the woods, reading both nature and books, and
waiting. Almost every aspect of my life was intellectualized so that I might
have some control over my immediate environment. Feelings are something I seemed not to have. Only in the past ten years have I even attempted to speak of things of the heart and soul with others, and still with
some difficulty. We need assistance in growing up and sensing the wide
world of which we are a part. One of the fascinations of Bernanos's work is
that his memory of childhood is so different from mine. I find his work
instructive for the very reason that his use of childhood—the opposite of
the priest's experiences—forces my steady revaluation of my own. As William
Bush writes:

> Regardless of where Bernanos begins . . . he invariably causes his crea-
> tures to look back to their childhood, as it were, to provide the needed
> balance to the destructive drama of daily existence as the author pushes
> them toward death. . . . [I]n the search for childhood man reveals both his
> present misery and his past—and future—glory, that lost glory which was
> once his in the first garden and which has been restored to him through
> the agony of Christ in another garden.[11]

For me, the calling has been away from my childhood and toward a life
lived with and for others: a steady growing away from dependence and the
sad need to try to please one who would not be pleased.

Faith. The search for a faithful life has been a long one, going back to that
lonely childhood. There has been a thread through my life, a calling to a
way of understanding myself, my work, and my world that I am confident
to label faithful. And I place this conviction firmly in my lifetime effort to
incorporate the biblical narrative of the struggle to learn the ways of God.
From those early Sunday school teachers and local pastors, through divinity
school, to present studies, the place of Jesus in my confidence in the reality
of God in this created order remains a constant source of question and reflection.
From Christmas stories to resurrection accounts, from ministry to the poor
to healing of the sick, this revealed and revealing life has drawn me to
question, to affirm, to witness, and to dare to believe the insistence of the
demand to follow him who calls me—Jesus of Nazareth. Faith is difficult to
describe. For me, it is the foundation upon which I build my life, a covenant
with a living God that sustains me when my abilities to cope with daily

trials are so obviously inadequate. For me, also, this covenant is established in and upon the life of a man, Jesus, who died twenty centuries ago after living a brief life in utter confidence in the God to whom he pointed. His teaching and his witness to a faithful life give me hope that I may be one who can be a follower, weak, selfish, and proud though I may be. I am joyfully aware that there are many religious faiths confessed by us as human beings, known to us at different times, in different places, and by varied names as revelations of a creative and redeeming spirit. There is an underlying belief that supports that faith and adjusts to the passage of time, to life experiences, to study, and to the deepening understanding that comes from prayer.

Faith and prayer. I accept my faith as a gift. It took me a while to realize that it was so freely given: it was mine, of course, before I knew that it existed. Faith is not an intellectual accomplishment, although thought and educated study enrich and modify the very nature of grace. I accept my faith as a child would a gift, yet I find it my responsibility to nurture it so that it can grow. As an avid gardener and a pediatrician, I appreciate the factors that make for sturdy and productive growth: an accepting soil, sunshine, nutrients, and water. These have their equivalents in the requirements of a maturing faith.

The struggle for me is to keep the reality of my faith in God alive in my thoughts and my actions. There are many distracting experiences that daily set that faith aside from the center of my consciousness. I do not lose my faith; I simply let it slip away for the moment. The priest in *The Diary*, writing about his own faith, says, "Faith is not a thing which one 'loses,' we merely cease to shape our lives by it.... An educated man may come by degrees to tuck away his faith in some back corner of his brain, where he can find it again on reflection, by an effort of memory." Noting that devastating events can induce despair and resignation, he still can say, "but my faith is still whole, for I can feel it. I cannot reach it now; I can find it neither in my poor mind, unable to link two ideas correctly, nor in my sensibility, nor yet in my conscience."[12] This faith is the grounding of my being, the foundation upon which I struggle to build my self-centered self, that transient dreamer who hopes for peace and justice, for grace and salvation. And it is faith that supports those hopes for the things unseen, the realities and the wonders of an existence that shine, often dimly, through the evidence of those deadly sins that are such a part of my day-to-day life.

Of course, this faith neither originates in me nor is it upheld by any effort of mine. As grace, as a gratuity from the God who brings all into being, I search for the connection to its source that will keep it alive, help it grow and ripen, presenting me with its fruits of peace and acceptance. The avenue to this source, to the God who has graced me with my life and its richness, is prayer. There is only one problem for me with prayer: I am not at all sure that what I am doing can be called by that name. I have read a number of books on prayer that detail the techniques, the goals, the deep spirituality, and the final peace that it encompasses; the experiences of a Trappist or Buddhist monk have certainly not been mine. It takes so little to distract me, no matter how desperate I may be for the focused introspection I imagine true prayer to be. The slightest stimulus from my immediate environment, the silliest thought, or the most insignificant bodily itch can effectively interrupt my efforts. But I am confident that prayer links me with that ubiquitous power, that profound depth of unconscious reality, that endless source of creative energy that I call God. The priest in *The Diary* says, at a time of near despair, "I know, of course, that the wish to pray is a prayer in itself, that God can ask no more than that of us." He continues:

> The usual notion of prayer is absurd. How can those who know nothing about it, who pray little or not at all, dare speak so frivolously of prayer? . . . If it were really what they suppose, a kind of chatter, the dialogue of a madman with his shadow, or even less—a vain and superstitious sort of petition to be given the good things of this world, how could innumerable people find until their dying day . . . sheer, robust, vigorous, abundant joy in prayer?

Prayer shows us more and more of the complexity of our lives and cannot be easily dismissed. "[W]hen has any man of prayer told us that prayer failed him?"[13]

I continue to pray in the hope that I will slowly learn its depth and find that center, that foundation in reality, that I know is there. I continue to pray for enlightenment, knowing how easily reason and thought are able to obscure, to hide in the shadows, those parts of me and my desires that I prefer not to acknowledge. Prayer is one of the keys that opens doors to understanding myself, revealing who I am and the effects of my choices on my future.

Social and political issues. The years 1954–75 were a period of clarification for me as I watched the turmoil over civil rights and the war in Southeast Asia spread across the country. The 1954 Supreme Court decision in *Brown v. Board of Education*, the bus strike in Montgomery in 1955, and the forced federal integration of school in Little Rock in 1957 awakened us to a reality that many had ignored, to the peril of others. Growing discomfort with the ways of government, the starkness of the antagonism to desegregation in the South, and the responses to the Freedom Riders forced our eyes open to what was happening. The divisive force of the conflicts was powerful, and I was compelled to decide who I would be by my hopes for the future of the United States. There was a close association in my mind and heart between my religious faith and actions of mine that would define who I was in those days of conflict. In our small New England town, the churches became places where these issues took on faithful overtones, where political anxiety, prejudice, and religious conviction suddenly became issues to be faced in ways not done before. As did many others, our town experienced confrontation, anger, and harsh words that would take years to resolve. A new and revealing age began. The year 1965 was one of those landmark years in my life. My reading of the experiences of those who took part in the Mississippi Summer of 1964 presented a challenge to be answered. Either I would take part in this evolving social and political contest, or I would not. Either choice would define me to myself forever. It was an opportunity, a gift that I would deny to my peril. As with my faith, there was no in-between position: I believed or I did not; I would commit myself or I would not. It would take another decade to reveal the intensity of racism and poverty in the North as well as the South, a lesson we learned from black activists.

In 1966, under the auspices of the Medical Committee for Human Rights, I joined a team from Tuskegee Institute that did a study—demographic and medical—of Lowndes County, Alabama. I was the physician for the group and examined some eight hundred children as part of the study. The findings were to be expected: lack of medical care, only one child wearing glasses, and evidence of serious accidents common to farming families. One finding that embodied the others was anemia. When I returned to my practice, I plotted the comparable hemoglobin results in the same number of consecutive children in my practice against those found in Lowndes. The bell curves of the two groups were distressingly different, that of the black children being much lower. These findings, in conjunction with the experience of living on Black Belt Road off Route 80 between Selma and Montgomery, determined part of my work for the next five years.

In 1967 the Field Foundation sent six doctors to Mississippi to evaluate the possibility of funding preschool education for black children. We were confronted, quite unexpectedly, by hungry children. Our alarm at this finding prompted a paper, "Hungry Children in Mississippi," and, that July, testimony before a Senate subcommittee cochaired by Senators Robert Kennedy and Joseph Clark. In its way, this initiated the War on Hunger, subsequent changes in food stamp policies, and other federal programs to alleviate hunger. I did some further work for the Field Foundation over the next few years, but the escalation of the war in Vietnam became the major issue. Also, growing pressure by black activists on the white population to focus on problems in northern cities helped reorient our activism to problems we had at home.

These activities in the two major movements of those years pushed me in a direction I had not intended. As I watched the political, economic, psychological, and sociological experts define the problems and outline the solutions to them, I became disenchanted. I found that intellectual foundations for change did not provide the foundation that I needed to sustain me. More and more I looked to my faith as a source for understanding who I was in these struggles and what were the reasons for my actions. In this questioning, I found, of course, that I was lacking in knowledge of my faith, its roots in the past, and its demands on the present. In part as a response to the immediate challenges, but also as a blossoming of a lifetime of longing for a deeper faith, I entered Yale Divinity School as a part-time student in 1972. My experiences there were revealing and instructive. Thanks to advisers and tutors, I was helped to realize the astounding fact that I was being called to be an ordained minister. I had no idea how this would occur, but I knew that it was inevitable. I have thought about this in depth over the years and remain convinced that there was a true calling that I sensed, an insistence on moving closer to Jesus as he calls us to follow him in our lives and loves. I needed to move from the crowd milling around him as he teaches, acts, and questions to a place nearer those disciples called by him to follow, as best as one can.

COMMENTARY

In 1982 I retired from my pediatric practice after twenty-eight years of demanding, rewarding, and exciting work to become chaplain at the Yale University School of Medicine. This move was made with a strong sense of fulfillment for me. I had been ordained in 1979 when called to be assistant pastor in my local church. One of the more memorable parts of that service was the moment when each ordained minister present came forward and laid a hand on my head as I knelt there, a symbol of the call, my entry into the ministry. Their touch was so light; my memory carried me back forty years when the elders did the same thing when I joined the church. I was filled with a sweet sense of arriving home, of having gotten to one of the destinations I had sought for many years.

The thread of the call to faith in the fabric of my life remains a palpable reality to me. From those early Sunday school days, through college and medical school, I have always sought a church, a pastor, a conversation about the direction of my inner life. My faith has been refueled many times during these years, most often by some event that refreshes the sense of calling so central to me. Certainly one of the strongest affirmations I have ever had of my need to struggle to be faithful was the work during those troubled years of 1960–75. The priest in *The Diary* places profound trust in his relations with the peasantry, with their lusts, their greed, their despair, and their hope of redemption. This ability to identify with others, although achieved only partially by me, is my gift from my work over the years. The transiency of my life and its accomplishments and the futility of much of my striving for personal recognition, if compared to the richness of loves, friendships, and work, are as dust.

I have described three times in my life when I was alert to a call to change, to grow, to listen. In increasing intensity they drew me to see myself and my life differently. Who knows how many calls are not heard because the static is so strong? I am grateful for having heard them and for having the courage to respond as best as I could. The need to know myself and my foundations was demanded by Thoreau as he drew me into an intense scrutiny of who I am in this world. The call to the ministry, coming out of my limited work for civil rights and peace, was grace indeed. I have had the opportunity to learn something of life and to study my heart and my ways.

The priest, as uneasy with himself as I am, wrote in his diary:

> How little we know what a human life really is—even our own. To judge us by our actions is probably as futile as to judge us by our dreams. God's justice chooses from this dark conglomeration of thought and act, and that which is raised toward the Father shines with a sudden burst of light, displayed in glory like a sun.[14]

I live in the confidence that grace abounds in my world, that God's gifts to us are many and rich. I am also acutely aware of the suffering and the misery everywhere, the powerlessness of many to control their lives, and the reality that evil is ubiquitous. This century has witnessed acts and intentions that are unqualified evils. Bernanos wrote *The Diary* when totalitarianism was spreading through Europe. The fascist power of Germany and Italy supported the victory of Franco, whose murderous policies were witnessed by Bernanos. His strong Roman Catholic faith was certainly refined by what he knew about the events of the first four decades of our violent century. The horrors of Nazism and fascism are frightening milestones in our treatment of one another as persons. I look next at the roles that faith plays in understanding these evils and to an ethic that determines my responses to them.

NOTES

1. *The Compact Edition of the Oxford English Dictionary* (Oxford: Oxford University Press, 1971), s.v. "calling."

2. Henry David Thoreau, *Walden*, ed. J. Lyndon Shanley (Princeton, NJ: Princeton University Press, 1971), 97.
3. Ibid., 17.
4. Ibid., 330.
5. Ibid., 323–4.
6. Ibid., 90.
7. Robert Coles, "Bernanos's *Diary*: A Country Priest as Everyman" [1968], in *A Robert Coles Omnibus* (Iowa City: University of Iowa Press, 1993), 133.
8. Georges Bernanos, *The Diary of a Country Priest* (New York: Macmillan Paperbacks Edition, 1962), 176.
9. Ibid., 76.
10. Ibid., 203.
11. William Bush, *Georges Bernanos* (New York: Twayne Publishers, 1969), 61.
12. Bernanos, *Diary of a Country Priest*, 109.
13. Ibid., 93–4.
14. Ibid., 80.

Chapter 4

Four

IN THE TIME OF THE
SILENCE OF GOD

Can faith resist meaninglessness? Is there
a kind of faith which can exist together
with doubt and meaninglessness?

—Paul Tillich, *The Courage to Be*

TILLICH'S QUESTION—IS IT possible to believe in God in this century
of doubt and loss of meaning?—is central to a serious study of the role that
faith plays in the development of an ethic of personal behavior. No other
era in Western history compares to the twentieth century in its challenges to
the classic Judeo-Christian model of God confessed as the creator of all that
is and characterized by the qualities of absolute love, power, and presence
in the world. If we add to these basic tenets of belief our conviction that
God has chosen a specific people as partners in a covenant, the concept of
God active in history is terrifying even to imagine. Theodicy—the justice of
God—is an overriding concern for believers in a biblical God. If we believe
that God is active in history, even controlling of it, these years challenge
our credence in that God. A century that witnessed 100 million deaths from
war, annihilation of political enemies, and the Holocaust provides a span of

human existence that presents the clearest possible assault on an orthodox understanding of the God known to us through the Torah, the prophets, and the Gospels. Perhaps the only theological lesson possible is the terrifying reality of a silent God absent from human affairs. To Jew and Christian confident in a covenant relationship with God, this is a threatening thought. Is it our behavior that isolates us from God? Is Isaiah speaking to my life and time when he announces, "See, the LORD's hand is not too short to save, nor his ear too dull to hear. Rather, your iniquities have been barriers between you and your God, and your sins have hidden his face from you so that he does not hear."[1] I ask the question, but I cannot explain the events of our time in a way that would satisfy a theologian. What I do is trace my own development during these years as one example of faith changing with experience, and a personal ethic derivative of it.

As a high school student, an only child in a family that I do not recall as being concerned about world affairs, I did not grasp the significance of the rise of Nazism in Europe. I knew little of the aftermath of World War I: its deadly conflicts between Communists and the emerging National Socialist Party in Germany and the collapse of the Weimar Republic. I suspect that the usual anxieties and concerns of adolescence effectively limited my awareness of the events in Europe. In the winter of 1938–39 I read a short story that opened my eyes and my heart.

ADDRESS UNKNOWN

In the fall 1938 issue of *Story*, I read a short story, "Address Unknown," by Kressmann Taylor. It is a collection of fictional letters written by Max, the Jewish owner of an art gallery in San Francisco, to his partner Martin, a German who returned to Germany in 1932. The affectionate correspondence includes mention of Max's sister Giselle, an actress who is in a play in Vienna. In 1933, Max asks, "Who is this Adolph Hitler who seems rising toward power in Germany?"[2] Martin replies with comments about the rise of nationalism, the surge of power that the people are beginning to feel, and the hope that is stirring for a strong nation. Martin, a banker, becomes an official in the new regime, and his family rises in social standing. Censorship of mail begins, and Martin says that he cannot correspond with a Jew. Giselle goes to Berlin to be in a play and is attacked and killed by Nazis as she approaches the house of Martin, who refuses to help her. When Max learns of his sister's fate, Martin's abandonment of her, and his support of the rampant anti-Semitism, he begins a series of letters to Martin that appear to be in a code and suggest persons and activities that are supportive of the Jews. Despite frantic pleas from Martin to stop, the letters continue. The final letter we read is dated March 3, 1934, and closes with a blessing by

Max: "The God of Moses be at your right hand."[3] The last entry in the short story is Max's letter returned to San Francisco stamped "Addressant unbekannt."

I recognized the anti-Semitism that was so apparent in the story but did not understand it. The small town where I lived had, as I recall, only a few Jewish families. I knew only one that owned a clothing store. To offer some idea of the isolation of my hometown from the hidden social plagues of the day, the first African American family moved to town twenty years after I graduated from medical school. But the story not only spoke of the obvious terror visited upon the Jews for being Jews but also showed the depth of the malevolence in the treatment of a "good" German and his disappearance into a concentration camp. This story remains a spur to my conscience: I carry the memory of it, grateful for that simple and powerful introduction to a persistent plague.

But there is an impressive difference between recognizing and decrying the social and personal destruction of a plague of human origin such as anti-Semitism, and interpreting and incorporating its significance for one's philosophical and theological understanding of self, world, and God. In my case, twenty years would pass devoted to education, professional training, starting a family, and beginning a medical practice, again, in a small town. Entering divinity school in 1972 initiated study and search for the significance of the Holocaust for me and for my faith. Several major questions surfaced as I struggled with what I was learning. Questions about faith and behavior, God and covenant, the meanings of the Gospels and the life and death of Jesus—all these were, and continue to be, sharply focused by what happened in Europe in my lifetime. The two world wars brought massive destruction of life, natural resources, and property to many parts of the world, East and West. But this has been a sad characteristic of human existence throughout recorded history. Defiling, killing, and destroying are defining features of our interactions with one another and with the rest of the world, animate and inanimate. The world history that I was taught emphasized wars, victories and defeats, treaties, political documents, empires, and the persons—mostly men—who accomplished the devastations. There was precious little about the artists, the peacemakers, and the lovers of this earth who nurtured and encouraged peace and that sense of oneness with the only world we know, which may be our only hope for survival.

THE HOLOCAUST

Only with a profound feeling of humility can I begin to consider the meaning of the Holocaust for me and my faith. What survivors tell me is understood only at a distance, and vicariously. And yet I must try to understand if I am to continue to study and interpret my life in this world. This unique event in our history teaches lessons that are stark and terrifying when we witness our potential for condemning others to hell on this earth. My study of writers who experienced the death camps and Jewish and Christian theologians who write of the agonies of doubt is a powerful determinant of the nature and the ongoing development of my faith. This study has forced me to confront the questions that have been asked for millennia about the existence, actions, and nature of deity. For a person of faith, there is no escape from this encounter in this century. Carl Jung, in *Answer to Job*, places his study in the context of the horrors of these years:

> We have experienced things so unheard of and so staggering that the question of whether such things are in any way reconcilable with the idea of a good God has become burningly topical. It is no longer a problem for experts in theological seminaries, but a universal religious nightmare.[4]

The coexistence of a loving God and the Holocaust is a paradox that will not go away; every faithful person lives with it. Richard L. Rubenstein states the question this way:

> Given the classical theological positions of both Judaism and Christianity, the fundamental question posed by the Holocaust is not whether the existence of a just, omnipotent God can be reconciled with radical evil. That is a philosophical question. The religious question is the following: *Did God use Adolph Hitler and the Nazis as his agents to inflict terrible sufferings and death upon six million Jews, including more than one million children?*[5]

My term paper for the Old Testament survey course at divinity school in 1973 was on Jeremiah, and in preparation for it, I read Rubenstein's book *After Auschwitz*, published in 1966. I knew what the Germans had done in the death camps—I had seen the British documentary that was required viewing in the United Kingdom after the war—but I had not thought through to the limits of my reason the implications of the Holocaust for faith in God. Certainly I had not argued through in my mind the question of the possibility of the "death of God." A corollary and sad question arises about the limits of the power of knowledge to influence behavior when one realizes that the outstanding scholarship in biblical studies—particularly in the New Testament—in the nineteenth and twentieth centuries was done in Germany, a country that prided itself on its accomplishments in the arts and the sciences. The Germans used scientific and administrative skills with expertise and economy in their attempted extermination of Jews, Gypsies, Slavs, homosexuals, the retarded, and the insane. All this was put into place with almost no objections from churches, governments, or individuals. My new learning clarified the "death of God theologies" of the late 1960s, which took on painful meaning for me as a divinity student learning the perplexities and the ambiguities of religious faith—in particular, my own. Of course, this awakening was exactly the hope that I had held for myself as I began my studies. Thoreau's call to be alert to the dawn that occurs in each moment affirms his belief that "Moral reform is the effort to throw off sleep,"[6] and I knew that I needed to be awakened. However, I had not expected to be shaken awake with such vigor. The Holocaust literature began a radically new phase in my personal journey of faith.

For any person who questions the bases of religious belief, regardless of which religion, denomination, or sect claims our allegiance, the Holocaust is *the* challenge to that belief. Religion was a dominant factor in determining the conditions and the rules under which the annihilation of European Jews was attempted by the Nazis. Twisted and corrupted as it was, the ideology supporting the final solution to the Jewish problem had its foundation in the Christian and Jewish religions. The ancient understanding of the covenant relationship between God and Israel and the living hope of Israel in a Messiah who will come and bring peace and justice in our world are beliefs that set a specific people aside from others. The Christian conviction that the Messiah has come in the person of Jesus and that the new church is now the chosen partner in the covenant with God established an antagonism that has never abated. In fact, the Roman Catholic Church's decision to officially remove its condemnation of the Jews as the killers of Christ was made only a few years ago. So the Germans appropriated the perennial religious anti-Semitism of Europe to their advantage as they constructed their program to eliminate Jews. In the words of a philosopher, Rubenstein writes:

> Religion was not a sufficient condition for the Holocaust, but it was a necessary one. What happened at Auschwitz is inconceivable without beliefs about God held first by Jews and then by Christians. For many who live after Auschwitz, however, it is God, not genocide, that is inconceivable. At the very least, the Holocaust makes both Jewish and Christian religious affirmations more difficult and problematic than they were before.[7]

The history of Hitler's emergence as dictator of Germany is fascinating and is required reading for anyone trying to understand the evil of those decades of the Nazis' rise to power. It is well documented in many sources, and I will not repeat it. Suffice it to say that the Germans were able to accomplish the killing of millions, including infants and children, totally within the law of the land. Medical experimentation, sterilization, and, finally, the gas chambers are the legacy of those years. One fact must be kept constantly in mind: the killing was done by citizens who knew and believed in what they were doing. Resistance to the destruction was rare, even in subjugated countries. The role of the French police in rounding up Jews for export is well known and is shameful in comparison with the responses of Scandinavians to German pressure for cooperation.

Anti-Semitism demands a response from any person who confesses a faith in God. For two thousand years the Jews have been persecuted for a number of reasons. They have been seen as a people without a country but with close and binding ties to one another that transcend the social and political environment in which they live. Their conviction is that a covenant relationship with God established them from earliest days as a people chosen by God to bring peace and justice to this world through obedience to laws handed down at Sinai and recalled in their history. The epitome of anti-Semitism is the long history of persecution as the people who killed the Christ. The Jews' refusal to recognize that a new covenant had been established after the death and resurrection of Jesus made them logical and recognizable subjects of defamation and vilification. The consequences were exclusion from professions, public office, and the military and denial of freedom to choose where to live and with whom. The history of the treatment of Jews by most of the nations in Europe is frightening. This plague of anti-Semitism is the most damning accusation that can be laid on Christianity, Western and Orthodox alike. Although I cannot literally know the incredible horror of the suffering of the European Jews in my time, I do attempt to understand, as best I can, the *Shoah* by reading and studying Elie Wiesel's *Night*. This short autobiographical work, published in English in 1960, is a wrenching description of life and death in the concentration camps. It was my baptism into terror—vicariously, of course—and my introduction to the experiences of another person that altered my understanding of plague forever, even as it continues to question the foundations of my faith.

NIGHT

Irving Abrahamson, in his introduction to a three-volume collection of Wiesel's lectures and selected writings, presents a succinct notation on Wiesel:

> For Wiesel, the deepest mystery of the Holocaust lies hidden in its religious implications: "The magnitude of the catastrophe, the absurdity of the tragedy, the silence of the world, the responsibility of the accomplices, the very fact that it could have happened, and the very fact that it could have been avoided—all these elements make it into a mystery, almost a religious mystery, with theological implications."[8]

Although I know the experiences of the victims of the Holocaust only through literature, it is imperative that I think through their implications for my faith and the source of that faith. I am alert to Wiesel's warning that we cannot talk about God. This provides a sense of relief when one is confronted by the almost infinite number of theological tomes that interpret and describe God for us. Also, any "theology of the Holocaust" is a farce; there is no explaining it in religious terms. Granted, this century has birthed a variety of attempts to explain the coexistence of a God of love and justice and the horrors we have observed and shared. But we would be wise to heed Wiesel's learned advice:

> I am reluctant to speak about God because no one should and no one can; when we do, inevitably we distort the idea and the concept of God. The injunction "You should make no image of God" includes "in words." It is better not to speak about God.[9]

Moche the Beadle, of the synagogue in Wiesel's small town of Sighet, was an early instructor for him in the need to question God:

> Man raises himself toward God by the questions he asks Him. . . . Man questions God and God answers. But we don't understand His answers. We can't understand them. Because they come from the depths of the soul, and they stay there until death. You will find the true answers, Eliezer, only within yourself.[10]

We are, however, required to educate ourselves to ask faithful questions in an attempt to find the correct ones that will support our faith in spite of experiences that counter it. The overwhelmingly present question to the reader of *Night* is the one that Wiesel asks repeatedly: where was God? Of course, as Moche tells us, there is no answer now.

As a reader, one is stunned by the horror of what happened to the prisoners in Auschwitz. It is impossible to even surmise what our response would be to seeing children thrown into the fire, as did the adolescent Wiesel. I shudder when I read one of the most searing pieces of writing I have encountered, the moment when Wiesel was facing the Angel of Death:

> Never shall I forget that night, the first night in camp, which has turned my life into one long night, seven times cursed and seven times sealed. Never shall I forget that smoke. Never shall I forget the little faces of the children, whose bodies I saw turned into wreaths of smoke beneath a silent blue sky.
> Never shall I forget those flames which consumed my faith forever.
> Never shall I forget that nocturnal silence which deprived me, for all eternity, of the desire to live. Never shall I forget those moments which murdered my God and my soul and turned my dreams to dust. Never shall I forget these things, even if I am condemned to live as long as God Himself. Never.[11]

I am struck dumb by this terrifying account. There is nothing to be said to relieve, to succor, to explain, to justify, to incorporate that experience.

But this is exactly what Wiesel tells us, in all his writings, we are *not* to do—remain silent. We all must learn from this moment of history that the Holocaust was a human act, the logical finale to a program of extinction directed at a specific portion of humanity united by a faith in God and committed to living out the commands of that God. The Holocaust was a human accomplishment. As a member of this human species, I must confirm my commitment to ensure that this will never happen again. One way to assist myself in this task is to fully acknowledge my identity with a long history that defines me through my own faith. I stand this day at a point in history preceded by so many shadows of persons who believed, who lived a life of faith and confidence and sacrifice, defining themselves by that community. And that community can be known through our history, through our faith, through our lives. Wiesel, speaking to teachers, says:

> No matter what we do, we must go back to the source. . . . You cannot see forward, you can only see backward. In going back to the beginning we find a kind of justification in our quest for life and survival. . . . [W]hatever we do, we must identify with our past. . . . That means that we are older than we seem. We are all part of a great memory, and we are responsible for that memory.[12]

Although Wiesel was speaking to persons of one faith, the warning applies to all who accept responsibility for being a human being on our earth. I look back to my inheritance as a collection of persons whom I accept as my ancestors. I have chosen them as my forebears and will live my life according to the promises I have in common with them. In matters of living a faithful life, I look to the past, to those who lived and died in a faith that I accept as my own. My parents are my biological predecessors, but I live my life according to the teachings and the examples of other preceptors. I cannot know now whether the foundation of the life I am living is as firmly based as I hope it to be. But there remains the imperative of Thoreau to push downward to as certain a base as I can find to support my life. There has been no Holocaust in my personal life to present that challenge, no experience like that first night in the camp after which Wiesel became an entirely different person. "The student of the Talmud, the child that I was, had been consumed in the flames. There remained only a shape that looked like me. A dark flame had entered into my soul and devoured it."[13] This is a conversion experience that most of us would decline.

Thinking through the implications of the Holocaust for those who believe in a biblical God raises questions, most of which strike at the very heart of faith. For a nonbeliever, the events of this century—indeed, of all human history—are actions derived from a mixture of fortuitous psychological, social, genetic, geographic, and many other factors; there is no goal for human history, either personal or as a species. As Ivan Karamazov says, "If there is no God, anything is permitted."[14] For a believer in the God of the Bible, however, our history is a tortured and sad story of painful separation from a happiness that could be ours if our acts showed forth our stated faith. Since I have little working knowledge of the many other religions that we human beings confirm, I cannot speak of them. But I do know that the characteristics of the biblical God, discussed earlier, are called into severe question by the Holocaust. Can any traditional belief in a just and loving God possibly withstand the death of millions of people committed to a faith that extols and worships that God? The overwhelming amount of gratuitous evil calls that God to the witness stand.

Two religious explanations are often offered to explain the Holocaust. First, in accordance with a long history of biblical exegesis in the rabbinic tradition, the tragedy is explained as punishment for the sins of the people in disobeying the laws given to Israel in the Torah. As Wiesel says, the Holocaust is "the other face of Sinai."[15] This is an ancient and traditional understanding of the persecution of the Jews. The sins of the people will be accounted for by the suffering of many. The second explanation of the Holocaust is an observation that has been made from time immemorial: the innocent suffer gratuitous evil at the hands of others without any reason at all. They are not being punished; they are merely in the wrong place at the wrong time, sacrifices at the hands of evildoers. It is sad, but that is the way the world is. The suffering servant presented by Isaiah, read as both the people of Israel and the person of Jesus, is a fitting illustration of this type of sacrifice, known so well to Jew and Christian. If, as Wiesel says, after the Holocaust we cannot speak about God but only to Him, what are we to say to one another about our condition? If we cannot know the ways and the purposes of God, we are condemned to suffer evil at the hands of others with neither hope nor courage. However, if—as so many believe—we live in a time of the silence of God, we can speak only to God and join with one another to stand against those evils we know. The devastations we witness are done at our hands. We shall not know why innocence is destroyed, why pain and suffering are ours to bear without explanation. The face of God, if such there be, is turned away.

JOB

The story of Job may well be the most demanding and challenging book in the Hebrew Bible. The narrative is well known and is the subject of innumerable commentaries dating back a millennium. The story begins with an ancient Middle Eastern legend about a virtuous and wealthy man whose faith is exemplary. The virtue of Job makes him a man of whom the King of Kings is proud. At a council meeting in heaven, Satan, a son of God, suggests that the piety of Job may simply be due to the generous gifts bestowed upon him. This God grants a wager in allowing Satan to test the faith of Job—without his knowledge—by a series of undeserved catastrophes: his children die, all his goods and flocks are destroyed, and he is afflicted with horrid diseases.

The profound arguments about good and evil and the nature of a just God begin when Job's friends visit him in his desolation and offer varied reasons for his trials. These include assurances that all will end well, that Job is suffering for sins he does not acknowledge, and that God is just in his dealing with us. In one of the most profound presentations of outrage against the immorality of our world, Job builds an astounding series of accusations against an *unjust* God. Job calls upon God to explain his pain and loss, defends his innocence, and asks for an arbitrator who will settle this dispute. Throughout his protestations of innocence, his questioning of the ways of God, and his demand for an explanation, his faith does not falter. Job refuses to believe the arguments of his supposed friends who deliver platitudes out of their own narrow faith. In the summation of his argument, Job "has become," according to Stephen Mitchell, "Everyman, grieving for all of human misery. He suffers not only his own personal pain, but the pain of all the poor and despised. He is himself afflicted by what God has done to the least of these little ones."[16]

In the concluding segment of the poem, the voice out of the whirlwind does not answer the pleadings of Job but questions him about his daring to interrogate the creator about things that no person can know or understand. Since this is a fiction—a story—and most of us do not hear voices, I suggest that Job has been alert to his own inner self. He has attended to his spirit and been informed of his temerity in questioning God and the things he cannot know. In any case, the view we are given is of a universe not comprehensible to the human mind. There is no moral or immoral God, no justice as we would see it. Before we were created, the world existed, and the experiences we have are what it means to be a person in the created order. There is no good or evil in the universe. As Mitchell writes, *"What is all this foolish chatter about good and evil*, the Voice says, *about battles between a hero-god and some cosmic opponent? Don't you understand that there is no one else in here?"*[17]

The result of this confrontation by the voice is Job's acknowledgment of the greatness of God, a creator who brought all into being and through whom all lives and dies. What we interpret as good and evil are examples of what it means to live. Suffering and pain, destitution and disaster, are examples of the driving force of the creator working in ways that we are not to comprehend. Good and evil, as we see them, are merely our understanding of the ongoing process of life and death. We are dust, and to that dust we shall return. The justice of God is not our justice; it is beyond our knowledge. God asks Job, "Will you even put me in the wrong? Will you condemn me that you may be justified?"[18] In a prose epilogue, we return to the flat and passive style of the prologue. God restores family, property, and health to Job; chastises his friends for their assumptions about punishment for evil; and compliments Job for understanding that good actions are not rewarded.

The issues raised by this gripping narrative are central to any discussion of faith within the defining limits of Jewish and Christian thought. The writer is, according to some critics, the epitome of a devout Israelite; for others, he is a Gentile from another country, perhaps Edom, Egypt, or another nation in the south. The suffering of Job with the direct permission of God has been condemned, justified, rationalized, and accepted as beyond mortal understanding. The nature of God has also been subject to the widest possible definitions, ranging from all-loving to vindictive, from uncaring to absent, from suffering with Job to ignoring his plight. This biblical account, highly praised throughout the ages for its beautiful poetry and poignant depiction of the struggles of a good person, remains an enigma to many. The intense drama of Job is, therefore, a logical but complex and complicated opportunity to understand the meaning of the Holocaust, the ultimate and final example of the ubiquitous presence of evil in our world—an order created, we assert, by a God of love, justice, and compassion. These very qualities, confessed by so many, are clearly brought under serious question by any study of Job. Mitchell notes that the theme of the poet is "the great Jewish one, the theme of the victim. . . . That is what makes Job the central parable of our post-Holocaust age and gives such urgency to its deep spiritual power."[19]

Not only is the credibility of faith in God a critical issue; the plausibility of ethical behavior based on the acts of a God of justice is questioned with utmost intensity by the author. As Robert Gordis writes, "Job's enduring significance lies in its theme, for it is concerned with the most agonizing issue confronting men—the mystery of evil. This central issue of the Hebrew Bible has remained the great stumbling block to faith for men through the centuries."[20] Gordis states the problem succinctly: "The axis on which all Hebrew religion turns has as its two poles faith in God as the just Ruler of the universe and the fact of widespread human suffering."[21] The prosperity of the wicked and the suffering of the righteous present an eternal dilemma not to be resolved by reason, perhaps by faith. The astounding fact about Job is that his faith in his tradition—as stated by his friends—is shaken, but not his faith in God. Despite his experiences, Job will not be an atheist; his faith persists. And of course it is this faith in God that forms his behavior, just as our faith determines our moral reasoning, our ethical actions. The

story of Job, in some ways retold in *Night* by Wiesel, provides other ways
to look at the relations between God and the created order. How does this
ambiguous and compelling story inform us in our century of trials and
persecutions severe enough to test any faith to its limits?

The story of Job and the experiences of Wiesel present us with the challenge to believe in a God who allows evil to flourish. The suffering of Job—as
it is invariably called—and the horrors of the Holocaust press us to seek an
understanding of God that is beyond our understanding of good and evil, or an
understanding of God that incorporates both good and evil. The label son of
God, applied to Satan, is often set aside as merely an ancient and anthropomor-
phic way of describing the family home life of God up in heaven. But it may
be better used to change our way of seeing God as an author who incorporates
both good and evil in the eternally evolving process of creation.

A provocative approach to thinking through the incorporation of good
and evil into our concept of God is found in the work of Jung. His *Answer
to Job*, written when he was seventy-seven years of age and published in
English in 1954, is a summation of his thoughts about God and suffering, a
condensation of his reflections on the structure of our personality in light of
the tensions that exist in all of us as we attempt to comprehend the meaning
of evil and its place in a world allegedly brought into existence by a God of
love. The question of theodicy is powerfully presented and answered in the
language Jung used in his work as a psychologist. For us, it provides another forum for debate about the nature of evil. Jung writes, "The Book of
Job is a landmark in the long historical development of a divine drama." He
continues with a brief description of the contradictory evidence in the Old
Testament about the nature of God in Jewish experience: jealous, angry,
cruel, loving-kind, and creative. His concern in his book is "with the way in
which a modern man with a Christian education and background comes to
terms with the divine darkness which is unveiled in the Book of Job, and
what effect it has on him."[22] Jung points out that Job does not doubt the
unity of God:

> He clearly sees that God is at odds with himself—so totally at odds that
> he, Job, is quite certain of finding in God a helper and an "advocate"
> against God. . . . Yahweh is not split but is an *antinomy*—a totality of
> inner opposites—and this is the indispensable condition for his tremen-
> dous dynamism, his omniscience and omnipotence.[23]

God is both justice and injustice.

In Jungian terms, God has a dark side that is necessary for our grasping
at all the concept of theodicy, the blatant evidence of evil in a world created and found to be good. God is inadequately understood as a trinity of
Father, Son, and Holy Spirit. To explain our experiences, there needs to be

a fourth element, the part of God that accounts for evil, although it need not actually cause it. The fourth component of God seen as quaternity is suggested by Jung at certain times to be the feminine part of reality and at other times as Satan, as evil. Any attempt to "describe" God is foolhardy and arrogant. But I believe that this approach to thinking of God, the ultimate reality of this universe, as beyond good and evil offers an explanation that is missing, and must be considered, in the many other attempts to describe God and make sense out of our lives. The polarities of good and evil, of male and female, and other opposites are defining for us. The symbols of the self that we encounter can express these oppositions. Wallace B. Clift, in *Jung and Christianity*, writes: "Particular images or symbols in an individual's experience may focus on one polarity rather than another. However, inasmuch as such symbols have a uniting, reconciling quality, they belong to the same family of salvific experiences." He notes:

> It is Jung, above all, who has taught us that to be human is to be the creature *par excellence* caught in the tension of opposites. This is the price we pay for being that part of nature that has become conscious of itself. Consciousness means awareness—awareness of a choice to be made. The tension of opposites is inescapable.[24]

Another opinion on the voice out of the whirlwind is offered by Jack Miles in *God: A Biography*. The voice is not addressed by Job as God, nor does the voice so identify itself. It speaks of power, whereas Job has persistently asked about justice, ignoring the entire substance of the horrendous trial Job has endured in his faithfulness. We learn from the writer of Job that God is both justice and power and seems quite unconcerned about suffering. In this story, it is Job who is moral and consistent in his faith. Miles, commenting on the opening scene, notes that, "In agreeing to a savagely cruel wager with the devil, the Lord has characterized himself by his own action."[25] After this encounter, this confrontation between God and his faithful servant, our understanding of God changes. This book radically alters our understanding of divinity. Miles writes, "God can never seem to Job after this episode quite what he seemed before it. More to the point, the Lord can never seem quite the same to himself. The devil is now a permanent part of his reality."[26] In this tragic encounter, Job wins: the voice concedes defeat, attempting to compensate Job for his losses by giving him a new family and estate. So in concert with the concept of God as a quaternary being—evil being a part of the creator—is Miles's note: "After Job, God knows his own ambiguity as he has never known it before. . . . With Job's assistance, his just, kind self has won over his cruel, capricious self just as it did after the flood. But the victory has come at an enormous price."[27] With the Book of Job we read the last words of God in the Hebrew Bible. God will be silent thereafter, only spoken of and about by women and men. God will now be absent as an actor.

FROM WHENCE COMETH FAITH?

In this chapter, I consider again the questions that are central to this study: In light of the events of my lifetime, is there a possibility for faith in God? If there is, what are the bases for it, and how will that faith inform my actions and direct my life? These questions are placed in startling relief in the Book of Job; this profound poem will be debated and dissected by generations to come, demanding ever deeper and more probing inquiries into the relations between faith and behavior. Job responds to the voice from the whirlwind: "I had heard of you by the hearing of the ear, but now my eyes see you."[28] Obviously Job did not see the voice—at least not literally. What he did do was *see* in the sense of understand. The events of his life could not be explained on the basis of retribution for sins, on the intentions of a god who provided vicarious suffering, or on human concepts of justice and love. He still had no logical explanation for the horrors he faced; he was awakened to the reality that his creator existed and demanded a faithful life from him. Thoreau warns us:

> Only great and worthy things have any permanent and absolute existence ... petty fears and petty pleasures are but the shadow of the reality.... By closing the eyes and slumbering, and consenting to be deceived by shows, men establish and confirm their daily life of routine and habit every where, which still is built on purely illusory foundations.[29]

We are to open our eyes. We, too, shall see God as Job did; we shall understand our lives and be both satisfied and grateful. These rather pious words can never explain the intense and unjust suffering in our world. But they start the process of a search for the foundation of our faith that we so desperately want. The Holocaust, in a way similar to the experiences of Job, forces us to examine our faith as the basis of our moral reasoning. A basic tenet of any contemporary theology, after the Holocaust, must be a cooperative effort between Jew and Christian to forge a foundation for living and working together in this hazardous world. Christian complicity in the death and the destruction of this time cannot be denied or excused. Certainly, for both faiths, this century has canceled efforts to explain the sufferings of Job in our day. Any promises devised by theologians to comfort us by projected hopes for a heaven with streets of gold and eternal light are to be distrusted. We must find a way to live in a faith that acknowledges the pervasive nature of evil and yet holds us to a commitment to the moral life.

Robert McAfee Brown writes:

> Christians are called to undertake a new appraisal of who Jesus is, and the starting point will not be a figure sitting on the right hand of God, Alpha and Omega; the starting point will be one Jeshua bar Josef—a first century Jew with the dust and grime of the road upon him, getting tired, hungry, and discouraged, a worker who cast his lot with the poor of the land, ... who would have been with the Jews in Auschwitz even if he had not been forced to be there. It will also be a Jesus possessed of a wild dream, a dream that justice and love and liberation and compassion could be real in the here and now, and need not be relegated only to another world in another life.[30]

The hope for the moral life in the here and now underlies the story of Job, of course. In the days of the author of that book, the expectation of a life after death was not a widely held belief. Job speaks:

> But mortals die, and are laid low; humans expire, and where are they? As waters fail from a lake, and a river wastes away and dries up, so mortals lie down and do not rise again; until the heavens are no more, they will not awake or be roused out of their sleep.[31]

The consolations of an eternal existence free of pain and filled with joy are not his. In fact, these words of Job remind us of Jesus' despair at his own death, when he recalls the words of the psalmist: "My God, why have you forsaken me?"[32]

Why did Job not curse God and die? How can Elie Wiesel still argue with God, debating forever the articles of his religion that sustain him? I continue to dig down into my heart and mind for the foundation that will support my moral life. I pray for the spirit that will illumine my way as I struggle with all that I am and hope to become. A study of the Holocaust and the responses to it of Wiesel and many others, the heartrending story of Job, and the brief question of Jesus on the cross combine to remind me of the bedrock upon which I set my convinced faith. Each narrative, in its own unique way, affirms God in these days of doubt and torment. There are three parts to my thought and my understanding of my faith that come from this work.

1. I do not understand the events in this life: the entire subject of undeserved suffering remains a mystery that cannot and will not be explained. Any attempt to explain or to justify suffering would be a travesty. The ancient observation that the wicked prosper and the righteous suffer is an experience that defies understanding. Certainly suffering without justification is not retribution for sin. The disparity between our actions and our pains

cannot be explained; can a child thrown into the fires at Auschwitz be expiating its or another's sin? We observe our world—microscopic and macroscopic—and develop theories about action and result that are scientifically valid, at least for the moment. But we do not *know* answers to the simplest questions about behavior, thought, creativity, art, or emotions. We are shaken by the happenings around and within us. We may well be destroyed by them without any comprehension of their meaning, intent, or purpose. But, like Job, we shall continue the dialogue with God. Wiesel writes:

> Job continued to interrogate God. By repenting sins he did not commit, by justifying a sorrow he did not deserve, he communicates to us that he did not believe his own confessions; they were nothing but decoys. Job personified man's eternal quest for justice and truth—he did not choose resignation. Thus he did not suffer in vain; thanks to him, we know that it is given to man to transform divine injustice into human justice and compassion.[33]

We, too, know a faith that, like Job's, can persist in and through arguments with friends, demands and anger directed to God, and a blunt refusal to surrender that faith. What is the source of that faith?

2. I have a history of faith that goes back to the creation of the world, as the powerful legends and fables relate it. Depending on our ancestors—the tellers of the tales—we have different sources for these stories that have been told, "time out of mind," about our beginnings, our places in this world, and our destinies. I accept the accounts of my history, fully acknowledging the mythic character of the story and the validity of other stories for other persons. I deny any exclusive right to correctness or even reality of the events noted. The plurality of these stories, these folktales we cherish, enhances their authority for all. Even in the simplest encounters, different accounts are recorded by observers and participants. So it is with our legendary beginnings, our revelations, our affirmations of truthful and reliable experiences upon which we establish our firmest faith. As we recognize the existence of differing, even contradictory myths, we affirm our own inherited faith. We live with cobelievers, with others who confirm our confidence in faithful coexistence in our given world. We do not abandon our faith.

An important corollary to this confidence in an inherited faith that is passed on from generation to generation is the chaos that ensues when the passage of the tradition falters. We live in a time that is labeled post-Christian by many serious theologians. Part of the reason for this lies in our failure to keep the faith alive in a functional manner. The relevance of biblical faith for contemporary living needs to be restated, to be brought up to date for our times. We are called to remember our past faith in its context, but we are also called to place that faith in terms that are readily understood by all—not only to recall the faith of the distant past, but also to suggest its ongoing significance for all times.

3. The importance of tradition as a channel of faithful response to the suffering we know is seen in the work of Wiesel and in the Book of Job. The learned and treasured beliefs are not abandoned when events make confidence in a loving God an apparent mockery to an outside observer. The chilling question of Jesus on the cross is still addressed to God. And it is addressed to God as a quotation from the scripture sacred to Jesus, a psalm of David. Also, at the beginning of Jesus' ministry, he goes to the wilderness, apparently to confirm the call that he received. In his simple replies to the temptations offered by Satan, we read quotations from scripture—no tightly argued sophistic language, no logical pedantic statements. All we know is that, in his extremity, Jesus calls upon the tradition he knows and obeys. The word of God to his people becomes the foundation stone for his commitment to the work he knows he must do. The walk down the long and dusty road begins with a confidence, with a faith founded on an old story of the covenant established between God and a rebellious people. This utter reliance on a God known through tradition and through personal identification with a people of like belief was witnessed by the Jews in the camps. Rebellion, in the mode of Job, became a firm component of the faith suggested by the work of survivors of the Holocaust. God is debated, engaged in argument, accused of wrongdoing, and blamed for the evils we know, but He is not denied. Acceptance of the apparent will of God, confidence in a justice I will not know here, and a strong sense of the personal nature of my relationship with my creator set my personal faith on a foundation that will not be moved.

How a faith like this informs and directs personal behavior and public action in times of pestilence is a question that will be asked as I look at the plagues we know, the responses we and others make to them, and the possibilities for an upright and valiant life in the midst of prejudice, persecution, and denial of human rights.

NOTES

1. Isaiah 59:1–2, NRSV.
2. Kressmann Taylor, "Address Unknown," *Story: The Magazine of the Short Story* 13, no. 73 (Sept.–Oct. 1938): 23.
3. Ibid., 32.
4. Carl G. Jung, *Answer to Job*, trans. R. F. C. Hull (Princeton, NJ: Princeton University Press, 1958), 91.
5. Richard L. Rubenstein, *After Auschwitz* (Baltimore: Johns Hopkins University Press, 1992), 162.

6. Henry David Thoreau, *Walden*, ed. J. Lyndon Shanley (Princeton, NJ: Princeton University Press, 1971), 90.
7. Richard L. Rubenstein and John K. Roth, *Approaches to Auschwitz: The Holocaust and Its Legacy* (Atlanta: John Knox Press, 1987), 290.
8. Irving Abrahamson, *Against Silence*, 3 vols. (New York: Holocaust Library, 1985), 1:31.
9. Abrahamson, *Against Silence*, 2:139.
10. Elie Wiesel, *Night*, trans. Stella Rodway (New York: Hill and Wang, 1960), 16.
11. Ibid., 43–4.
12. Abrahamson, *Against Silence*, 1:293.
13. Wiesel, *Night*, 46.
14. Fyodor Dostoyevsky, *The Brothers Karamazov*, quoted in Rubenstein, *After Auschwitz*, 38.
15. Abrahamson, *Against Silence*, 1:31.
16. Stephen Mitchell, *The Book of Job* (San Francisco: North Point Press, 1987), xvi.
17. Ibid., xxiv.
18. Job 40:8, NRSV.
19. Mitchell, *Book of Job*, vii.
20. Robert Gordis, *The Book of God and Man* (Chicago: University of Chicago Press, 1965), 7.
21. Ibid., 135.
22. Jung, *Answer to Job*, 3.
23. Ibid., 7.
24. Wallace B. Clift, *Jung and Christianity* (New York: Crossroads, 1986), 134.
25. Jack Miles, *God: A Biography* (New York: Alfred A. Knopf, 1995), 326.
26. Ibid., 327.
27. Ibid., 328.
28. Job 42:5, NRSV.
29. Thoreau, *Walden*, 96.
30. Robert McAfee Brown, *Elie Wiesel: Messenger to All Humanity* (Notre Dame, IN: University of Notre Dame Press, 1983), 185.
31. Job 14:10–12, NRSV.
32. Matthew 27:46b, NRSV.
33. Elie Wiesel, *Messengers of God*, trans. Marion Wiesel (New York: Random House, 1976), 235.

Chapter **5**

F i v e

A DIVIDED AND TROUBLED LAND

How many a man has dated a new era in his life from reading a book.
—Henry David Thoreau, *Walden*

MY FOUR YEARS IN medical school were a delight. For the first time, I was able—indeed, expected—to do what I wanted to do without distraction: study to become a doctor. The medical school at Johns Hopkins was quite a surprise for one who had just finished the usual college-level studies, where readings were assigned and examinations were given regularly: chapter 10 for Monday, chapter 11 for Tuesday, a ten-minute quiz on Friday, and so forth. The school has changed over the years and is now similar to so many others in examining and ranking students, but we were blessed with the freedom to figure out for ourselves how to learn. Examinations were rarely given. I realized quickly that I was responsible for my education; I had to determine what was to be memorized, what was essential. We soon learned to appreciate the absence of competition, our developing collegiality, and the rewarding, nearly palpable presence of a prestigious past that radically altered medical education in the United States in the early twentieth century.

77

The painting *The Four Doctors*, by John Singer Sargent (1905), which hangs in the Welch Medical Library, was a constant reminder of the four men— Welch, Osler, Halsted, and Kelly—who started the school on its amazing course. I have a copy of the painting in my office to refresh my memory when my perspective falters and I need to recall my training.

Osler, a chosen mentor from the past, continues to inform my life as a physician. His spirit, his demands for accuracy in diagnosis and research, and his awareness of his call to an honored profession are present at the school. Osler transformed medical education in the United States, worked to mold the state licensure system, and upgraded both the training and the practice of medicine to an amazing degree. I read his essays and varied addresses that show his developed sense of what physicians are called to do and to be in their relations to patients, to the public health, and to the profession. There is a characteristic, yet delightful, Victorian tenor to his writing, and he is renowned as a writer of clichés. His dedication to work; his demands for study, scholarship, and commitment to the profession; and his focus on virtue as a defining trait of the physician have remained goals in both my personal and my professional careers.

I return to class reunions with some regularity to see classmates, recall the high points and moments of inspiration of the past, and see the remarkable changes taking place in a leading medical institution. Reunions are grand affairs. A buffet luncheon with good food and wine in one of the newer buldings in an expanding complex, talking with friends and teachers, admiring recent additions to the collection of faculty portraits—all are delights. The old hospital, dwarfed by new facilities, still recalls the hopes we had and the promises we made for compassionate care of the sick and the dying. But there is a sad note to reunions, and that is provided by the drive to the medical school through one of the more deplorable slums in the United States. I look at the children in the street, the elderly sitting on doorsteps, and the general decay typical of today's cities, and I wonder about the university's role in using its astounding resources to make life livable. We work separated from the very ones for whom we are called to be advocates and witnesses.

One of the secondary gains from the system of instruction at Hopkins was freedom to take an evening off and go to the ballet or the symphony or escape into a book that had nothing to do with medicine. Personal accountability was assumed and, I think for most of us, accepted as a foretaste of what was to come in our professional lives. It proved true for me as a physician, and even more so as a person. I realized that I could not memorize all the factual material presented by instructors in the basic sciences. This has turned out to be important, since what is assumed to be true one year may be incomplete, even erroneous, the next. What I must know, even today, is where information can be found; what are the methods for solving the inevitable, difficult, and confusing problems in diagnosis and treatment; and what are the personal characteristics of a good physician. The marked changes in medical education and the environment of health care make it more important than ever to master the skills needed to remain learned in the expanding scientific and social milieus in which we practice and study.

My childhood and college years were lived in a homogeneous environment. We all looked alike and seemed to live in the same social and political system: white, middle class, and more or less comfortable, even during the Great Depression. There were obvious economic differences among us in college; I was impressed with the money that some of my fellow students sported. I accepted as inevitable, and did not question, the inequalities that were so apparent in society. As a medical student, I was also quite accepting of what I saw in East Baltimore. Poverty and racial discrimination were everywhere, yet I remember no anger or shame at what I saw. I assumed that Baltimore was a southern city and that local customs such as public rest rooms labeled "white men" and "colored women," the balcony of the movie theater called "nigger heaven," and segregation of the hospital wards by race and gender were norms for that society. I must admit to being somewhat startled when I saw the slave auction blocks near the harbor.

Inside the entrance to the Johns Hopkins Hospital, in a classical rotunda memorable to many of us physicians, is a copy of the statue of Christ in the Cathedral of Copenhagen by Bertel Thorvaldsen. A beautiful piece, it has a calm face and open hands and arms that welcome the sick and their visitors. I, and many others, would touch the hem of the robe as we walked by as a gentle reminder and a source of strength for the day. Often persons would kneel before the statue in a posture of humility and hope that I sensed revealed not only confidence, but also a consolation that I was yet to know. As a young man in his early twenties, I had a way to go and a lot to learn. This new culture was accepted by me without criticism or evaluation; I assumed that differences were inextricable parts of diverse social orders and were not particularly relevant to a medical student from a different one.

An important discovery in Baltimore was the Mount Vernon Methodist Church, where Harold Bosley was the senior minister. Later to become dean of the divinity school at Duke University, Bosley was a superb preacher and a person whose faith was apparent. His writing and preaching pointed to another dimension of the faithful life not accented in the small-town Methodist church I had joined years before: the intellectual one. Vigorous study of literature for hints of the life of the spirit, attention to philosophical forms of analysis, critical examination of the thought and the argument of others, and an ongoing surveillance of my own beliefs and convictions were hallmarks of a newer and livelier faith, particularly for one about to become a physician. I knew that the practice of medicine would certainly require more than clinical skills: a sensitivity to matters of spirit and mind would be essential. But the years of residency training and postdoctoral study left little time for churchgoing, theological study, or reflection on the health of my spirit.

In 1948, while an intern at Bellevue Hospital in New York City, I read *Cry, the Beloved Country* and began a new chapter in my life. The book awakened me, or a part of me, to the perennial and tragic racism that is a plague upon us. The sense of awakening was similar to that I experienced when I read *Walden*, with its insistence on the need to attend, to be awake to what was actual all around me. The novel by Alan Paton is beautifully crafted and written with a personal passion that captured me immediately. The story takes place in South Africa at a time when apartheid is law. It tells of two fathers, two sons, two themes of the presence and the absence of God, and two ways we understand *land*: the people and the soil they live upon. Here is a brief summary of the story: the Reverend Stephen Kumalo, a Zulu Anglican priest, goes to Johannesburg to search for his sister and his son, who left the tribal community to find new lives in the city. Kumalo is guided in his search by another priest, Msimangu, who lives in the mission house. While in the city, Arthur Jarvis, a young white man active in the struggle to end segregation, is killed during a robbery. Jarvis is also, with novelistic license, the son of the large landowner in Kumalo's village, and the murderer is Reverend Kumalo's son. The young Kumalo is caught, tried, and sentenced to death. The writings of the murdered Jarvis are found by his father and disclose a man and a cause previously unknown to him. The tragedy brings together, for the first time, the two fathers, and they share their grief, their love of the land, and their hopes for the future. The beauty of the writing, the intensity of emotion called forth, the clear exposition of an active faith, and the strong hint of hope combined to make this novel widely read in the United States, five years before *Brown v. Board of Education* began the U.S. activist movement.

I knew enough about myself to realize that when writing struck me at such a deep level, it was speaking to a need that was there but obviously not understood. Just as I must ask myself why I cry at a certain moment in a film or can sing no farther in a certain hymn, so must I pursue the significance of writing that catches me by surprise, from my "shadow side," as Carl Jung would put it. My knowledge of South Africa was limited, and my acceptance of life in East Baltimore as a given for that society left me ignorant of the impact of racial segregation on all persons, oppressed and oppressor alike. I had not understood and incorporated the implications of what I had seen as a student. My easy acceptance of social stratification, with its heavy toll on life, shocked and sobered me as I read this hauntingly written novel about men and women far away in South Africa. Comparison with life in the United States nearly half a century later shows distressing similarities. Although the status of the poor in the United States is better than in many other countries, it is not acceptable. Adequate educational and work opportunities, minimal health care guarantees, and participation in government at all levels are beyond the reach of many of our people for reasons entirely beyond their comprehension or alteration. The plague of racism damages, distorts, and destroys lives before they begin.

The reading of this novel was a turning point in my life. I accepted it as a gift to have the personal aspects of racial discrimination opened for me and to have the influence of faith and commitment on building a life displayed clearly and without sentimentality. I use this novel to point out my struggle to enrich my faith and look at the impact of that faith on a life lived in the declining years of this century. My quest is for sources of courage and wisdom sufficient to carry a fragile and anxious person through these days.

FEAR IN THE LAND

"Have no doubt it is fear in the land. For what can men do when so many have grown lawless? Who can enjoy the lovely land, who can enjoy the seventy years, and the sun that pours down on the earth, when there is fear in the heart?"[1] We are beset by fears. Life in inner cities is hazardous; even the suburbs, formerly considered safe places, are troubled by crime and violence. We accept as commonplace situations we never imagined before: dead bolts on doors, alarms on cars and in houses, security guards and escorts everywhere, identification cards, private ownership of guns, and instructions on how to avoid being robbed, raped, or killed. There is fear in the land, indeed. And much of this fear has deep roots in racism, a ubiquitous plague through time. How to hold to a faith that will overcome this pestilence and provide courage to act in all things as if blind to race will remain a challenge forever. Certainly, the we-they position that many of us take runs through our human history like a thread. The differences that we recognize at a glance become shortcuts to define one another and place persons unknown to us in categories that we use for social interaction or rejection.

Although differentiation by color and race is the most blatant form of discrimination, we use other criteria as well. The bloody history of nationalism in the Balkans and the Middle East, tribal warfare in Africa, killings in Ireland in the name of nationalism and religion, and subjugation of native peoples around the world by European colonists are examples of our distressing interactions with those easily recognized as different. In the United States, black-white polarization is paramount; this by no means dismisses the subjugation of Native American peoples, prejudice against Latinos, or the treatment of Asians earlier in this century. It provides an overt example of fear stemming from racial prejudice.

Fear cuts both ways in racial discrimination. The Ku Klux Klan was a visible and powerful force for maintaining white supremacy in the South for nearly one hundred years after the Civil War, and it was certainly a source of fear for persons without the civil rights that many of us take for granted. The heritage from the days of slavery could only be abiding fear of what white persons could do to powerless black ones. Living a demeaned life is hardly an avenue to richness and fullness of experience. An older man I met in 1966 on Black Belt Road in Lowndes County, Alabama, put it this way: "As a Negro, you go from being a 'boy' to being an 'uncle.' You never get to be a 'man.'" A truncated life lived with fear around the edges and a future without hope is hardly one to be desired. The underclass, by definition, lives in fear of the power of the upper classes. And by a cruel irony, this suppression leads to revolt, which creates the fear that white people know and is so apparent in our cities today: fear of black and Latino gangs that disrupt urban culture, making city living frightening. The result is, as Paton writes, that:

> We shall live from day to day, and put more locks on the doors. . . . We shall be careful, and knock this off our lives, and knock that off our lives, and hedge ourselves about with safety and precaution. And our lives will shrink, but they will be lives of superior beings; and we shall live with fear, but at least it will not be a fear of the unknown.[2]

The conditions of our lives these days are tragic. The poor and dispossessed are just that: people whose past histories and ancient cultures were dismissed and not replaced or renewed. Violence in the streets, disintegration of the value of sexuality for enriching our lives, fascination with the moral corruption of others, commitment to litigation as a way of resolving differences, and definition of self by goods and power—these cultural characteristics present nearly insurmountable barriers to bringing about a just and fulfilling society. Passivity is a social trait that lacks therapeutic power in our disintegrating communities. In our world—where political and social power and influence seem paralyzed, or at least weak and ineffectual—personal responsibility assumes a central place in reclaiming our lives as fellow citizens.

It is easy to list the sins of society and decry the loss of virtue and value. It is another thing, indeed, to find sources of hope and power to heal this sad and sick world. Church and state are unable to muster the strength to meet the demands of these days. Prayers ask God to do something to correct the inequities, to heal the sick and comfort the dying, and to end famines and wars. Sermons admonish, chide, encourage, and interpret texts for the hearers. Words, not acts and deeds, are the hallmarks of most church services. In the 1960s, we said that eleven o'clock on Sunday morning was the most segregated hour of the week. Although there are some striking exceptions to the rule, churches are not known for their witness to a free and open society, with equality before God an accepted belief to be acted upon. The state is so beset by political maneuvering for personal and regional gain, by corruption, ineptitude, and bureaucracy, that it will not, and cannot, assure the rights and the health of its citizens. After all, both church and state show forth the power of those who control them. There seems to be little hope for either to alter the existing patterns of our lives. While we pray to God and voice our hope that salvation will be ours, the work can be done only by us.

GOD TURNED AWAY FROM US

The first night that the Reverend Kumalo is in the city, he has dinner at the Mission House. The newspaper account of the murder of Arthur Jarvis is read aloud; it states that three native men are suspect.

> A silence falls upon them all. This is no time to talk of hedges and fields, or the beauties of any country. Sadness and fear and hate, how they well up in the heart and mind, whenever one opens the pages of these messengers of doom. Cry for the broken tribe, for the law and the custom that is gone. Aye, and cry aloud for the man who is dead, for the woman and children bereaved. Cry, the beloved country, these things are not yet at an end. The sun pours down on the earth, on the lovely land that man cannot enjoy. He knows only the fear of his heart. . . . There are times, no doubt, when God seems no more to be about the world.[3]

The perennial question, posed by Job and by the prophets about a God who is absent or whose face is turned from us, is presented again. Gratuitous suffering and devastation, with no apparent relation to punishment or justice, are perennial and definitive tests of faith in God.

The most disturbing example of gratuitous suffering is that of children. Powerless in every way, without a vote or a voice, they die by neglect, abuse, and exploitation. I do not mean those whose deaths are caused by things that we do not understand and that affect all ages, such as cancer, genetic anomalies, unavoidable accidents, and natural disasters, but those who die from starvation, preventable infections, and lack of immunizations. In these cases, it is we adults who bear the responsibility. Because of our failure to act as surrogates and caretakers, children suffer. It is not a question of the absence of God; it is our absence that permits these devastations.

THE HAND OF GOD

Paton's novel, in gentle and delicate ways, pursues this theme of God absent from our affairs, setting the stage for both an apparent affirmation of this abandonment by the construction of the plot and a final confirmation that God is present to our suffering. It does this by defining the ways of God in a specific way. Msimangu is the priest who helps Kumalo in his search for his son. "Kumalo said, 'In all my days I have known no one as you are.' And Msimangu said sharply, 'I am a weak and sinful man, but God put his hands on me, that is all.'"[4] This simple, yet powerful, image of God putting a hand on us to do certain work recurs in the story as a fine balance to the seeming desolation that the characters endure. The hand of God is a compelling image; there are times when we know that we are called to a task, to accept a commitment, to awaken. The ceiling of the Sistine Chapel comes to mind, with the outreached finger of God enlivening Adam.

I return again to the sense of calling to a task, to a role, to a way of being, because it is an abiding part of my own experience. Frederick Buechner is an informed writer who is alert to the working of the spirit in our lives. In *The Sacred Journey*, he says what I point to in my own life. Through the work of writing, he developed "a sense that perhaps life itself has a plot— that the events of our lives, random and witless as they generally seem, have a shape and a direction of their own, are seeking to show us something, lead us somewhere. . . . [I]n the midst of our freedom, we hear whispers from beyond time, I think, sense something hiddenly at work in our working."[5] Whether we know this direction through a "whisper" or by the conviction that we have been touched by God matters little. What I emphasize is the confidence we sometimes feel that we are to go on this journey, not that one; that we are to do this and not that; and that we are instructed— for our own health—to attend and to obey.

It is with caution that I recount similar experiences in my own life. Is it possible that I could be "touched by God"? Could I have had the distinct sensation, at a given moment in a certain place, that a question had been put to me, a hint given, a suggestion offered that freedom to become and to define my self by action and word was being presented? Freedom is a key word here and must be interpreted with care. As we know so well, much of the damage and horror inflicted on our world has been done by people "called" to a special task, to a saving mission that results in catastrophe for us. It is with hesitancy and reserve that I claim this experience as mine. And yet, similar to the accounts of the two priests in the novel, the memories of encounters with the hand of God are realities in my life.

I expect that we all struggle with prayer in its myriad forms, uncertain about how to pray, unsure of to whom we are directing our words, and perhaps even questioning the existence of a hearer. In *The Alphabet of Grace*, Buechner comments on a long quotation from an early novel of his, *The Final Beast*, in which a young clergyman lies stretched out on the grass near his father's barn in the warm summer sunlight. Suddenly, with his heart pounding, he thinks that Jesus might appear to him. All is still as he asks Jesus to come to him there, in that place. A single leaf twirls in the stillness, and then:

> Two apple branches struck against each other with the limber clack of wood on wood. That was all—a tick-tock rattle of branches—but then a fierce lurch of excitement at what was only daybreak, only the smell of summer coming, only starting back again for home, but oh Jesus, he thought, with a great lump in his throat and a crazy grin, it was an agony of gladness and beauty falling wild and soft as rain. . . . Maybe all his journeying, he thought, had been only to bring him here to hear two branches hit each other twice like that, to see nothing cross the threshold but to see the threshold, to hear the dry clack-clack of the world's tongue as the approach of splendor.[6]

Buechner comments on this autobiographical experience as the substance of his writing:

> The clack-clack of my life. The occasional, obscure glimmering through of grace. The muffled presence of the holy. The images, always broken, partial, ambiguous, of Christ. If a vision of Christ, then a vision such as those two stragglers had at Emmaus at suppertime: just the cracking of crust as the loaf came apart in his hands ragged and white before in those most poignant words of all scripture, "He vanished from their sight"— whoever he was, whoever they were. Whoever we are.[7]

I, also, have had revealing experiences like the "clack-clack" one just recounted. On a fall afternoon a dozen or so years ago, I was walking alone in the stillness of a cove beach. I was at a major crossroads in my life, with a decision to be made: do I leave the practice of medicine and become chaplain at the medical school? The decision would also involve the dissolution of a marriage. I was completely at a standstill in my life, unable to find a reasoned course of action. In deep distress, alone on that beach in the warm silence, I asked God for a sign: Am I called to the chaplaincy? Do I leave all and start a new life? Suddenly, from out of nowhere and in the utter silence, came a brief and strong gust of wind aross my right ear that I knew to be "yes." The sure knowledge of a call to the ministry as a student in divinity school, the conviction that I must do something in the days of the civil rights movement, the varied times at which self-definition was clearly laid out for my acceptance or rejection—these have been instances of revealing experiences that I am confident were responses to deeply internal questions that required answers if I was to be as true to myself as I hoped.

Living as I do with a certain confidence that my words, spoken and unspoken, are heard, I also pray. Basically, my prayers consist of grateful thanksgiving and hope for a sense of direction in the days ahead until death. I have thought a lot about what my expectations are for a response to my prayers. Informed in part by an interest in Jungian psychology, I make an effort to be responsive to those moments when a dream, a surprise synchronicity of events or words, or an unexpected meeting occurs. Perhaps more importantly, I try to listen to that part of my mind that carries the religious and moral guidelines that are founded upon my faith. The effort to be true to these continues. I find that answers to prayers surface to my consciousness in what I call "nudgings." I seem to become aware of a course of action, a way to write some words more clearly, an obvious need to approach another with a painful apology or a request. The unexpected tears, the startling sense of presence, the unprovoked feeling of acceptance and peace that occasionally descends, these are experiences that I interpret as signals. Discomfort and embarrassment alert me to question who I am and what I am doing and suggest the need for prayerful attention. All these experiences are reflections of core questions for me: Who am I, and who am I becoming? What acts, what thoughts tell you who I really am?

Arthur Jarvis, the murdered man in the novel, left some writings that surprise and inform his father of the thoughts and hopes that defined him in uncertain and difficult times. I would also affirm my writings as defining of my aspirations, if not my works. Jarvis wishes to be free to be the man he hopes to be in his devotion to South Africa. He writes:

> I shall no longer ask myself if this or that is expedient, but only if it is right. I shall do this, not because I am noble or unselfish, but because life slips away, and because I need for the rest of my journey a star that will not play false to me, a compass that will not lie. . . . Therefore I shall try to do what is right and to speak what is true. I do this not because I am courageous and honest, but because it is the only way to end the conflict of my deepest soul. I do it because I am no longer able to aspire to the highest with one part of myself, and to deny it with the other.[8]

How to end the conflict of my deepest soul? With the sure knowledge that we are defined, finally, by what we do with our lives, this question is ever present to me and repeatedly colors my thought, my prayer, my questions of identity. There is a certain moment when it is a relief to say that one takes a position on an issue and can take no other, as Martin Luther might say. Finding the courage to do the defining work and the wisdom to know how was a difficult task. It is in this work that the creativity and the promptings of prayer encourage and reassure me of the goals. Often, the strength and the vision appear coincidently. Two aspects of prayer are thus combined. The defining nature of a calling to a career, to an act, to a sacrifice is combined with the assurance that freedom has been granted to do the work. Both the action and the freedom to act are self-revealing conditions and, for me, are consequences of prayer. This freedom requires, as a coordinate, courage to act. One of the boons that have been recorded throughout our history is the relief felt after a decision has been made on a moral issue and the way is cleared for action that will define the self. This freedom allows one to resist forces that would imprison and destroy the weak and the powerless and to stand for a course of action that will not, in all probability, overcome evil but will state a commitment to resist it. We are defined as distinctly by what we resist as by what we support.

A NEW FREEDOM

The other novel published in the same year that addresses these issues, albeit in an entirely different context and from a distinctly different point of view, is *The Plague* by Albert Camus, discussed previously. A similar structure allows one to identify certain roles with specific persons and to find oneself in the story. Obviously, both novels have helped me understand my own calling, declare the foundation of my life, and disclose the resources that I require for comprehension, affirmation, and support in the hours of failure. Dr. Rieux, the hero of *The Plague*, like Arthur Jarvis, finds his strength to confront pestilence in the sure knowledge that he is acting out his defining alliance with sufferers without an underlying theological or philosophical context. Neither man has a stated basis for belief and action outside the self. For my own life, I have found myself to be an inadequate guide and interpreter of the way I should go. The temptation always persists to understand the world to my own advantage and to sidestep the clear call to act according to a standard nearer the absolute that I profess to accept.

The two priests, Kumalo and Msimangu, derive their courage to act in a time of travail from their faith in God, the God who put his hand on them. Kumalo is carried through his pain by his confidence in a God who holds him. "I believe," he said, "but I have learned that it is a secret. Pain and suffering, they are a secret. Kindness and love, they are a secret. But I have learned that kindness and love can pay for pain and suffering."[9] The call to work for the people and for the land must be answered by the women and men who inhabit it. God does not act or do anything to alleviate our condition; we are the responsible ones, committed to the care of the earth and its peoples as our response to our faithfulness. If we do not act, nothing interrupts the work of those who destroy after they use the earth for their own purposes. We are called to two basic stances by faith: union with the oppressed in resistance to the means and the persons of the oppressors, and stewardship of the land on which our lives depend. There are two lands: (1) the actual soil and water, flora and fauna that support all the living, and (2) the land as an ideal, the corporate body we know as the people of a country with laws and customs. Both of these lands must be preserved by our common efforts, by our firm understanding that we are but sojourners upon and in them and are held responsible for their viability.

WHY WAS IT GIVEN TO ONE MAN?

Cry, the Beloved Country closes with the Reverend Kumalo climbing to the top of a mountain to await the sunrise, the hour of the hanging of his son. He rehearses the events of the past weeks, which include the coming restoration of the land in the valley, the building of a new church for his people, the deep personal losses of two fathers, the gifts without price of friendship and support, the intensity of fear in the land, and the fervent hope for change in a troubled place. His return to his home is such a joy to his people. Their support for him in his tribulations, the new project to renew the land, the love of his wife and family—all these ease his pain. "He pondered long over this, for might not another man, returning to another valley, have found none of these things? Why was it given to one man to have his pain transmuted into gladness? Why was it given to one man to have such an awareness of God?"[10]

The importance of this book for me is centered in awakening and in awareness. The gift of insight into the ubiquity of racism in all its guises and the power of discrimination to destroy any hope for personal fulfillment was a literal awakening for me. I am sure that I knew, intellectually, about the impact of racial discrimination, but the heart was unknowing. I was able to look back to my childhood, to my years in college and medical school in Baltimore, and learn better who I was and what would be needed for my true maturation. Why was this awareness given to me? Then and now, this question can be answered only through faith. The long road back to childhood is one marked by milestones of awakening and of awareness of a call to a faithful life. I certainly do not understand how this has happened, but I am grateful for the times when I interpreted events, words, dreams, coincidences, and doubts as certain signs that there was a call by God to a different life, an awakened life. My responses to these times of awakening have been meager, as one would expect. Yet they have called me to change direction, to make new promises, and to gently renew my daily moments of thankfulness.

At a recent Sunday service at church, a nervous and awkward group of adolescent confirmands joined the church. As a sign of their acceptance into the body of the church, a deacon and the pastor lay a hand on the head of each kneeling person, blessing and welcoming him or her. I carry with me to this day the sensation of those hands upon my head more than half a century ago. That awareness, that sense of both a beginning and a continuation of earlier teaching and calling, was to be repeated at my ordination. It is with great humility and a keen sense of thankfulness that I, too, can ask, Why was it given to me to have an awareness of God?

As the sun rises, Stephen Kumalo prays for Africa:

God save Africa. But he would not see that salvation. It lay afar off, because men were afraid of it. Because, to tell the truth, they were afraid of him, and his wife, and Msimangu, and the young demonstrator. And what was there evil in their desires, in their hunger? That men should walk upright in the land where they were born, and be free to use the fruits of the earth, what was there evil in it? Yet men were afraid, with a fear that was deep, deep in the heart. . . . And such fear could not be cast out, but by love.[11]

Our histories of these current days are replete with evidence of fear and the violent responses we make to it. A persistent challenge is to translate a faith in God and in our future into a working scheme for living a life that is consistent with that faith. The work goes on, both in the heart and mind and in our social settings. We live in hope, and that hope is a sure one; so we have been promised.

The sunrise has come, the hour of the hanging of his son. The Reverend Kumalo stands facing it as the sun rises in the east. "For it is the dawn that has come, as it has come for a thousand centuries, never failing. But when that dawn will come, of our emancipation, from the fear of bondage and the bondage of fear, why, that is a secret."[12] It is a secret, however, that we must try to bring to revelation, both of the will of our God and of the hopes of our own hearts and minds for peace and fullness in the land.

NOTES

1. Alan Paton, *Cry, the Beloved Country* (New York: Charles Scribner's Sons, 1948), 75.
2. Ibid., 79.
3. Ibid., 73–4.
4. Ibid., 215.
5. Frederick Buechner, *The Sacred Journey* (San Francisco: Harper & Row, 1982), 95.
6. Frederick Buechner, *The Alphabet of Grace* (New York: Seabury Press, 1970), 6.
7. Ibid., 8.

8. Paton, *Cry, the Beloved Country*, 175.
9. Ibid., 226.
10. Ibid., 274.
11. Ibid., 275–6.
12. Ibid., 277.

TO SEE NO EVIL

The sin of Dives [the rich man] was that he could look on the world's suffering and need and feel no answering sword of grief and pity pierce his heart; he looked at a fellow-man, hungry and in pain, and did nothing about it. His was the punishment of the man who never noticed. . . . It is a terrible warning that the sin of Dives was not that he did wrong things, but that he did nothing.

—William Barclay, *The Gospel of Luke*

THE PARABLE OF THE rich man and Lazarus is told in the Gospel of Luke (16:19–31). A rich man, dressed in purple, feasts sumptuously every day. Lying outside the gate to his house is Lazarus, a cripple, covered with sores that the dogs lick. Lazarus survives on the bread that the rich man and his guests wipe their hands on and throw away under the table. Both men die. The rich man goes to hell, and Lazarus goes to the bosom of Abraham. The rich man was condemned, not because he had done anything evil, but because he had done nothing. He did not see Lazarus as a fellow traveler on this journey of life: he accepted the existence and the misery of the poor man as part of the order of things.

The lesson of this teaching of Jesus that trips us up is that we do not have to do evil acts to be in danger of judgment; to ignore the distresses of

91

others is sufficient. If we accept the injustice and the suffering of our times as part of the scheme of things, the way the world has always been, we miss an opportunity to define ourselves, to witness to the foundations of our personal lives, to declare our position as members of an endangered species. As Thoreau tirelessly tells us, we must awaken to the dawn, see what lies before us and the part we will play in the drama that is unfolding. This part of my study of the role of faith in defining a personal ethic for the time of plague focuses on awakening, on seeing the nature of the social order and the possible roles I could play in the drama.

In 1954 I opened my pediatrics practice in a small New England town. After two years as a naval medical officer and a year of postdoctoral training in pediatric oncology, I was ready to begin the practice of medicine. It was a major step for me, containing all the anxieties—professional, social, financial—that such a step entails. As it turned out, all went well: the practice was successful and grew steadily to include five physicians.

In 1954 another event occurred that carried greater national significance: the U.S. Supreme Court, in *Brown v. Board of Education*, declared racial segregation in public schools illegal. Although many of us did not realize it, this was the beginning of a new era in our lives and in our understanding of ourselves, personally and politically. There would develop a clear distinction in many social, interpersonal, religious, and community relations between those supportive of and those opposed to desegregation. Personal friendships were strained, new relationships established, affiliations shifted, and new promises made as we began to understand what was happening in our country. The drama unfolded, gradually and inexorably, with a bus boycott, lunch counter sit-ins, Freedom Riders, essays from prison, violence, and sermons. The time was upon us for self-determining decisions.

A personal and local intermission occurred. In May 1960, the House Committee on Un-American Activities held a hearing in San Francisco to which known Communists were called to testify. There were student protests attended by mounted police, and at one point, the students, sitting on the ground, were soaked by fire hoses. Some five hours of committee hearings were filmed and edited commercially to create one film, *Operation Abolition*; two thousand copies were made available for circulation around the country. The film was deceptive; it was cut and spliced to develop a documentary about the widespread infiltration of communism in our country. The editors were unscrupulous. They eliminated scenes of police brutality, presented demonstrations that occurred at other times as if they had occurred at the hearing, substituted taped answers to questions asked in other situations, and provided interpreters whose intent was to provoke anger in viewers. It was a fraudulent film produced for a House committee to show that its many vocal opponents were either Communists or dupes of Communists. Strong

support for the film was provided by the John Birch Society and other severely conservative groups. Major newspapers and *The Christian Century*
criticized the film for its misleading presentations and inaccuracies, its dishonesty and outright lies; the National Council of Churches advised against
showing it, as did several Roman Catholic publications. The film became a
national issue at an inflammatory period in our political history.

A showing of the film at the local high school was sponsored by the
Junior Chamber of Commerce, at the urging of a U.S. Naval Reserve officer
who was a resident. A group of us, alerted by the published articles, organized to prevent its showing, or to at least provide intelligent and honest
appraisal of its content. For the first time in my life, I was confronting a
community upon which I was dependent for my livelihood, making enemies,
co-leading a committee labeled subversive and un-American, and staking
my personal reputation on this action. Indelibly imprinted on my memory is
an image of our minister and me kneeling in my house after a meeting,
praying for the courage to continue our opposition. There was a palpable
experience of Presence with us that night that carried us through with patience and without anger. At the public showing of the film—with a much
larger audience than was expected—we debated the issues of the film. Fortunately for our group, the speakers brought from out of town—routinely
provided by the distributors of the film to support it—were obviously wild
and foolish. The controversy died out, but personal animosities persisted
and increased as a profound political and religious movement, based on a
different agenda, was organizing and demanding a response from us. The
controversy around *Operation Abolition* was the first round in our town, a
time of testing, a search for a center of the moral and ethical bases by
which many of us would define ourselves for the next twenty years.

I cannot provide a broad perspective of the two decades 1954–75. The
diorama is too wide, my experiences only a small corner of the whole. But
I can detail my development and my struggles in those years as they affected
my faith and my behavior in response to the turmoil in our country. There
were milestones along the way—some associated with suffering and pain,
some associated with a heightened sense of purpose and commitment, some
associated with humility and grace. They had an impact on many of us as
we watched the struggles of southern blacks to achieve some measure of
freedom and realistic opportunities to effect changes in their lives and offer
hope for their children in the future. The aspect of those years that I focus
on is the inner one, the somewhat startling recognition that choices must be
made by the self, and the dramatic realization that these choices would define who I was both to myself and to others. Events, local as well as national, set the stage for actors who would declare their roles in a most serious
drama, make their promises, and live out the consequences. There are two

parts to the tale: (1) recognition of the choices offered when the conditions demanding moral decision become known, and (2) the moral and ethical values that we rely on to make decisions and live out the life. I was awakening to a new dawn.

A FIRST AWAKENING

Around the year 1960, many of us began to see what was happening in the United States. The struggles for racial equality in the public spheres dated back to the late 1940s, but I was minimally aware of them, if at all. The profoundly conservative political movements of the 1950s—epitomized by the John Birch Society and slogans such as "Better dead than Red"—were dying out, and a more hopeful decade began, romantically captured in the election of John F. Kennedy to the presidency. In my town, we organized a Human Relations Council to educate ourselves about the civil rights movement and methods we could develop and use to encourage integration in the suburban towns around New Haven, Connecticut. We held well-attended meetings and wrote letters to the local newspaper, but our activities were primarily political and social in nature. I think that this time of awakening was based on intellectual curiosity and personal feelings of self-righteousness about what other persons were not doing to bring about change in our country. It was a beginning.

The powerful and courageous action by a child, Ruby Bridges, to integrate the public schools in New Orleans dramatized the need for political and social action. The event was presented hauntingly in the painting by Norman Rockwell and was used by Robert Coles in his early writings about the effects of segregation and efforts at integration on children. Her calm determimation moved me to attend more carefully to current events that were shaping me by my responses, whether I was aware of it or not.

By the time of the Mississippi Summer of 1964, it was apparent that momentous events were under way; a radical effort was in progress that looked to change the very face of the United States by extending civil rights to all persons. An integral part of this awakening was the realization that who I was—how I defined myself as a citizen and as a Christian—would be clearly determined by my involvement in the movement or my remaining on the sidelines. I was again at a point in my life when what I did would tell me and others who I was. It became a critical time for me, sharply outlining the role that my professed religious faith played in determining my ethical response to an obvious social crisis. After searching my heart, praying for guidance, and talking with my family and friends, it became obvious to me that I was at a crossroads; what I did in the present crisis would characterize me. As one of our great poets noted, there are roads that we take and others that we do not. Who I was becoming would be determined by the road I chose.

In July 1966, I went to Alabama as a volunteer physician for the Medical Committee for Human Rights. This organization was established in 1964 as the medical arm of the civil rights movement and supplied medical and paramedical assistance to the movement in a variety of ways: medical presence for the civil rights workers, general counseling services for young people far from home, consultation in improving health services for rural people, and help in documenting segregation in health and welfare facilities. I was assigned to work with the Tuskegee Institute Community Education Program (TICEP) in Lowndes County, Alabama, as part of a team that would conduct a survey to determine the health needs of this rural area. TICEP, begun in 1965, was federally funded by the Office of Economic Opportunity and the Office of Education, originally for the purpose of providing tutorial services in the public schools, using Tuskegee students as tutors. The program was expanded to include medical, library, social work, and recreational studies.

Lowndes County lies between Montgomery and Selma, some seven hundred square miles of farmland. According to the 1960 U.S. Census, the population at the time was 15,500, of which 81 percent were black. The basic demographic figures for the county were characteristic of the times. The median income for white families was $4,400; $935 for black families. Of the 3,800 housing units in the county, 3,000 had no sewage disposal. Infant mortality was disproportionately high for blacks—a finding common in the rural South. Two white physicians practiced in the county, and there was one drugstore. One of the disturbing sentences in the orientation packet advised the removal of the overhead lightbulb in the car so that we would not be visible targets at night. The pervasive presence of pickup trucks without license plates but with guns across the rear windows was sobering.

In preparation, I had read enough about life in the rural South to consider myself professionally educated to interpret the relationships between poverty and health. I was, however, quite unprepared for the intense personal experience of living and working intimately with southern blacks. I was fortunate to have Laura Reed as my landlady during my stay on Black Belt Road off Route 80 in Haynesville. She was a strong, independent, and fearless black woman who affectionately remembered a hug and a kiss from Martin Luther King Jr. on the famous march from Selma to Montgomery. With a serious commitment to improving the health and the education of her community, she was my teacher. Her house had no window screens; the housefly was the connecting link among outhouse, kitchen, and farm animals. Water for most houses came from shallow wells or rain barrels. The latter source was a dangerous one; airplanes sprayed pesticides on the farms indiscriminately, including the roofs of the houses. I thought of this as I washed and shaved each morning in a bowl of warm water out on the porch.

Segregation by race was strict, and rigidly imposed. I was amazed and embarrassed to learn that the thirty-eight black physicians in Alabama had been denied membership in the State Medical Society, a component member of the American Medical Association. Of all the professions, medicine should be least susceptible to the debasement of racial discrimination.

School buses for white children were heated, and there was a seat for every student. Black children rode in unheated buses that permitted standees. The books for black children were ones that had been replaced in the white schools by updated editions. Tenure for teachers was discontinued; black teachers were fired for registering to vote or for teaching literacy to others who were preparing to fill out the two-page registration form.

White supremacy was maintained, often by "crackers" who received no benefit from their positions. Sitting on the courthouse porch, standing in front of the stores, or driving in ever-present pickup trucks, the white man maintained control with a rudimentary type of power: of the 800 white men in the county over the age of twenty-one, 550 were deputy sheriffs legally permitted to carry arms. It was astounding to hear the ends to which whites would go to avoid calling a black man "Mister." A teacher, who obviously cannot be called "boy," was addressed as "Professor," a rather impressive title in the North.

These few illustrations of my experiences are not new revelations; they merely provide some background to the milieu in which I worked. One of the more impressive experiences I had was on my first Sunday morning, when Mrs. Reed asked me to go to church with her. She got all dressed up—including a straw hat—and we were ready to leave. Calmly, as if picking up an umbrella, she reached up to a shelf, took down a pistol, and put it in her pocketbook. "Ready to go?" she asked.

The findings of the survey were depressing, but expected. It is important to keep in mind that these children were "well school children," not ones brought to the doctor because of health problems. We did a hemoglobin test and urinalysis, determination of visual acuity, and complete physical examination on each child. Nine out of ten children had never seen a doctor; most did not know their birth dates or addresses; four out of five children were anemic; one child in seven hundred had glasses; the only evidence of dental care was extraction; congenital defects were untreated; lacerations and farm-related injuries had not been repaired. I was struck by the poor language the children used: incomplete sentences, severely limited vocabulary, primitive speaking skills. My findings in adults were equally distressing. Anemia, uncorrected vision, hypertension, and obesity were common. One woman in seventy had heard of self-examination of the breasts. Vaginal examinations showed the results of poor obstetrical care: cervical lacertations and erosions, vaginal tears, and prolapse of the uterus. Adults had minimal knowledge of prior illnesses and therapies. Many had received blood transfusions before common and simple surgical procedures, confirming widespread anemia. In a sense, none of this was a surprise—frightening and sobering, but not unexpected. All I was missing were the details. Another telltale finding was the existence of burial insurance but no health insurance—a finding now common among youth in inner cities.

Not unexpectedly, living and working with the people was its own awakening. The birth of political power and the hope for change was beset by intra- as well as interracial problems. "Uncle Tom" and "cheese-eater" were terms describing the personal issues vigorously discussed by organizers. "Uncle Tom"—the teacher, government employee, or rare large landowner who had achieved some status by white standards—was threatened by the possibilities of change. The name "cheese-eater," usually used to describe someone of lower social status, derived from the practice of white store owners giving pieces of cheese to informers. These issues were on the agenda each Sunday afternoon at a meeting held in one of the county churches. The meeting began with prayers and the singing of hymns and then proceeded to address the issues of the day. I noticed that there were four ministers present, but they seemed *ex officio* rather than community leaders. Clergy had come lately to the civil rights movement, apparently because many churches received mission funds from white city churches, and financial anxiety was a reality. Ministers who were not active in the movement often found themselves preaching to empty churches.

All the fears, hopes, anxieties, and dangers of the people were opened for me at this first meeting. It was my initiation into the impact that centuries of debasement and denial of humanity had had on a people. Feelings of apathy and urgency coexisted, as those active in the movement spoke of being "halfway across the river," at a point of no return. As they talked of alienation, aloneness, and love of others, I sensed that I was in the presence of a knowledge of God and other people that sophisticated theologians had stifled. Those present—individuals who had suffered at the hands of white authority—gave testimony to the evil possible in the hearts of men. But they also seemed exquisitely sensitive to all those with bad thoughts and evil hearts, regardless of race, gender, or social position. They spoke to the many conditions that separate us from one another, to loneliness, and to the love of others in words that would have moved Camus. One speaker compared the contemporary political situation to that of the Israelites in the wilderness. Ignoring the negative reports of earlier scouts, Israel was encouraged by Joshua and Caleb to move forward into freedom and history.

As I watched the people practicing their new art of faith defining politics, and as I stumbled through a few words of greeting, I was acutely aware of the paleness of my heart and soul.

A SECOND AWAKENING

As I labored—and labor it was—to crystallize my personal and professional experiences, to correlate my participation in community meetings and the findings of my brief but intensive medical survey, I was surprised at my optimism for Lowndes County. As I brought order to my thoughts and feelings, I saw that the black people in that isolated rural area were at a historic crossroads in their development of racial consciousness and political maturity. Using traditional methods of U.S. politics, refusing to meet violence with violence, and receiving only token assistance from white citizens and the government, blacks were entering American life. Witnessing the unfolding of yet another part of the American Dream had the same effect on me as had earlier readings about the founding of the Republic. In Lowndes County, I watched the Founding Fathers, 1966 style, hammer out techniques of politics that could lead to a representative government for all.

As I thought through what I was seeing and hearing, I knew that it was a new dawn for me. I recall a rueful smile as I realized that I would change in ways that I could not yet know. And the reason lay in these poorly educated people's reliance on the power of their religious faith to produce change. There was no doubt that their church communities were the sources for their confidence and their courage. I began to rethink my own religious perceptions and the bases for my faith, even searching out—yet again—what I would define as my faith. After all, it is an ongoing process that begins in childhood. We mature in thought and experience, influenced by so many factors: teachers; readings in history, biography, and religion; dreams at night; chance conversations and events in our days.

The first response I was aware of in myself was humility before the witness rural blacks made to their faith. This faith was religious, in the traditional Christian definition of confidence in God known to us in life, the teachings of Jesus Christ, and the workings of the Holy Spirit among us. But another type of faith, a belief in the basic human kindness of all persons—black and white—was also apparent and expressed in a way that I had not seen in the North. I was surprised and startled, humbled and brought down by the lived-out faith of these people and the firmness of their convictions about the successes that lay ahead.

My second response was uncomfortable but essential for any hope that I might grow in faith and in the works stemming from that faith. My training in medicine was, by nature, strongly intellectual, with a firm work ethic attached. My discernment of my religious faith was attained along similar lines: studying my Protestant background by reading history, the Bible, and theology; a fascination with my Puritan heritage; a certain wariness around emotion evidenced in religion; and a strong certainty in the force of intellect. All this was put to the test by my contact with the black communities. My second response to this experience in Lowndes County was a distressing awareness of former feelings of superiority based on education, language, knowledge, and experience. I became painfully alert to a distinct strain of self-righteousness and boasting in both my personal faith and my daily living. Because of my knowledge and my control of language, a feeling of superiority came quite easily to me. I did not realize this until the lived-out faith of my new teachers humbled me.

These two awakenings—the recognition of my ignorance of what was happening in my country and the humility I felt before the people I worked with and for—were signs to me that a new life would have to be forged out of the experiences. How this would be done, I had not the slightest idea. I returned to my medical practice and my life in family, town, and church to reflect on the work of the summer. The magnitude of the problems I had seen was overwhelming, and I had neither ideas nor plans—real or fanciful—for action. I was fortunate in having a mentor at the Yale University School of Medicine. Milton J. Senn was director of the Child Study Center, former chair of the Department of Pediatrics, and a man who had worked in the South and knew its problems. He suggested that I contact Leslie Dunbar, director of the Field Foundation in New York, a philanthropic organization with a continuing concern for the Child Development Group of Mississippi, a Head Start program for poor rural children, predominantly black. Re-funding of this group by the Office of Economic Opportunity had been derailed by Senator Stennis. A private organization, Friends of the Children of Mississippi (FCM), was successful in restoring some of the funding. The Field Foundation wished to study the feasibility of establishing a health program for the two thousand children in FCM. I was one of a team of five physicians who went in May 1967 to interview people and evaluate the possibilities for a health program. I visited twelve centers in four counties, observing the children, their teachers, and the facilities; talking with mothers; and studying the programs.

"There's no food and there's no jobs." This quotation from one of the mothers summarizes our findings. I thought that we would be considering health education, immunizations, and other public health measures to upgrade the health of the children. What we saw is difficult to grasp. The teachers told me that the children came from such deprived homes and were so fearful and withdrawn when they entered the centers that they required constant loving care for days before they would join activities. They described one boy who sat and rubbed his hand across a windowpane over and over again. He had never seen glass. Others turned the water faucets on and stared at them. Painstaking efforts were taken to teach children how to use drinking glasses and forks. The social handicaps were obviously considerable, but the finding that overwhelmed us was hunger. Intellectually, I suppose we should have expected to find hunger, but I had never really seen it. When we doctors met that first night, our immediate conversation focused on this, and we decided that the plight of hungry children in Mississippi must be the message we brought back to our sponsor.

Our findings were published by the Southern Regional Council. We also presented them to the secretary of agriculture, who was unimpressed and disbelieving. Finally, we were interviewed by Senators Joseph Clark and Robert Kennedy and were asked to present our findings to the Senate Subcommittee on Employment, Manpower and Poverty, which we did in July 1967. The hearing received nationwide attention, and we were pleased that it helped initiate a federal program to feed the hungry in our land, which is still in operation. This work with FCM and the people awakened me to yet another dawn.

Another Lazarus

Late one morning, I sat in a small, unpainted, dilapidated church in Waynesboro talking with a deacon about life in his town. I listened as he spoke about the problems of being black in the rural South and about the expectations that so many had for change in the social and economic poverty that plagued them. We spoke about some of our basic faithful beliefs and the role that faith played in our lives, in our behavior, and in our hopes for ourselves and our children. As we sat quietly in concert with the buzz of the fly and the hum of the mosquito, he began to tell a story that he thought could explain his views on how justice could be accomplished. He said that he knew a man who was sick. I assumed him to be a friend. As his friend got sicker, the man's sisters sent for a healer in a nearby town—not an unusual medical practice in rural America. The healer was delayed, and the man died a few days before he arrived, to the dismay and sorrow of the sisters. But when the healer came to where the dead man was laid, he told the people to roll away the stone, and he called to the man to come out. The way the deacon told the story, I was taken by surprise when I realized that he was retelling the story of Lazarus in the Gospel of John. He explained what the story means for today.

God can heal and bring new life to our world. The various miracle stories in both the Hebrew Bible and the New Testament show that faith can bring rebirth, new life, even resurrection. But we must attend to the lesson that the story of Lazarus tells. Before the healing and a recovered life can be accomplished, the stone must be rolled away, and that is not the chore of God. Jesus instructs those present to do that work. We are the ones who must remove the barriers to the full life that we have erected in our nation. Only we can open the way for love and the power of creation to bring new life to our sad world. We can do the work, we must do the work, if there is to be any hope for us.

I have carried this story in my heart all these years. It is a biblical lesson as clear as any I know. There will be no dramatic act of God that will bring about change. God works through us, and we must prepare the way for that holy work. One could say that God is powerless to produce change except as faith, hope, and love are instrumental in altering our visions, our relationships, our commitments. Perhaps we could say that the divine will can be known only in and through understanding our own calls to heal, to mend, to save, to care. If we do not roll away the stones, death in its many guises will hold us in its firm and unrelenting grasp.

LOOKING FOR THE FOUNDATION

During the next few years, I was active in my own town and church in speaking about my experiences in the South, the religious and political power I had felt there, and the hopes we held for change. We raised funds and collected sewing machines, food, tools, and other items needed by the people I had met there. A visit to Kentucky showed me firsthand how the land is devastated. The manifold problems with the mining of coal are evident in the poverty, the broken limbs, the damaged lungs, the despair of the people. But I also met a nurse who, wearing her flour sack dress and carrying her shoes and the $50 check she had won as a high school senior for her essay on America, had walked to the bus that would take her to Berea College. I met doctors who went to practice in rural areas and others who, through faith and struggle, moved on to a full life.

In 1970 I went to south Florida with two other doctors for the Field Foundation to visit farms, labor camps, homes, and schools in six counties. There were significant differences between the rural black southerners and the children, women, and men exploited on large farms in Florida. "Stoop labor" has its own special hazards—physical, chemical, social, and psychological—that have been documented thoroughly. What was striking was the ethnic and racial tensions among the various workers: Chicanos picking leaf vegetables, Jamaican blacks cutting cane, whites from Appalachia working with cattle, and local blacks picking citrus fruits. Exploitation was of a different and more malignant type than I had seen in Mississippi and Alabama. Housing for migrant workers was the most miserable imaginable, unfit for a despised dog.

Change was taking place as the 1970s began. Black Power was a reality, and we were told, in no uncertain terms, to stay in the North and solve the problems there—the problems that had their reflections in the South. I think that this was good advice. There is no question in my mind that the work I did always had the potential to induce pride and a covert, if not actually overt, self-righteousness. Both of these characteristics are well known to me. I can point to the good works I have done, hint at the risks I have taken for others, all without acknowledging that the very problems I am addressing are present, perhaps to a lesser degree, in my own backyard.

The war in Southeast Asia escalated rapidly, and a distinct peace movement was forming. Many of us switched our efforts to trying to stop the horror that we were perpetuating in Vietnam. I was active in local efforts to mobilize opposition to the war. Meetings and teach-ins were organized. I was occasionally awakened at night by obscene phone calls, and church meetings were often painful. Yet, with this, it was my learning of the relationship between faith and action in the South that brought about the next move in my life. There is a connection between what we believe and what we do that is undeniable. The letter of James, to the distress of Martin Luther, tells us that "faith by itself, if it has no works, is dead."[1] My two awakenings— my realization that self-definition was occurring, and my humility before the lives of others—forced me to examine thoroughly the roots of my faith.

In keeping with my professional training and my confidence in the intellect, I began studies at Yale Divinity School as a part-time student while continuing my practice of pediatrics. It seemed important for me to learn more about my faith so that I would better understand what I was called to do in this world and how to do it. I registered and attended the orientation sessions with the other students, who seemed quite young. I was surprised, and a bit annoyed, to learn that my faculty adviser for the first year was a nun. I could not believe that an older man, a Protestant at that, would be assigned a Catholic woman adviser. But it was only for the first year; I could make my own choice thereafter. In keeping with my interest in learning about my religious tradition and the role that faith played in my life, I enrolled in a two-year program for those not headed for ordination into the ministry.

I met, off and on, with my adviser, Sister Margaret Farley, a professor of ethics. I had none of the usual student concerns about courses or tuition or student activities; I was quite busy with my practice and with my studies at night. Conversation and some specific suggestions for courses were a major part of our meetings, except for one question that she put to me several times that year, "Alan, why are you here?" As I thought through an appropriate answer, I realized over time, with her guidance, that there was a severe reality to what is referred to as a "call" to the ministry. I had thought that the word was a euphemism for taking a job as a minister or priest. I learned otherwise. Of course, Margaret Farley became an admired, respected, and trusted adviser, teacher, and friend.

In my early enthusiasm for the work we were doing in the South, and later in the peace movement, I anticipated radical changes in our country that would reflect a new awareness and a new understanding of the common needs we have for food, shelter, education, and worthwhile work to do: a *Walden* basic curriculum for a good life. Entrenched social, economic, and political forces are not moved easily, and when they are, they have a distinct tendency to return—like a gyroscope—to their earlier position of self-interest. A lot was accomplished in expanding the food stamp program, assaying the health of our people, and broadening educational opportunities for all ages. For my own development, I realized that I required a motive force beyond indignation and anger at the failure of representative government to fulfill its many roles as advocate for the people. I was saddened by another inner experience that came from these years. Our national flag, which I had always associated with freedom and justice and a guide to where one could go in times of trouble, became for me a symbol of oppression and injustice.

What I was searching for in my work, in my living and practicing in a community, and in my attending divinity school is that foundation I have spoken of frequently, that certainty of a reality that transcends the ordinary in my experience, a source of confidence that will not be shaken by the terrors and the heartaches of life. Whatever that is, it is the focus and the source of faith. That faith, in turn, establishes the code of ethics, the determinant of my behavior. The ground for my faith will define the rules by which I live out this life. Occasionally, when people hear that I am a minister, they tell me that they are atheists, that they do not believe in God. I smile and counter gently with the observation that everyone has at least one god to worship. Be it money, the face in the mirror, power, fulfillment of sensual desires, creative artistic or literary skills, or other idealized things and concepts, we do have at least one god. The question is, of course, which god is ultimately the object of our enduring faith?

I learned the elements of my Christian religion in school and remain grateful for a fine education that gave me some knowledge of those centuries of Judeo-Christian experiences. Fortunately, my years in school stimulated as many questions as they answered, encouraging me to continue my studies. But it was the question of why I was in divinity school that led me to a peace and an acceptance that remains. The long road from childhood finally led to the sure knowledge of a call to the ministry, to ordination. An integral part of our intellectual history is the attempt to create a schema that explains all. Philosophers, theologians, scientists, historians: all are tempted to construct a comprehensive picture of life as it has been, and should be, lived over time. Their contributions rank with the highest scholarly accomplishments and deserve our attention. All cultures and all peoples have texts that are revered for their insights into human nature and that plumb the depths of our experiences in this cosmos. Many make valiant efforts to explain all of human experience to us, uniting their observations and hypotheses into rational constructs that make sense to an orderly mind. A basic knowledge of these writings is important for an appreciation of the breadth of intellect and sensibility that the human being is capable of expressing. But they have not provided a center to my life.

My faith, admittedly Christian, has developed through the years as a result of two active forces upon my life. The first is a persistent pursuit of teachers and preachers who detail the nature of faith, our call to it, the strengths of it, the weaknesses of those who seek it. Some inner part of my being urged me to pursue this search for the holy, for evidence of the divine in the mundane, for sources of hope in a world of devastation. A key factor in this search is my confidence in a God known to me as a creator and a sustainer of life, a God who can be known in meditation, in prayer, and through sensibility to the nuances of the subconscious and the conscious experiences we all know. This "knowing" has called for hard work in learning to understand my own person in all its vagaries. One of the key elements is a willingness to know oneself. A line I hold in my heart and mind is by Samuel Hoffenstein, an American poet of the 1930s: "Everywhere I go, I go, too, and spoil everything."[2] A clear knowledge of my self informed by confidence in a God revealed in many ways and times is the foundation of my life.

The second force that has been effective in determining my faith and my behavior are the experiences recorded in this chapter. Working with faithful persons who believe in the possibility of community and service, who decline to give credence to prejudice and hate, and who wish their avowed enemies well—these experiences confirm my faith in their faith. My confidence in economics, politics, and social psychology remains low. Unless there is a sea of change in us through a faith that transcends our capacities and knowledge, we will continue on the road we are on. Faith, even a weak one like mine, empowers by placing my hope and my confidence outside the self I know so well. Living life in a faith that upholds an ethic of concern for the weak and the lonely, the sick and the hungry, is possible. I know of no other support that will not fail us.

NOTES

1. James 2:17, NRSV.
2. Samuel Hoffenstein, *Complete Poems of Samuel Hoffenstein* (New York: Random House, 1954), 281.

Chapter 7
Seven

SMOKESTACKS, SWEATSHOPS, AND CIRCUMLOCUTION

Hell is a city much like London—
A populous and smoky city.

—Percy Bysshe Shelley, "Peter Bell the Third"

OUR HUMAN CHRONICLE RECOUNTS many and varied plagues, and suffering is a common ingredient of them all. We respond in varied ways to this ubiquitous affliction. Whether it be the closing out of a life with painful disease, the loss of a newborn baby, the horrors of ethnic cleansing, or the misery of a life lived in poverty and hopelessness, undeserved ordeals and adversities are present to us daily. We react to these events in ways that are too numerous to detail and quite individual in their characteristics. Anger, compassion, disregard, social and political actions, sacrifice, acceptance, pity: we know them all in our histories and in our selves. The theme of this study—the relationships between our faith and our personal ethic of behavior in times of plague—finds a fine model in the life and the writings of Charles Dickens. He is, therefore, required reading for this work.

My introduction to his writings was reading *A Christmas Carol* as a boy, an annual habit that persists to this day. Sentimental and hopeful, not religious, and written in his remarkable prose, this story filled an empty spot in my personal life at a season when sentiment and hope were not evident at home. Over time, I have read his novels and other works that interpret his life and his writings. He was the most widely read novelist of his day, and it is astounding to realize the intensity of the personal impact of his writing on millions of readers. I am awed to read of the crowds standing on the dock at Boston, eagerly, yet anxiously, awaiting the current installment of *The Old Curiosity Shop* that would tell them whether or not Little Nell died. Dickens appeals to most levels of class and education then and now; more importantly, he presses the central questions of his and our times: faith and family values, wealth and social class, poverty and abuse, crime and punishment. All this is done, of course, within the limits of his own personal and social borders.

Dickens offers us an opportunity to study the life and the work of a person who was persistently and, occasionally obsessively, involved in the multiple social and religious concerns of his time. More important for the purpose of this study, he was involved without the supporting structure of a religious faith to provide reliance, personal assurance of forgiveness, and a solid conviction of hope. He lived and worked frustrated by an absence of a strong and abiding response—his and others'—to the social and economic revolutions occurring in his day. The years of Dickens's major writings, 1836–70, saw profound changes in England that produced the world as we know it today in the West. Radical alterations and conflicts that beset England and caught Dickens's attention were (1) the Industrial Revolution, characterized by the advent of the railroad and the factory and the rapid growth of the city, with its attendant poverty and misery; (2) Parliament's inability to institute reform legislation; (3) the paralysis of bureaucracy; (4) powerful conservative forces of evangelism and strict Calvinism; and (5) the shift of economic power to the middle class. These socioeconomic events characterize the Victorian Age, a time in our history when the destructive nature of human greed and vanity was detailed in poetry and prose of enduring excellence.

Dickens described in his writings and lived out in his life a disturbing and unsettling discovery: an acknowledgment that the principles on which he based his life could not withstand the unrelenting attacks of the pestilences we know. One aspect of Dickens that is important to this study is his frustration with the failures of others—his fellow citizens—to right the social wrongs that were so evident. But he had no basis for encouraging good works by himself or others besides urging responsible persons to behave toward the distressed the way that the good teacher, Jesus, would have done. He did not have a religious or philosophical faith that could interpret evil, provide power to confront it with courage, and offer a community that would share the suffering and the hope when facing the demands that dreadful times impose on us. What motivates us to meet the challenges of plague with courage and confidence? This aspect of his work—the role that faith plays in the hour of plague—will be developed.

I noted that both Defoe and Camus suggest that the plagues described in their fictions can be interpreted as metaphors for the cities of their days. Were they merely regretting the passing of the "good old days" of bucolic pastoral life? It seems more likely that each saw the concentration of people within the limits of a city to be the cause of social, psychological, and health problems that were severe and threatening enough to warrant the name plague. The English city, particularly London, became a major focus for Dickens. It was the incarnation of social and political evil. The rapid growth of the city attendant upon manufacturing and the railroad—complicated by disastrous secondary effects of inadequate sanitation, housing, education, and security—made it a new symbol for the plagues of an earlier day.

Dickens's writings are filled with narratives, parables, and thinly disguised figures that have their origins in the Bible. He was well acquainted with the Bible and the Book of Common Prayer, both of which were ready and well-used sources for his stories. More than any other popular writer, he created characters easily recognized by his readers, adding to his amazing popularity at home and abroad. He remains one of the most popular novelists in the English language. The vision of a Vanity Fair, a serious model for Victorian social critics, plays a role in his work and in our study. London, that "populous and smoky city," fascinated Dickens for many reasons. It was the Vanity Fair of Victorian England. The Dickens novel I use in this study—*Little Dorrit*—has a firm base in the biblical author whose focus on vanity remains so influential: the teacher Quoholeth, author of Ecclesiastes. As the Book of Job is the foundation for *Bleak House*, so Ecclesiastes is for *Little Dorrit*.

Ecclesiastes stands out in the Bible as an oddity. Dating from the third century B.C.E., it belongs to Wisdom literature, although it attacks the concept of rewards to be had for a faithful life. Whatever we gain in our lives is voided by death. What lies before and after life is unknowable and has no meaning for the way we live. We should, instead, enjoy the pleasures of youth—food, wine, love, work, play—in full recognition that these will pass with aging and death. Wisdom, the perennial goal of the searching, faithful sage of Israel, is confronted by folly and the hedonism implied—indeed, explicit—in the absurdity of the reality that the good die young and the evil live to old age. There is an inherent unfairness to life that many of us agree to without regard for religious or philosophical views. Injustice and suffering are rampant in all societies, and the word *plague* encapsulates that reality. From nowhere appear desolations that destroy alike the good and the evil, the young and the old, the saint and the sinner.

The opening lines of Ecclesiastes set the stage for our interpretation of *Little Dorrit* as a story about plague:

> The words of the Teacher, the son
> of David, King in Jerusalem
> Vanity of vanities, says the
> Teacher,
> vanity of vanities! All is vanity.
> What do people gain from all
> the toil
> at which they toil under
> the sun?[1]

The author searches prophetic vision, psalmist hope and confidence, and, most importantly, Wisdom literature and finds no compensation for faith shown forth in rewards, in virtue, in an enriched life. He sees, instead, futility and unfairness. Victorian novelists writing about the vanity of their age had a primal source for their work in the masterpiece of John Bunyan, *The Pilgrim's Progress*. Written two centuries earlier, in the 1670s, this powerful allegory is firmly entrenched in our culture. The author describes a new town:

> Then I saw in my dream, that when they were got out of the wilderness, they presently saw a town before them, and the name of the town is Vanity; and at the town there is a fair kept, called Vanity Fair; it is kept all the year long; it beareth the name of Vanity Fair, because the town where it is kept is lighter than vanity; it is also because all that is there sold, or that cometh hither, is vanity. As is the saying of the wise, all that cometh is vanity.[2]

It is the Vanity Fair of his day that Dickens addresses in his darkest novel, *Little Dorrit*. Lionel Trilling, in his landmark essay on this novel, writes, "*Little Dorrit*, one of the most profound of Dickens' novels, and one of the most significant works of the nineteenth century, will not fail to be thought of as speaking with a peculiar and passionate intimacy in our own time."[3] This relationship between the novel and our own era is the focus of this chapter. As does the author of Ecclesiastes, Dickens bases his novel—its settings, its goals, and its characters—on personal observations. The work is an intense reflection on life in London, the "capital of the world," the city Dickens knew as well as the back of his hand. He was an inveterate stroller, known to walk as many as thirty miles at a time; in particular, he was a night observer of the entire city. His contemporaries commented that few people knew London as well as he did. Dickens saw and incorporated all of London into his writings and into his bitter struggles with religious faith and organized religion and its observances. He saw and pitied its abandoned and homeless, its squalor and blind alleys; he hated its wealthy and powerful, its vistas of endless toil, its limited opportunities for fun and pleasure, its polluted waters, houses, and people, and the hopelessness of its children. All this forms the background of a novel with its roots in the words of the preacher of Ecclesiastes: "all is vanity."

Little Dorrit presents my concerns directly through metaphor and analogy. The novel is threaded with themes that illustrate them: what are the plagues of our history, and what is the faith that determines our responses, defining who we are in that hour? Dickens is very clear in telling us what the plagues of his day are: he so labels the central social issues of his day. How his fictional characters respond to them can help us understand the options available to us in our day. I look at the following social institutions that concern Dickens in his writings: the city, prisons, industry and wealth, bureaucracy, and observance of the Sabbath. Our personal and societal responses to these fixtures of our lives reveal the moral ground on which we elect to stand.

THE CITY

Little Dorrit is a novel about London. That city, in its multilayered complexity, is described by Dickens in words that do not flatter the metropolis. As F. S. Schwarzbach states, "Whenever the city is described, certain words and images recur. Words like 'wilderness,' 'grave,' 'dark,' 'smoke' and 'labyrinth,' and images like the desert, the tomb, the unnatural forest or garden, and of course the prison, are used over and over again." City life for many of its present-day inhabitants can be described with the same language. Violence and poverty are common, and a sense of isolation from the rest of the world is certainly present. But the city of London in the mid-nineteenth century was much worse. Schwarzbach continues, as he describes the London in *Little Dorrit*: Dickens's "view is of London as a hostile and alien environment in which life is virtually no longer possible. Its leitmotifs are an overriding atmosphere of suffocation and oppression, the surrounding wilderness of buildings, and the dark and dank, mysterious river running through it. It is a view of London as a tomb."[4] Public health measures to provide clean water and disposal of sewage and garbage were almost nonexistent—cholera was a reality—and both the national and the city governments were incapable of legislative acts to provide relief. The problems were overwhelming. A powerful sense of foreboding and incorrigible evil associated with the city permeates this novel. We have a picture of a city and its major institutions collapsing under the rapid influx of too many people. Young unmarried people and children flee the impoverished country to come to the deadly cities. The indisposed and inhospitable nature of London is pressed upon the reader. A sense of hopelessness is succinctly presented in the use of labyrinth and dead-end streets to describe the oppressive maze of impenetrable alleys and byways. Dickens uses these synonyms for roads as metaphors for the paths of life that we travel, detailing the difficulties we have in finding our way.

This association of evil with the city developed in the early 1800s, with the influx of people looking for work. The sheer size and confusion of the city produced feelings of mystery and anxiety that could be overwhelming. There grew out of these sensibilities the classic interpretation of the city as terra incognita—an unknown world. Loneliness in the midst of millions of people and the strangeness of the crowds produced feelings of frightening alienation in immigrants from rural England. Almost every other person was unknown. In his novels, particularly in *Oliver Twist* and *Little Dorrit*, Dickens presents every variety of wickedness and depravity. Most of the vices known to us are there and are deemed to be characteristic of city life. One of Dickens's accomplishments is his penetration of the mystery of the jungle of the city and the presentation of his findings in such powerful prose.

It is of interest that Dickens is almost alone as an author concerned with English city life. The Romantic writers that followed him "took to the country," along with the wealthy city bankers and merchants who bought estates there, although their business empires remained in the city. Also important to Dickens's interest in the city and in prisons are his childhood experiences in London when his father was imprisoned in the Marshalsea for debt and Dickens worked for a number of months in a blacking factory. He saw his family only on Sunday, when he visited his father. Most critics emphasize these experiences as being formative for his entire literary output. They certainly flavored his use of the city as a negative cultural force. Dickens's work is of a pioneer character; some of the mystery and confusion about our city experiences were lifted, and the modern world became an expression of metropolitan life.

A fascinating sidelight to Dickens's vision of the city as evil and oppressive is his practice of equating the house with the personality of the character described. Language that we equate with physical and emotional functions of living are applied to houses: sadness, anger, boredom, joy, fear, and dying. Not only the city is morally and spiritually bankrupt; the places where people live—from the wealthy on Harley Street to the prostitutes in Covent Garden—are equally deteriorating and dying. The image of London as a tomb that holds the corrupt dead in their coffin houses recurs.

At this point, I add a corrective note to these comments on Dickens's descriptive skills. For all his astounding accounts of collapsing houses, blind alleys, foul dunghills and gutters, the Thames as a sewer, and questionable professional and personal practices, Dickens did not fully describe the evils that were present. His writings were popular in an era when novels were read to the family, when anything written must be presentable during the "children's hour." With this in mind, we find that the true nature of life in London is hinted at but never fully detailed. Prostitution, alcoholism, all kinds of physical violence and abuse, and the utter disintegration of people before the social anarchy of the large city are censored by the author. In a sense, his novels usually end with the good people pursuing their lives—living happily ever after—and the bad people punished in one way or another. This fact about his work is related to his religion or, perhaps better, to the determinants of the religious convictions he held. I discuss this in detail later.

PRISONS AND PRISONERS

Little Dorrit is dominated by the image of the prison. The metaphor of imprisonment permeates the story in all its possible variations. Robert Barnard begins his critique of the novel with these words:

> To many critics *Little Dorrit* is the crowning achievement of Dickens' maturity. Born out of personal depression and disillusion, it is a hideous vision of imprisonment and disorder, a despairing plea to a whole people to find out how it has gone astray, how it has entrapped itself in decaying institutions and perverted modes of thinking.[5]

Not many years had passed since the fall of the Bastille. That symbolic event—regardless of the many subsequent negative results of the French Revolution—was interpreted by many as opening a new age of creative abilities, freeing both bodies and wills so that we could realize ourselves as individuals. The flowering of Romanticism followed quickly on this new and radical concept of freedom. Revolutions and struggles for independence in the nineteenth century were expressions of this attempt to acquire universal freedom.

Dickens offers few examples of freedom in *Little Dorrit*. Regardless of class or occupation, the characters are held captive by external forces as well as by personal desires, hopes, prejudices, and lies. This setting of the novel finds a base in the psychological depression and personal despair that Dickens experienced at the time of its writing. But it also has a base, I believe, in the inadequacy of his faith as a driving force for understanding his cultural environs and the role that religious faith can play in providing insight and strength for working in that setting. Close to the center of this work is the debtor's prison, the Marshalsea, where Dickens's father was jailed. Perhaps, as some critics suggest, the writing of this novel finally freed him from the anger and shame he apparently carried with him through the years. The heroine of the story, Amy Dorrit, was born in the Marshalsea and, following her mother's death, cared for her father, who became so well adjusted to his life there that he lived as a "prisoner" long after his release. Most of the characters in this novel are prisoners: captives of wealth, position in society, power over others, conviction of their own worthlessness, and other sections of their own personal penal codes. The superb correlation between social and personal sources of imprisonment is developed by Dickens in *Little Dorrit* and is a plague that tests faith. Much of Dickens's writings, lectures, and speeches used the powerlessness of the people and the spiritual paucity of their lives as texts for exegesis.

The prisons in which many of us find ourselves, knowingly or not, are omnipresent; there is no escape. In the second part of the book, William Dorrit, released from prison, travels abroad with his daughters, meeting other English travelers. Dickens writes:

> It appeared on the whole, to Little Dorrit herself, that this same society in which they lived, greatly resembled a superior sort of Marshalsea. Numbers of people seemed to come abroad, pretty much the same as people had come into the prison; through debt, through idleness, relationship, curiosity, and general unfitness for getting on at home. . . . They had precisely the same incapacity for settling down to anything as the prisoners used to have; they rather deteriorated one another . . . and fell into a slouching way of life: still, always like the people in the Marshalsea.[6]

Dickens, over and over again, stresses this point: we are prisoners of ourselves and of our society. As A. O. J. Cockshut puts it, "the fundamental point, which is essential to the book's whole conception, is that a man can travel anywhere and carry his prison with him."[7]

The prison is a structure we use to illumine our struggle to become individuals in a restricting society. In *Little Dorrit*, Trilling notes, "the prison is an actuality before it is ever a symbol; . . . it is the practical instrument for the negation of man's will which the will of society has contrived."[8] This novel addresses the relationship between the will of the individual and the needs and demands of society as a whole. It is at this point of our intersection with society where freedom versus restraint and the determination of the self are issues that define us. In Dickens's dark writing, at a time in his life when he had serious doubts about both his professional future and his personal relationships, he saw few persons who were free to be themselves as inner-directed and developed human beings on their own journeys. He also saw what we know so well in the world of today: the self-destruction of talented and useful individuals bent on their own annihilation for reasons that, although understandable, are not valid. In our captivity to society's demand for capitulation to its definition of who we are and will become, we are victims of a plague, a pestilence so widespread that most of us are infected, knowingly or not. This is an aspect of plague to which religious faiths speak with clarity and assurance, from centuries of experience.

INDUSTRY AND WEALTH

An emerging middle class was a major social development of the Victorian Age. Spawned and influenced by a host of interdependent factors, this new class became a powerful force in Western countries because it managed money. Wealth, in *Little Dorrit*, is tainted by the means of acquiring it and the purposes to which it is applied. Dickens mistrusted wealth, and those who possess it are not admirable characters in this novel. For many of the characters in *Little Dorrit*, it is impossible to find out how their money is earned; the questionable moral texture of both money and its acquirers and managers is, however, clearly expressed. Arthur Clennam, the hero of the novel and perhaps a model of Dickens at the time, is walking toward the disintegrating house of his mother:

> As he went along, upon a dreary night, the dim streets by which he went seemed all depositories of oppressive secrets. The deserted counting-houses, with their secrets of books and papers locked up in chests and safes; the banking-houses, with their secrets of strong rooms and wells, the keys of which were in a very few secret pockets and a very few secret breasts; the secrets of all the dispersed grinders in the vast mill, among which there were doubtless plunderers, forgers, and trust-betrayers of many sorts, whom the light of any day that dawned might reveal; . . . he thought of the secrets of the lonely church-vaults, where the people who had hoarded and secreted in iron coffers were in their turn similarly hoarded, not yet at rest from doing harm.[9]

A desperate and puzzling character is Mr. Merdle, an apparently fantastically wealthy financier who is honored, even worshipped, by masses of people of all classes. He is a shadowy figure, and we never know much about him except the astounding power of his money. Standing, as he does, at the center of the financial world, we are surprised to learn that he is powerless. He understands his own insignificance in comparison to the power of those who have placed him where he is for their benefit. In showing the rapid growth of the apparent financial power of Merdle, Dickens establishes the metaphor of plague:

> That it is at least as difficult to stay a moral infection as a physical one; that such a disease will spread with the malignity and rapidity of the Plague; that the contagion, when it has once made head, will spare no pursuit or condition, but will lay hold on people in the soundest health, and become developed in the most unlikely constitutions: is a fact as

firmly established by experience as that we human creatures breathe an atmosphere. A blessing beyond appreciation would be conferred upon mankind, if the tainted, in whose weakness or wickedness these virulent disorders are bred, could be instantly seized and placed in close confinement (not to say summarily smothered) before the poison is communicated.[10]

Merdle is, we learn, a forger and a thief who destroys the fortunes great and small of investors who have blindly accepted his advice and given him their money to invest. It is to him and his work that Dickens attributes a plague. Pancks, a friend of our hero, joins the multitude in investing all his money with Merdle and strongly recommends that Clennam do likewise.

Of whom Mr. Pancks had taken the prevalent disease, he could no more have told him than if he had unconsciously taken a fever. Bred at first, as many physical diseases are, in the wickedness of men, and then disseminated in their ignorance, these epidemics, after a period, get communicated to many sufferers who are neither ignorant nor wicked. Mr. Pancks might, or might not, have caught the illness himself from a subject of this class; but in this category he appeared before Clennam, and the infection he threw off was all the more virulent.[11]

One of the biological characteristics of some infectious diseases is increasing virulence as the causative agent reproduces rapidly in the early days of an epidemic. Dickens picks up on this aspect of the spread of infectious diseases, noting the near hysteria that accompanies an opportunity to invest one's life savings with Merdle. A subtle note is added to Dickens's presentation of the wealthy: they gather wealth by using the money of the working poor, but they themselves do not appear to work. We find them in their houses—residences that resemble them—at dinner parties, in Venice, at resorts; they are not described at their offices. The clearest descriptions we have of their workplaces are the observations of Arthur Clennam during his evening walk through town.

The financial empire of Merdle collapses; the destruction he wrought is widespread, and he is a suicide. The work that he did is a visitation of a plague. Dickens picks up on an ancient prohibition regarding the use of money: injunctions against using money to make money go back to early Hebrew law, although they were rarely observed. Ezekiel considered charging interest to be evil, and he praised those as pious who loaned without a fee. The wisdom literature cautioned that wealth increased by interest was fleeting. Certainly, in our time, we see the potentially disastrous results of market manipulation, junk-bond dealing, and using the investments of others to increase one's wealth. The warning in the first letter of Paul to Timothy, "the love of money is a root of all kinds of evil,"[12] is well demonstrated in our history. More descriptive of the effects of our striving for riches, amply illustrated in *Little Dorrit*, is the warning in the letter of James:

Listen! The wages of the laborers who mowed your fields, which you kept back by fraud, cry out, and the cries of the harvesters have reached the ears of the Lord of hosts. You have lived on the earth in luxury and in pleasure; you have fattened your hearts in a day of slaughter.[13]

The collapse of the Merdle empire is inevitable, based, as it is, on greed and deception.

Dickens observed the profound changes in the economy of his time and the damage that industrialization brought to the poor drawn to his city. He documented his distress and his sense of hopelessness in *Little Dorrit*. His response to his concerns was to urge his fellow citizens to do better, to look to the devastations in their nation, and to correct them by legislation and by doing good works. He offered no motivation to counter this epidemic other than his plea that we should be better people, following the teachings of Jesus to care for the poor and the miserable. A faith that could empower action in the time of plague is as absent in his writings as it was, apparently, in his life.

BUREAUCRACY

Chapter 10 of Book the First of *Little Dorrit*, "Containing the whole Science of Government," begins with these words:

The Circumlocution Office was (as everybody knows without being told) the most important Department under Government. No public business of any kind could possibly be done at any time without the acquiescence of the Circumlocution Office. Its finger was in the largest public pie, and in the smallest public tart. It was equally impossible to do the plainest right and to undo the plainest wrong without the express authority of the Circumlocution Office.... This glorious establishment had been early in the field, when the one sublime principle involving the difficult art of governing a country, was first distinctly revealed to statesmen.... Whatever was required to be done, the Circumlocution Office was beforehand with all the public departments in the art of perceiving—HOW NOT TO DO IT.[14]

This invention of a governmental office that obstructs and confuses both the public and the elected Parliament is one of the more humorous Dickensian constructs. Or it would be, were it not descriptive of a plague that we recognize: the corrosive and paralyzing power of bureaucracy in government. Those elected on platforms to change the duties and functions of government soon learn from the office how *not* to do things, preserving the reign of the Office over the nation. Through methods we know so well—forms, applications, summaries, minutes, reviews, memoranda, delayed correspondence, and board meetings—the office assures all that no changes will be made in the government. The Tite Barnacle family, which runs the office, is firmly entrenched. Coming from educated and wealthy families, solidly established in the old-boy network, subtly careless with their power and their largess, the Barnacles are not bound by rules. As Cockshut says:

> The Barnacles are not unfeeling bureaucrats; they are lazy, humane, selfish, privileged people, sheltering behind a weak barricade of minutes and forms. Incompetence, irritation, even kindness . . . are continually breaking through. Dickens was doing something important here, he was showing how all this lovable absurdity . . . could have consequences that were harsh and irrevocable.[15]

The consequences are the strengthening of the concept of imprisonment that is so central to *Little Dorrit.* Not only are we prisoners of our personal desires and ambitions (the seven deadly sins); we are also prisoners of the bureaucracy that we employ to maintain our governments. A second response to this office that does nothing is that, although we appear to object to it, we still evidence admiration for it. This is true of elected as well as appointed officials. National anthems, parades, religious services by popes, State of the Union addresses, and oaths of office all warrant our attention and deference; we justify this by calling it respect for the office. We may, however, differ decisively with the persons involved. In Dickens's public statements about Parliamentary inadequacy, he made a clear distinction between his confidence in the People and his wariness of the people who governed. Bureaucracy, a plague that is ever present to us, is a direct challenge to faith because there is rivalry for our adherence to an organization, to a creed, to a constitution, to a way of life, to a secular or a religious view of life, public and private. A distinct challenge of faith is the demand that we choose the final authority for our life and work. Many calls to faithful attendance are to worship of the transient, to products of our fancies and our wishes, tempting and delightful figments of our imaginings and our hopes. A faith that transcends these, that provides a firm base for committed action and confident assurance, can free us from the prisons, real and imagined, that Dickens so clearly describes.

OBSERVANCE OF THE SABBATH

Strict observance of Sunday as a day of worship and biblical study— sabbatarianism—was a national issue in England that Dickens found abhorrent and opposed both in his public writings and speeches and in *Little Dorrit.* Dennis Walder writes:

> Sabbatarianism is a kind of idolatry; but the basis of Dickens's opposition to the Sabbatarian view is primarily a moral and social one, and it is hardly surprising that many contemporary Christians took exception to it,

especially as the Sunday issue had long since become one of the touch-stones by which one could distinguish "real" or evangelical faith from the merely "nominal" brand purveyed by latitudinarians.[16]

An unsuccessful attempt was made to close down public entertainments on Sundays, such as concerts in the park; to prevent trading; and generally to limit community activities to observances of worship. For those who worked a full six-day week, this was a severe, class-driven restriction. The poor could have no social life on the Sabbath, while the rich, served by them, enjoyed the day according to their desires. This proposed imposition of hollow religious regulations was, in itself, a sickness and a form of imprisonment. The despondent and melancholy city on Sunday is described by Arthur Clennam:

It was Sunday evening in London, gloomy, close, and stale. Maddening church bells of all degrees of dissonance, sharp and flat, cracked and clear, fast and slow, made the brick and mortar echoes hideous. Melancholy streets, in a penitential garb of soot, steeped the souls of the people who were condemned to look at them out of windows, in dire despondency. In every thoroughfare, up almost every alley, and down almost every turning, some doleful bell was throbbing, jerking, tolling, as if the Plague were in the city and the dead-carts were going around. Everything was bolted and barred that could possibly furnish relief to an overworked people.[17]

Scrupulous evangelical and fundamentalist Christians, fiercely interpreting their Calvinism, had a strong influence on education and public policy and upheld teaching methods and curricula that we read today with amazement. The focus was placed sharply on the evil inherent in humankind, a separation from God going back to the original sin of Adam and calling for rigid self-denial and a restricted sense of salvation.

In our novel, Arthur's mother is a prime example of the type Dickens is exposing. Mrs. Clennam is exquisitely and joyfully self-righteous, convinced of the sins of others and of the vicious judgment of God that will be visited upon them. In the descriptions of her, as well as in sermons and other writings of the time, there is a repressed sexuality, a projection of the power of unacceptable feelings into the damning of others. The power of tract teaching of children about sin and depravity and the misinterpretation of the Old Testament as a legal document proscribing bad behavior combined to immunize many people against the possibilities of a saving grace available in both testaments of the Bible. Not only is the house of Mrs. Clennam a prison; her erroneous interpretation of the Bible and confidence in her own salvation imprison her and those like her. Dickens, aware of the coexistence of good and evil in all of us, has Mrs. Clennam substitute evil for good as her idol. For her, as for Dickens in his presentation of biblical faith, a simplistic and incorrect distinction is established between the Old Testament focus on justice and the New Testament one on mercy.

A VISION, NOT A FAITH

"One of the features of English Liberalism in the nineteenth century that most distinguished it from its counterparts in other countries in Europe was the habitual use of Christian language." With this sentence, Humphrey House begins his chapter on religion in *The Dickens World*. He continues: "the whole movement was saturated with religious, Christian feeling. Speakers in every part of the country drew their quotations and their imagery from the Bible. . . . But these reformers were not theologically minded."[18] There was abroad a vague and warm sense of the goodness and the moral rightness of Jesus found in the Gospels. Quotations extolling Christian neighborliness and concern for the less fortunate were rampant. Missing from much of the writing and speaking was a reasoned theological basis for the language and the ideas set forth so warmly and righteously in the movement for reform. This pseudoreligious environment was perfect for an author such as Dickens. Not only was he talented in the use of the English language; he was able to tap in to this cozy morality with his vision of social salvation coming forth by the doing of good works.

Dickens presents a picture of human beings in which our natural state is characterized by virtue and happiness. Dickens uses biblical language more than any other writer of his time; his knowledge of the Gospels is quite extraordinary. However, there is virtually no mention of worship or of the varied doctrines of Christian faith that are central to believers in that faith. House writes: "the Church was for Dickens a repository of good-feeling: its establishment allowed for a kind of ancestor-worship, its creeds began with the Fatherhood of God. The more mysterious doctrines of Redemption and Grace concerned him very little, the technique of worship not at all."[19] One cannot make any judgment on the beliefs of another, but I feel a deep sadness in reading Dickens's later novels. Although he is convinced of the innate goodness of the world and of humankind, and he rejects the concept of warfare against evil, the reader rarely has a sense of power and conviction based on anything other than that innate goodness. As noted earlier, Dickens disliked and distrusted evangelicalism. At a time when anti-Catholic feeling was running high in England, he also hated that religious faith. It seems that doctrine of any type was highly suspicious. The intensity of a united and committed community of like feelings, convictions, and dedicated faith was unacceptable. What Dickens wanted was a Christianity that was practical in its moral concerns and actions, provided a vision of the good life without faith as a foundation for that life, and avoided doctrine.

There is no question that Dickens uses religious language and imagery to deal with tragedy and loss. But, as House writes:

[I]t is difficult not to feel that it is a mask to conceal some inability to control or express his emotion. . . . He accepted certain religious opinions, and thought that they were the proper adjuncts of any emotional crisis; but the emotions were more powerful than the beliefs, and the two could never coalesce. . . . There is a failure to assimilate and dignify the fact of suffering and waste; and the pity . . . is merely self-pity transferred.[20]

Dickens appropriates Christian language, symbol, and teaching but does not avail himself of the faith that provides the power to act in a definitive mode. Sentiment remains the atmosphere for the severely driven encounters in his novels. Hope, subdued as it is by the oppressive prison milieu of *Little Dorrit*, is offered by Dickens in a characteristic Christian setting. Near the end of the novel, in a Dickensian coincidence, Arthur Clennam is in the Marshalsea for indebtedness. Amy Dorrit visits him.

[T]he door of his room seemed to open to a light touch, and, after a moment's pause, a quiet figure seemed to stand there, with a black mantle on it. It seemed to draw the mantle off and drop it on the ground, and then it seemed to be his Little Dorrit. . . . He roused himself and cried out. And then he saw, in the loving, pitying, sorrowing dear face, as in a mirror, how changed he was. . . . Little Dorrit, a living presence, called him by his name.[21]

Here we read a description that could match a sentimental Victorian description of Jesus—quiet, compassionate, and gentle; a visitor of prisoners. I am reminded of a typical portrait of Jesus hanging on many a Sunday school wall: a soft upward gaze, long hair and a beard, an Anglo-Saxon face, and warm brown eyes—a sensitive hippie of the 1960s. Amy Dorrit offers Arthur the most profound religious experience a Christian could know: she, like Jesus Christ, calls him by name. In this scene, Little Dorrit represents the path of hope for the marginal and the castoffs of society. Acceptance of others as they are and the gift of charity—love—are Dickens's prescriptions, his gospel for a damned world.

PHYSICIAN

It is unlikely that we could find another author with Dickens's inventive capacity for creating names that we will never forget. His novels abound in delightful, descriptive, humorous, and cutting labels for his characters. A second person in *Little Dorrit* is unique in this respect. Dickens places three unnamed men close to Merdle, the unscrupulous financier. We know them only as Bar, Bishop, and Physician. The first two receive Dickens's usual ridicule. Not so with Physician. Both in language and in deed, he is a Christ figure. There is no reference to family, to intimate friends, or to religious affiliation of any kind. But the language describing his work is biblical:

> Few ways of life were hidden from Physician, and he was oftener in darker places than even Bishop. There were brilliant ladies . . . who would have been shocked to find themselves so close to him if they could have known on what sights those thoughtful eyes of his had rested within an hour or so, and near whose beds, and under what roofs, his composed figure had stood. But Physician was a composed man, who performed neither on his own trumpet, nor on the trumpet of other people. . . . [H]is equality of compassion was no more disturbed than the Divine Master of all healing was. He went, like the rain, among the just and unjust, doing all the good he could, and neither proclaimed it in the synagogues nor at the corner of streets. . . . Where he was, something real was.[22]

Physician is extraordinary, the ideal doctor in the time of plague. A healer with the highest professional standards of personal behavior, confidentiality, and true benevolence, his presence is a reality among the most despised by society. He is identified as one who does the work of salvation. When science fails, when hope is lost—as in the suicide of Merdle—Physician persists in his care, living his life for others, disregarding social standing, creed, gender, race, personal habits, or any other qualifier. What Dickens does not tell us—because he does not know it in himself—is the source of Physician's strength and the foundation for his untiring efforts to heal and to be present for all beset by the plagues of his day.

A FAITHFUL FOUNDATION

Amy Dorrit, the Christ-like figure in this novel, has been interpreted by some critics as a personification of the teachings in the Sermon on the Mount in the Gospel of Matthew. But as Janet L. Larson points out:

> Dickens' Jesus, a wronged hero, does not die for the sins of the world but is merely victimized by evil men. Amy belongs to a long line of suffering Dickensian innocents whose strength of renunciation is hard to judge morally, to distinguish from the weakness of submission to powerful circumstances or the stronger will of others.[23]

The identification of Amy Dorrit with the sermon is a weak one, because it distorts the central concern of faith; the call is not for better behavior, for leading a more moral life, or for revision of Old Testament faith. The sermon is Jesus' demand that we undergo a conversion of our hearts, that we change and place our confidence only in God. The gospel makes it clear that there is no possibility of living by the dictates of the sermon. Jesus sets up criteria that cannot be met by our actions because our thoughts convict us before we can act. We cannot save ourselves; we must turn to God for the courage and the wisdom to live that life for others, fully aware of a sinfulness uncorrectable by our own efforts.

The life of Dickens is an amazing story of the overcoming of his personal fears and anxieties by the inventiveness of healing storytelling. We are gifted with his exquisite skills in describing us, our foibles, our sins, our foolishness, and our hopes. But there is a despair in his writings that is quite clear in *Little Dorrit*, with its gentle heroine confronting the imprisoned of the world with her message of hope. There are losses that accompany our recognition of that despair. As Larson says:

> The losses that attend the process of experiential learning accumulate unbearingly for hero and heroine, as though to learn is virtually to lose and nothing more. Whatever new birth of being or advance in knowledge is possible in *Little Dorrit* must contend with the bitter awareness that even the noblest motives, aspirations, and actions partake of "vanity" in several senses of the word.[24]

Dickens, in his rejection of a religious faith, was left with hope for a new world only in the good works of people. He watched as the horrors of his time unfolded, and all he could offer was encouragement to do good.

Dickens had no confidence in a transcendent reality that provides motive power to do the good works so desperately needed. Jesus was only a good man who taught us to care for one another, even at the risk of personal losses. His life, death, and resurrection were not realities that Dickens could use as a sure foundation for his personal behavior and his pleas to others to change. It would be hard to find a more skilled writer in the English language, one whose characters practically walk off the page and are known throughout the world as typical of the varied persons we are. Finally, however, we sense in his writings a hopelessness about the human venture that points, I believe, to laying the foundation of hope for life on the sands of human wisdom, skill, and knowledge rather than on the rock of confidence in a God of love, justice, and mercy.

NOTES

1. Ecclesiastes 1:1–3, NRSV.
2. John Bunyan, *The Pilgrim's Progress* (New York: Heritage Press, 1942), 102.
3. Lionel Trilling, *The Opposing Self* (New York: Viking Press, 1955), 50.
4. F. S. Schwarzbach, *Dickens and the City* (London: Athlone Press, 1979), 151.
5. Robert Barnard, *Imagery and Theme in the Novels of Dickens* (Atlantic Highlands, NJ: Humanities Press, 1971), 91.

6. Charles Dickens, *Little Dorrit* (New York: Viking Penguin Classics, 1985), 565.
7. A. O. J. Cockshut, *The Imagination of Charles Dickens* (New York: New York University Press, 1962), 43.
8. Trilling, *Opposing Self*, 51–2.
9. Dickens, *Little Dorrit*, 596–7.
10. Ibid., 627.
11. Ibid., 640.
12. I Timothy 6:10, NRSV.
13. James 5:4–5, NRSV.
14. Dickens, *Little Dorrit*, 145.
15. Cockshut, *Imagination of Charles Dickens*, 149.
16. Dennis Walder, *Dickens and Religion* (London: George Allen & Unwin, 1981), 177.
17. Dickens, *Little Dorrit*, 67–8.
18. Humphrey House, *The Dickens World*, 2d ed. (Oxford: Oxford University Press, 1942), 106–7.
19. Ibid., 111.
20. Ibid., 132.
21. Dickens, *Little Dorrit*, 824–5.
22. Ibid., 768.
23. Janet L. Larson, *Dickens and the Broken Scripture* (Athens: University of Georgia Press, 1985), 271.
24. Ibid., 181.

E i g h t

THE SEARCH FOR MEANING

[T]he way leads from innocence into guilt, out of guilt into despair, out of despair either to failure or to deliverance; that is, not back again behind morality and culture into a child's paradise but over and beyond these into the ability to live by the strength of one's faith.

—Hermann Hesse, "A Bit of Theology"

MEANINGLESSNESS IS A UBIQUITOUS plague of our twentieth century, evident in signs and symptoms of loss of purpose for living, insignificance of work, cynicism concerning politics, questions about the value of truth-telling, boredom, and a visible disintegration in public and private morality. There do not seem to be obvious relationships between this ennui and class, wealth, occupation, or church attendance; outer circumstances appear to be inconsequential. A widespread sense of loss of purpose and meaning for the acts and the commitments of life has been apparent in Western culture for a long time, increasing in significance and hazard for that culture. We are losing an image of the responsible self in relationships and in work that was part and parcel of being a person in the past. This serious loss in the inner person is interpreted by some psychologists and theologians as a catastrophe for the human spirit in our time.

Despondency and anxiety are consequences of loss of meaning. In *The Courage to Be*, Paul Tillich writes:

123

> The anxiety of meaninglessness is anxiety about the loss of an ultimate concern, of a meaning which gives meaning to all meanings. This anxiety is aroused by the loss of a spiritual center, of an answer, however symbolic and indirect, to the question of the meaning of existence.[1]

The reasons for this loss of life's meaning and its pleasures and responsibilities are many, and they certainly include the failure of traditional religious beliefs and dogmas to explain, to justify, and to encourage a life of purpose and serenity. Meaninglessness is portrayed by Tillich, as it is by Carl Jung, as a spiritual problem, resolvable only by an intense search of the psyche—the soul, the unconscious, the home of the spirit—for a true knowledge of the *telos*, the goal, of our lives.

I suggested that Charles Dickens, in the middle of the nineteenth century, suffered from feelings of frustration and depression caused by the impotence of the people and the government to correct blatant social injustice and corruption. The lack of a spiritual foundation to life, the reliance upon doing good works without an empowering and centered faith to uphold it, caused Dickens to despair of social change to benefit the poor and the imprisoned. This sense of anomie, of loss of meaning for life and work, began with the Industrial Revolution, but it received its greatest impetus from the existentialists of the next century, whose creative impulse was the work of Friedrich Nietzsche. Coincident with the startling decline in the power of the Christian Church in Europe, these philosophers filled the vacuum with their thesis that we are not "essentially" anything; we are constantly in the process of defining and determining ourselves during our brief time here. We are always in the process of becoming what we will be by our decisions, our actions, our work: we create ourselves by our "existence." There are no gods, no ultimate laws for our mutual living. We are alone in the time between birth and death, and there is no way out of this world, as Sartre's play *No Exit* depicts so powerfully.

A central tenet of existentialist thought is our aloneness in a world known as hostile. Kenneth Keniston calls this

> a sense of existential outcastness, of "throwness" into a world not made for man and indifferent to his fate. In previous centuries in Western society this same sense of cosmic outcastness was usually expressed as a sense of religious outcastness, as a fall from grace, as loss of faith, or as estrangement from God. In the twentieth century, however, this sense is probably best expressed in existentialism, with its denial that the world has essential meaning. Human life is in this context "absurd," lacking inherent purpose: "meaning" must be artificially manufactured by men in the process of existence. And since any one man's answers to the riddles of life are individual and private, they will often be irrelevant and meaningless to other men.[2]

In past centuries, the meaning of life was supplied, in large part in our Western culture, by the doctrines and the symbols of Christianity. The rapid decline in religious faith in our time brought a mixture of rage, anger, anxiety, and aloneness that is paralyzing for many of us. Concomitant with these feelings are boredom and an emptiness that can lead to estrangement from the self, the very core of our being. Our deepest needs are unrecognized or denied, our fantasies and wishes foreshortened, and our dreams become as nightmares. It is the separation from our selves that is debilitating and alienating and destructive of the need to know that our lives have meaning. For many persons, loss of meaning is translated into futility in the workplace, casualness or antagonism in relationships, and, for many, hatred.

In this century, the loss of meaning previously supplied by religion and the church was corrected for many by the advent of a violent nationalism in the form of fascism and communism. We cannot do without some center to our lives; the offering of the state, of a certain nationalist people, of an economic salvation system, became a new religion in many European countries. The causes of our despair and our anomie were shown to be capitalism or the Jewish problem or other concerns outside of the self, and solutions to the experienced sense of historical loss of meaning for Western civilization were presented to people eager to fill the void in their personal lives by surrender to nationalism in its worst constructs. It is frightening to recall the profound excitement, even elation and jubilation, in Germany when the Great War began, signaling a new and glorious era for that nation.

THE RIDER ON THE RED HORSE

When he opened the second seal, I heard the second living creature call out, "Come!" And out came another horse, bright red; its rider was permitted to take peace from the earth, so that people would slaughter one another; and he was given a great sword.[3]

War is certainly a plague, one of terrible and overwhelming magnitude. As devastations visited upon the people, wars have swept across our world with awful frequency. Our history is filled with wars; for many of us, history was taught as a series of dates delimiting wars and the terms of their treaties. Inventions and discoveries were added, almost as an afterthought, but the real human record was one of battles: victories, losses, and their political aftermath. We have a long parallel narrative that details memorable literature, art, music, scientific discoveries and medical and public health advances, lives of sacrifice for friends and enemies, and an endless and seamless garment of billions of ordinary lives lived in hope and love. These pale, however, before accounts of persecution, killing, and destroying—persistent themes in our tragic biography. We are one of the few species of animals that kills its members with intent, a sad commentary on our avowed commitment to community and common purpose in a world of want and sadness.

This twentieth century is our bloodiest yet. Although the years of the Black Death in the fourteenth century may have recorded a higher percentage of the population dying of bubonic plague, this century is the winner in deaths caused by war. As the ultimate expression of an absence of meaning for our lives—personal and corporate—war is the classic example. The human, economic, and ecological costs are beyond calculation, and the hopelessness experienced cannot be measured. Perhaps we are witnessing the final expression of the costs of a lost faith. The loss of meaning centered on religious faith leaves us with no gods but ourselves and the constructs that race, government, property, pleasure, and pride offer as limited goals. Lethal ethnic hostilities, deadly religious conflicts that distort the meaning of faith, persistent economic depression, and seething racial animosity follow upon our sense of aloneness in the universe.

No law, decree, papal bull, or poll of voters will restore the loss of meaning to our lives. The externally apparent religious consensus of past centuries is gone and will not return. We are in a post-Christian era in terms of the influence of organized churches upon private or public morality and political action. Is there any way that a faithful foundation for our lives can be found that will empower the realization of a vision of peaceful coexistence? We certainly cannot live others' lives, but we can be responsible for our own, accepting the challenge of living in accord with universal principles of love, justice, and mercy. But the courage—perhaps even the wish—to do this is one of the gifts of faith, a faith that informs and supports an ethic of mutual acceptance and obligation within a belief in an ultimate spiritual reality binding us together. A sense of the holy in our lives—indeed, in all of creation—can be recovered and may restore confidence that we can achieve a harmony only dreamed of by the mystics of another age. When we are in the depths of despair about the human condition, new concepts and new interpretations of the human experience appear, and we find hope.

An intensely analytical theologian who is important for my understanding of our times is Paul Tillich. Although perhaps now out of fashion, his writings on the nature of being and the characteristics of our concerns in this life—preliminary and ultimate—inform many of us. His studies are global in style, including all possible alternatives and options, and they can be difficult to understand. Like many other theologians, he uses a vocabulary that often requires translation into our common language; I cannot pose as a critic of his work. But his writings on faith and meaning, on courage, on the nature of Christ as he understands him, and on the ultimate concern we are called upon to respect and submit to are seminal studies for me and my construction of a faithful ethic for the time of plague. Faith in an ultimate reality that commands our allegiance is required if we are to confront and not be defeated by the potentially overwhelming power of estrangement and the hopelessness of total loss.

Tillich writes:

> Faith is the state of being ultimately concerned; ... man has spiritual concerns—cognitive, aesthetic, social, political. Some of them are urgent, often extremely urgent, and each of them as well as the vital concerns can claim ultimacy for a human life or the life of a social group. If it claims ultimacy it demands the total surrender of him who accepts this claim, and it promises total fulfillment even if all other claims have to be subjected to it or rejected in its name.[4]

We can see in this definition the destructive power of the nationalisms of our century, with their demand for total surrender to goals that pervert the very meaning of being human in their claims to preeminence. For Tillich, our "ultimate concern" as Christians is God. "Ultimate concern is the abstract translation of the great commandment: 'The Lord, our God, the Lord is one; and you shall love the Lord your God with all your heart, and with all your soul and with all your mind, and with all your strength.'"[5] Jesus' answer to the questioning scribe in the Gospel of Mark is a variant of the Deuteronomic commandment to Israel, the powerful Shema we read in the second account of the law.[6] The center of ultimate concern is the God of Israel, the God of Jesus Christ.

The unconditional demand of this concern defines the believer; the nature of the ultimacy of the concern brings doubt along as an inevitable, if unwanted, companion. The coexistence of faith and doubt is the challenging and defining nature of belief and of commitment. It is inevitable that we live in a psychological state that holds belief and doubt in tension; it is also creative, since it forces an ongoing evaluation of both the object of faith and our ways of showing forth that faith. The tension that we sense between belief and doubt is illustrated in the Gospel of Mark, when the father of an epileptic boy asks Jesus, "'if you can do anything, have pity on us and help us.' And Jesus said to him, 'If you can! All things are possible to him who believes.' Immediately the father of the child cried out and said, 'I believe; help my unbelief!'"[7] Doubt and faith, and the courage to persist in faith in an ultimate concern—the God of our fathers and of Jesus Christ—are the components of our willingness and our ability to build a personal ethic that faces the plagues of our days with confidence.

Inherent in the writing of both Tillich and Jung is confidence that God is made known to us in our inner selves as a spirit that informs, directs, and determines us through our responses to the ultimate. The holy is an actuality that is separate from us yet is knowable to us. Rudolf Otto, whose 1917 classic text *The Idea of the Holy* develops the theme of the numinosity of the holy, of God, uses words such as *aweful, mysterium tremendum, fascinating*, and *transcendent* to describe our sense of the holy. He notes that "the essential nature of the numinous consciousness . . . cannot be taught, it must be 'awakened' from the spirit. . . . What is incapable of being so handed down is this numinous basis and background to religion which can only be induced, incited, and aroused."[8] The experience of the holy is acknowledged within us; we are "grasped by God," in Tillich's phrase. He writes, "The feeling of being consumed in the presence of the divine is a profound expression of man's relation to the holy. It is implied in every genuine act of faith, in every state of ultimate concern."[9]

Coincident with the pervasive sense of existential estrangement and emptiness of the early 1900s, a countermovement appeared that discovered a latent and powerful force in the psychological and religious centers of our being. The origin of this novel religious and spiritual resurgence is found in the work of Sigmund Freud, who "discovered" and described the unconscious components of ourselves that determine much of our behavior and our self-understanding. Freud considered religion to be an illusion, but one of his early pupils was Carl Jung, whose lifelong study of the roots of the meaninglessness common to his patients provides insights into our religious needs and our spiritual anatomy and offers hope for our reinstatement as bearers of peace and concord. His insights into the makings of the modern person must be studied and taken seriously as the work of a creative and observant man. They add immeasurably to any consideration of the relationships between faith and an ethical and meaningful life. A deeply religious man, Jung disclaimed any church affiliation. His wide-ranging studies of other religions and philosophies and his fascination with the symbolism of alchemy gave him a broad faith based in a God known to us within our selves as well as in the created order. His work as a physician, his learning of the workings of spirit from his patients and from his own experiences, and his careful scholarship offer profound insights into our personal lives in the spirit and our understanding of concepts of God among us. Some of his ideas and constructs are powerful modifiers of my own religious and personal growth over the years. As before, the reading of a book and the study of its genesis in the life of its author proved instrumental in my developing faith. I look at some of the theses of Jung that bear on religious faith and commitment through a novel, *Narcissus and Goldmund*, by Hermann Hesse. It was published in Germany in 1930, and the first good English translation appeared in 1968. Hesse was a writer whose life and work are open testaments to the meaning of religious faith for an examined, faithful, and ethical life.

DISCOVERING THE SELF

Hesse was a popular German author in the beginning of this century. A stormy childhood in the home of Pietist Protestants, a desultory and incomplete education, and severe doubts about his life and its goals made him a restless man, dissatisfied with his work and himself. The onset of World War I was a turning point for his writing career; he found unbelievable the elation of Germans who saw the war as the birth of a new era. Marital problems, the painful antagonism of his former German readers precipitated by his pacifism, his restlessness, and his uncertainties about his writing prompted referral to a therapist, Josef B. Lang, a disciple of Jung. They became friends, each benefiting from their relationship. Hesse, through the introspective self-study characteristic of therapy, changed the course of his career. Theodore Ziolkowski writes:

> Hesse perceived that his ever more frantic flights, in the years 1904 to 1914, had been flights from himself, projections into the outer world of his own torments. And his writing had been correspondingly subjective. . . . Renouncing his mandarin pose of detachment, he proclaimed his own complicity in the events of a world gone insane.[10]

Again, we see the pervasive meaninglessness that became increasingly apparent in European culture, not only in artistic works—painting, music, literature—but also in the lives of persons perceptive of the radical social and political changes occurring across the continent. The growing influence and importance of psychotherapy for neuroses attest to the loss of a valid center of purpose for living for many people. Wallace B. Clift notes:

> Jung was perhaps the first psychotherapist to focus on what has become widely recognized as *the* problem for individuals today—the problem of meaninglessness. It is, in traditional language, a religious problem. . . . Jung himself so understood his psychology, that is, as dealing with the religious question. . . . It did not matter whether his patient was rich or poor, had family or social position or not.[11]

Jung became convinced that healing—giving meaning to life—is a religious question, one that the usual cultural sources cannot answer. Education, involvement in sociopolitical activities, even churches failed to provide a conviction that life had meaning for his patients. Clift continues:

> Jung called the world religions the world's great psychotherapeutic symbol systems. He said that for all his patients in the second half of life their problem in the last resort was that of finding a religious outlook on life. They has lost what the living religions of every age gave their followers. . . . In the paths which they charted, the seeker could find a balance in life and a sense of oneness or wholeness.[12]

It is interesting that both Jung and Hesse were raised in families that were professionally religious: Jung's father was a minister; Hesse was raised in a family of Protestant missionaries who served in India. Both men professed a belief in God, but neither was a member of a church. For both, faith that God was active and knowable in their psyches—their selves—was a reality that determined their lives and their work. Both shied away from dogma and ecclesial constructs that formalized belief.

To what sources do we turn as we search for meaning for our lives? What is our "ultimate concern" that will provide a sure foundation, a consistent, reliable, and knowable base on which to build a faithful life? How and where will we find it? For Jung and for Hesse, this source is the unconscious within us, that part of our selves that—beyond any direct connection with the conscious ego—makes itself known to us by dreams, visions, and revelations about ourselves. This unconscious segment of ourselves is similar to Otto's numinous quality of God—the Other—and to the confidence Tillich expresses in an ultimate concern that directs our lives. The analytic psychology of Jung is complex and, expectedly, not always logically consistent, developed as it was over a lifetime of experience and published in some twenty volumes in his *Collected Works*. In this work I emphasize the religious nature of universal symbols and the personal assurances that both Jung and Hesse held that God—affirmed by us in many and varied ways— is a reality that we can know.

THE TWO PERSONS WHO I AM

After the end of World War I, and as a consequence of his psychotherapy, Hesse developed a theme for his novels that presented what he considered to be the two basic types of human beings: the rational and the pious, or, sometimes, the person of spirit and the person of nature. These two types are not absolutes; rather, they inform us in the ways by which we understand ourselves and the world about us and how we manage our lives in the meaninglessness we see and know. In his 1932 essay "A Bit of Theology," Hesse lays out an extended comparison between the two types. "The man of reason believes he possesses within himself the 'meaning' of the world and of his life. . . . He believes the man of today to be a higher evolvement than Confucius, Socrates, or Jesus because the man of today has developed certain technical capabilites to a higher degree. . . . His most feared enemy is death." In contrast, "The basis of the pious man's faith and attitude toward life is reverence. This expresses itself in two principal characteristics: a strong sense of nature and a belief in a suprarational world order. The pious man treasures reason, to be sure, as a precious gift, but does not see in it an adequate means of understanding the world, still less of mastering it."[13] Hesse is quick to note that he, and many of us, vacillate between these poles; they are simplified models for his literary creations.

Another construct central to understanding Hesse's later novels is his division of the developed and mature life into three stages, a characteristic of the psychology of Jung and Eastern religious thought. The first stage is one of childhood innocence and a lack of responsibility for the world and for others. (This stage poses an interesting question for our time: in the light of our new and frightening knowledge of abuse of children throughout the world, is there ever a time of innocence?) The path of development leads to a second stage, "to guilt, to the knowledge of good and evil, to the demand for culture, for morality, for religions, for human ideals." He notes that serious attention to this stage leads to disillusionment and to acknowledgment that perfect virtue cannot exist. Despair at our failure to achieve goodness "leads either to defeat or to a third realm of the spirit, to the experience of a condition beyond morality and law, an advance into grace and release to a new, higher kind of irresponsibility, or to put it briefly: to faith."[14] These extended quotations are essential to understanding Hesse's novels. The plots follow the developmental path just described; the characters exemplify one of the personality types, or both patterns are incorporated in the same person, invariably a man. Our polarization between body and spirit and our journey of development from the innocence of childhood to a realized life in the spirit and in faith are the lessons Hesse offers us. As Walter Sorell writes, "What mattered so much to him was to add meaningfulness to existence, and beauty to meaningfulness. He rejected the idea of living a life for the sake of mere living, or of loving for the sake of mere loving a woman."[15]

The influence of Jungian psychology is quite evident here. A valued life is understood to involve introspection and honest evaluation of the self. But who is this self that I am? How can I know it with confidence? First there is my persona, the *I* known to others as spouse, parent, worker, citizen, friend. Many of us, over time, accept the persona as who we really are. We also have a shadow, as Jung calls it, that represents aspects of our personality that we may not honor or accept and are quick to project on others. Characteristics of our shadow are not necessarily negative, but they are aspects that we deny as definitive, although they are alive and well. Understanding and acceptance of this other part of our psyche lead to a richer life, one aimed at achieving a higher level of individuation—becoming the whole person we can become. We must also be aware that there is an unconscious part to our selves perceived through dreams and symbols, through the "Ahaah!" experiences we discern. Attempts to understand this vital part of our lives, to be alert to the messages that are sent to us, will provide meaning and worth to our ventures. For Jung, as for Hesse, the unconscious part of the psyche is often equated with God, with that primordial knowing, loving, creating, and judging force that supports all activities and enriches all thought and art. In Jungian language, this is referred to as the Self, to which we all have access through reflection on the language of our hearts and minds, the symbols we endow with meaning, and the knowledge of our selves we gain by attention to our dreams and fantasies.

NARCISSUS AND GOLDMUND

This novel is set in the Middle Ages; the central section of the book—the story of Goldmund—takes place in the time of the Black Death. Although there are direct references to the death, abandonment, and dereliction obviously related to the plague, the story could as well describe World War I, which Hesse decried. I see the plague as his metaphor for the state of Europe in the grip of an epidemic of meaninglessness epitomized by the massive killing and destruction of a disintegrating culture. The central question, according to Hesse and the psychology of Jung, which he exploits so well, is, does life have meaning despite the evidence we see about us? What is the meaning, and how are we to be cognizant of it, realize it, feel it? Hesse's answer will bear heavily on his own convictions concerning the role of art in clarifying and offering his readers the promise of the eternal in our transient lives as sojourners. In Hesse's earlier novels, the two types of persons—those of the spirit and those of nature—are presented as two aspects, two faces, of the same man. In *Narcissus and Goldmund* there are two men, each representative, more or less, of these same types. They are the two types that thoughtful readers recognize in themselves, one of them being the shadow side.

Narcissus is an ascetic and brilliant monk, a master logician and teacher, absolutely committed to his life of obedience to the will of God. Goldmund, an adolescent, is brought to the school at the monastery by his father. His mother, a beautiful and sensual woman, abandoned her husband and son to find fulfillment elsewhere. Goldmund, aspiring at first to be a spiritual man like his teacher, is helped by Narcissus (as a Jungian analyst) to realize that his consummation lies elsewhere in the world of art, of love, of life and death. The polarities of the two men are not quite so simple. Narcissus is not completely a father figure; he is intuitive, aware of his pride, anxious to serve others and help them toward realization of their own selves. Goldmund is also a teacher, enlightening Narcissus about the role of art and the function of the mother figure in achieving a full life.

Goldmund leaves the monastery to search for what he will finally call his mother, the Eve-Mother. His adventures include loving, killing, attending to the ever-changing seasons (which tell us of the passing of time), learning of art and life, and finally returning to the monastery and Narcissus to do his sculpture. The two men are the artistic representation of me, the reader, looking for meaning for my life. There is a holding together in tension of the lives, the promises, the growth of the souls in the two men placed as father and mother figures, each in search of a center for life. Edwin F. Casebeer writes:

> Between the world of the mother and the world of the father, as seen by the primitive and the child within all of us, exists many contrasts: hers is the world of matter and nature, his the disembodied spirit joining God; hers the cycles of life and death, his immortality; hers the transient, his the permanent; hers the unconscious, his the conscious intellect; hers the primitive, his the civilized.
>
> As both Narcissus and Goldmund realize, there are many ways to the mystic center, as many ways as there are beings. But there is only one true guide, the Self. One must follow it through horror and ecstasy, good and evil, life and death.[16]

Critics express widely divided positions on this novel: some find it flawed in its structure and ending; others praise it as an exquisite work, developing with great finesse many symbols and concepts that we must know and consider as we search for centers to our own lives. One compliment they all share: the role of art as the mediator of the spirit, the bearer of the symbols that declare ourselves to be centered, is succinctly and lovingly presented by Hesse in this novel. This is so because it is Hesse's own understanding of the function of art for us. Art is presented as a way to knowledge of our selves, a learned sense of enlightenment and of mystery that most of us find only in our dreams. As Theodore Ziolkowski states, "Art emerges as the supreme mediator in the novel: the foe of death and the synthesis of the apparently irreconcilable poles of nature and spirit." He continues, as he notes Hesse's use of art:

> Hesse is describing . . . the process through which his own composition takes place. His works always emerge from an initial compelling image of a central figure—in this case, of Goldmund. Through this conception of the creative spirit both Narcissus and Goldmund find their way out of the chaos of the world of experience, for it is the responsibility of the creative mind to treat the ideal spirit as though it were eternally present.[17]

As the story ends, Goldmund dies in the arms of Narcissus, who has confessed his love for Goldmund, his other self. Narcissus is challenged by Goldmund to find his own "mother," so that he will be able to die when his hour comes.

We must be alert and read Hesse as a novelist whose polarized characters are presented to inform us of who we are. In this novel, the two men are *me*. I am Narcissus *and* Goldmund: one is more obvious as my persona, but the other will appear unexpectedly as my shadow. My goal, maturing as a person with meaning for my life, requires me to recognize the man of nature and the man of spirit coexistent in me, each striving for recognition and fulfillment. This maturation occurs as I find and create meaning for my life, meaning that will bear up under the crises and catastrophes—the plagues— that are certain components of life. In the novel, the ascetic monk shows us his own artistry in the intensity of his search for the meaning of the divine call he knows. His careful crafting of prayer, the stripping away of the external accoutrements of his daily life, his artful dissection of his sin of pride and his desire for power are certain signs of his virtuosity. It is craftsmanship of the spirit, not of watercolor, woodcarving, or collage, but artistry just the same.

Meaning, Faith, and Ethics

A polarity exists in my life between the meaning I give to that life and the faith that supports it. These two poles—meaning and faith—and the energy that flows between them determine my behavior, the ethical basis to my life. Of course, the actuality of that life will never approach my expectations for it of an ethical and faithful existence. But the meaning and the faith abide. The authors I have discussed so far—Tillich, Jung, and Hesse— offer me distinct and articulate evaluations of choices in my search for defining aspects of faith and of meaning for living. In a vital way, each tells a story, partly fictive and imagined, that enlightens the path we are on as sojourners. Essential to these stories are the myths that lie behind them, the ancient and recurring dramas of human insight and certainty of being and knowing that urge us on in our travels.

The role of myth is central to understanding meaning and faith. As our knowledge of other cultures and religions expanded in the latter nineteenth century, we became aware that there are many religions, many deeply held belief systems explaining our creation, our being, and our destiny. To recognize only one revealed faith, to acknowledge one religion as ultimate and definitive, became a doubtful enterprise. Herein lies the appeal and the strength of the works of Jung and Hesse. Convinced of the reality of God active in our lives, both men declined acceptance of a specific religion as primary or exclusive. Tillich certainly is to be read as a Christian, but even his theological construction is not typical of most church affirmations. Myth and legend tell us more than eyewitness accounts do. Jesus' birth announcement in the local paper, a photograph of Buddha sitting under the Bo tree, a tape of Ezekiel describing the wheel—none of these could have the power of the myths developed from those symbolic events. Toward the end of his memoir *Memories, Dreams, Reflections*, Jung writes:

The need for mythic statements is satisfied when we frame a view of the world which adequately explains the meaning of human existence in the cosmos, a view which springs from our psychic wholeness, from the co-operation between conscious and unconscious. . . . Meaning makes a great many things endurable—perhaps everything. For it is not that "God" is a myth, but that myth is the revelation of a divine life in man. It is not we who invent myth, rather it speaks to us as a Word of God.[18]

Awakening to these revelations is our task, for they can be the beginning of a new phase in life, an experience that Thoreau affirmed. "If one listens to the faintest but constant suggestions of his genius, which are certainly true, he sees not to what extremes, or even insanity, it may lead him; and yet that way, as he grows more resolute and faithful, his road lies."[19] Although for each of us these suggestions of our genius will be different, we search for a common foundation upon which to build a faithful ethic of living with one another. History tells us that we are rarely successful in this chore, but we persist. It is seeking that common ground that is important, and we find it in the visions that most religions profess of a unity of being, a commonality of purpose, a hope for peace and prosperity. I have a sharply limited faith as a Christian, determined as it is by birth, nurture, and choices made, usually in ignorance of other options. Yet I delight in my faith as I interpret it broadly upon my understanding of its history, its modes of transmission, and its very human tales of wonder and presence. I see Christianity as one of a number of deeply held religious faiths capable of inspiring sacrificial actions toward the sick, the helpless, and the hopeless. I know my faith as a way of life, as an assurance that despair can be overcome, and as a statement of my best dreams and hopes for us all, even though I know that I am unable to truly live the Christian life as I understand it. The assurance of forgiveness permits—demands—that I forgive. The confidence that God is with me in my innermost being and is known to me in varied ways is a comfort that encourages me to accept others into my life. Jesus' teaching about the duties we have to heal, to feed, to attend to others as our equals, encourages me to try to do likewise, although I often fail.

I am a man of nature *and* a man of spirit. I am Narcissus and Goldmund, inheritor of the traditions of Job and of Jesus, admirer of followers of other faiths that I understand poorly, if at all, yet accept as revelations of the prospects we have for a future together. Faith in my ultimate concern—God—is confirmed for me by the symbols, the dreams, the "nudgings" I receive in my daily life of listening to the language of my head and heart. I am confident that the source of my being, the hope of my life, and the promise of my future are revealed through careful attention to the search for meaning. Harold A. Bosley, minister of the Mount Vernon Methodist Church, which I attended as a medical student in Baltimore, writes that revelation is God speaking to man, whether by dreams and visions, as he was thought to do in Old Testament times, or through the church, or through the Sacred Word, or through the sudden indwelling of the Holy Spirit yielding a holy ecstasy. Whatever the medium, the fact of communication *from* God is the distinguishing mark of revelation.[20]

We are sought by God, called to attend to the inner spirit that speaks of the Holy Spirit, ever mindful of our deep and profound need for meaning for our lives.

For many of us, particularly those in professions that require years of education and specialized training to become competent to teach or practice one's skills, education in matters of the spirit ceases, for all intents and purposes, when we are too old to be forced to go to Sunday school. In adults, a developed sense of the spiritual aspects of human nature is often as poorly evidenced as appreciative knowledge of art, music, or literature. It is a truism that we cannot do and learn everything. An unfortunate result of this stalled development in things of the spirit is unawareness of the depth of meaning and fulfillment that can be a part of daily living. The search for an ultimate concern, an awakening to the power of the unconscious to inform and guide our lives, and the discovery of the bonds that can be established between the self and the rest of the created world—these are the gifts that faith offers. The search for meaning for our lives is a rigorous journey inward as we learn to communicate with ourselves and the source of our being that seeks us out.

There is no map for this journey, although many signposts have been placed during these centuries. Some are indistinct, partly hidden from casual view; others are shiny and new. There seems to be a variety of paths to follow, but the common component is that they all point to the inner person. What we are to learn about our purposes and our goals will come from trained and informed introspection. The search within leads ever deeper and yet clearer. We commonly call this search prayer, although there is no magic in that or any other word. What I speak to is an opening of the heart and the mind to revelations about the self, about our actions and feelings that well up in moments of quiet reflection. These can be painful, disgusting, joyous, or grateful. But there are messages there about courage, honor, gratitude, thankfulness, the need for redirection, a call for change, and commitment to promises. Even as Georges Bernanos's country priest tells us, to want to pray, to try to pray, *is* prayer to God.

Introspection, that searching of the heart for an understanding of who I am and would be, sensitizes me to assess with care the occurrences of my life, looking as much for their interrelations as for their independent meanings. I am alert to synchronicity, the meanings sought in and learned from the coincidence of circumstances, conversations, ideas, and actions—mine and others'—that determine me. Studying to understand the significance of coexistent happenings and thoughts enlightens and directs my search for the meanings not only of events but also of the totality of my life. Prayer, that looking inward for the informing influence of the unconscious upon the conscious, is a reliable source for interpreting the meaning of my life and empowering actions that define it.

METAPHOR, ILLUSION, AND FAITH

The plague of meaninglessness can be faced in all its ambiguity and hiddenness by a developed and whole person who unites the inner spirit and the outer nature in one self: the result of the process of individuation presented by Jung. Religion, in all its varied nuances and belief systems, is also an accessible and effective mode for thinking through the significance of our lives. Considered by many to be mere superstition, primitive and naive, religions meet deep and permanent needs we have for meaning in our personal and social lives. Jung points out that the lack of a cohesive sense of what we are about in our collective life—a sense of ultimate meaning for our existence—opens for us "all sorts of private idiocies and idiosyncracies, manias, phobias, and daemonisms whose primitivity leaves nothing to be desired, not to speak of the psychic epidemics of our time before which the witch-hunts of the sixteenth century pale by comparison."[21]

Robertson Davies exploits the psychology of Jung with consummate skill. *Fifth Business*, the first novel in his Deptford Trilogy, offers a scholarly, witty, and profound study of the search for meaning in life and for understanding the nature of what it means to be a person. For Davies, as for Jung, the human search is for a lively and feasible knowledge of our identity as human beings. Grasping the meaning of our lives is dependent on understanding what it means to be a self: to be a person who recognizes and acknowledges the multiple aspects we present to the world. Davies asks two questions to inform this understanding: what roles am I playing in my life, and who is the real me, my true identity? The journey of discovery occupies a lifetime and takes us down a winding road with curves that can, at times, effectively obscure our vision. Significant intersections will require fateful decisions. Time is a crucial factor, for my reading of the map is dependent on the time of day: am I in the morning, noon, or late afternoon of my life? In the thought of Hesse, am I in the time of innocence, of despair, or of faith?

Fifth Business is the autobiography of Dunstan Ramsay, a seventy-year-old retired teacher who recounts both reflections on his past and current discoveries about his self. With skill and impressive knowledge of Jungian psychology, Davies offers us characters and occasions that illustrate both the illusory nature of religious faith and our profound need for those illusions as metaphoric bridges between reality and us, the observers. Since reality is perceived by us only through our prejudiced and ignorant senses, we recognize truth in varied and individual ways; metaphor becomes the way of communicating these partial truths. Patricia Monk, in describing one aspect of the faith of the hero of this novel, writes:

> Religious beliefs (as expressed in religious art, saint's legends, and so on, as well as religious language) are metaphoric expressions of religious reality (the numinosum). A metaphor may be taken either literally (without understanding that it is a sign for something else), which leads to delusion, or symbolically (understanding that it is a sign for something else), which makes it a form of fantasy; the former is the way of the "simple," the latter the way of the "truly sophisticated." Both fantasy and delusion, however, are, in Davies' terms, forms of illusion. Consequently an apprehension of the numinosum is possible only through the medium of illusion.[22]

Delusion is shown to the reader in a woman gone mad, a person whom the hero, Ramsay, mistakes for a saint. Only in time, with the skilled help of others, does he understand that she is a fool-saint. He has been deluded. Thoreau warns us about the dangers of delusion, telling us to be cautious in our defining of reality. He suggests that illusion, in the form of fable, offers us the truth about ourselves and the world.

> Shams and delusions are esteemed for soundest truths, while reality is fabulous. If men would steadily observe realities only, and not allow themselves to be deluded, life, to compare it with such things as we know, would be like a fairy tale and the Arabian Nights' Entertainments.[23]

The journey of Dunstan Ramsay to faith begins in childhood, when he notes a close relationship between the *Arabian Nights* and the Bible in their tales of wonder. He comments that he reads the Bible "not from zeal but curiosity and that long passages of it confirmed my early impression that religion and *Arabian Nights* were true in the same way. (Later I was able to say that they were both psychologically rather than literally true, and that psychological truth was really as important in its own way as historical verification.)"[24] This realization draws him into a long and fruitful search for the sources of religious faith. This source is located in the psyche. Faith, or religious belief, has its ground, its defining revelation, in the psychological self. In turn, the source of faith is the unconscious, that part of our psychological being that is informed by the self, the unconscious that can be equated with the ultimate reality that we know and call God.

Ambivalence is a key factor in learning about faith and truth, words laden with intensity and significance in this novel of evolving revelation of the personal nature not only of the characters but also of the reader. The hero, in his attempt to understand himself, his friends and enemies, and his world, delves deeply into the recesses of his shadow, that dark and hidden aspect of the personality that surprises us with its unwanted and painful awakening to who we really are. In this suppressed other reality, Ramsay, as does the reader, learns of the equivocal nature of realities, the physical and the psychic totality that is this man. In brilliant and creative writing, Davies presents characters who represent the mandala, the fourfold symbol Jung employs to depict our total selves, with the ego in the center. This fourfold symbol recalls the quaternity of God as Father, Son, Holy Spirit, and Evil developed in the discussion of Job. Ramsay's persistent search for self-understanding, for individuation, leads him to a developed and sure knowledge of the nature of faith as revealed to us through metaphor—through our acceptance of illusion as our only source of certainty about reality.

Ambivalence in life, particularly the inner moral life of ongoing self-definition, runs through the novel, informing the reader of the ways employed to recognize truth. The use of symbols to comprehend the spiritual reality of the numinous in our lives points us to the necessity of accepting metaphor to be as revelatory of faith as it is explanatory of the inner self. Discrimination between fact and illusion, light and dark, good and evil, truth and falsehood, the ego and the shadow—this lifetime work is work for a developed self. If we act unconsciously, we will court evil, for the Devil—its symbol—is readily present to us as the unexamined part of our lives. This unveiling of the evil within is essential to finding meaning for life. The evil within is sufficient for us; we do not require a Devil in Hades—we have our own. Monk writes:

> Jung points out: "everything begins with the individual" (CW 10:45:27), and a man who takes on the evil in himself takes on as much as he can or needs to of the evil in the world: "Such a man knows that whatever is wrong in the world is in himself, and if he can only learn to deal with his own shadow he has done something real for the world. He has succeeded in shouldering at least an infinitesimal part of the gigantic, unsolved social problems of our day" (CW 11:140:83).[25]

Davies, through his hero, Ramsay, calls on us to acknowledge our responsibility for our guilt and not project it on to others. We must recognize the persona that is ours; study to learn to be reconciled to the evil inherent in us; and attend to our shadow, which can, at any moment, level us from behind.

Faith: A True Illusion

Religious faith is an illusion. There is no certain knowledge of the nature of a divine being, of God, of an ultimate reality. But the symbols, the myths, and the legends that have been ours since antiquity attest to a spirit that can be believed. We all have a god in whom we place final confidence, even if it is our persona, our sexuality, our possessions, our intelligence, our social and political power. Finding the God beyond the other gods is the work of a lifetime, not easily accomplished in youth. Ramsay, the hero of *Fifth Business*, finds that his late years give him the retrospection needed to understand his life. The "afternoon" years can suggest—may even force—reconciliation of opposites and admission of our polarized and conflicting psychological components. This can be the entry point for the ancient, ubiquitous, and constant tales of the Other, of the *numinosum* so longed for, so hoped for, in our lives. In the work of Jung, discussed briefly in this section, I hear the demand that I attend to what happens *around* me; I also know that I must attend to what happens *within* me, the perpetual signals that come through my interactions with others, my dreams and fantasies, the gentle but persistent urging and reorienting that I sense as answers to prayer.

Using the powerful and heavy-laden imagery and symbolism of the past—ancient and modern—I am able to construct a faith that abides. As do many others, I accept the metaphoric language that describes God as being just that—a language of metaphor for a reality that I cannot know except through symbol and image. Art is a major transmitter of the Other. Painting and sculpture, poetry and scripture, music and dance—these are intermediaries that transmit the words of the holy, the messages of our meaning. The plague of meaninglessness is everywhere today. On city streets, in internecine warfare among brothers, in the economics of buying and selling, and in many hearts and homes there is that profound sense of loss and betrayal we know as abandonment, as loss of meaning to life, as worthlessness in the human endeavor.

As with our two novelists and their source in the psychology of Jung, we can turn within and seek the sure and knowable signals that the unconscious provides for our instruction and our well-being. There can be confidence in, even faith in, an infinite and eternal psychic reality that seeks us out to respond in love and justice to the glory of the creation and the potential greatness of human efforts to achieve peace and equity. But it requires introspection of a magnitude not easily acquired, a searching of the heart and the mind to find the sources of strength and revelation that will carry us through to an hour of understanding. If we understand ourselves and the created order in which we are transients, meaning for our lives becomes not a possibility but a reality: a reality of faith made known to us in words and thoughts that can be transfigured into acts that show forth that faith.

The plague of meaninglessness, endemic to our time, must be faced by us as individuals first. We receive the gift of meaning for our lives when we learn who we are and what roles we play and acknowledge the presence of an ultimate and transcendent reality—the illusion of faith—as our guide for living. This experience of the transcendent within our own lives provides a new and sure foundation for behavior. Our irrevocable relatedness to others, our commitment to preserving the environment for the future, and our gratitude for the life we have been given—these are to be interpreted in the context of thanksgiving for gifts we receive without price and will form the skeletal structure of our ethics. We are to awaken to each day in the sure knowledge of our brief tenure here, the definition of our selves that we write out in acts and thoughts, and the certainty of our death. This knowledge of the self, coupled with a sense of the *numinosum* as informant of the unconscious to which we must be alert, can ground an ethic that can be lived with confidence. The Socratic advice to examine ourselves if we are to have a good life is also found in the first letter of Paul to the church at Corinth. Instructing those who would partake of the Lord's Supper, he writes, "Examine yourselves, and only then eat of the bread and drink of the cup."[26]

NOTES

1. Paul Tillich, *The Courage to Be* (New Haven, CT: Yale University Press, 1952), 47.
2. Kenneth Keniston, *The Uncommitted* (New York: Harcourt, Brace & World, 1965), 455.
3. Revelation 6:3–4, NRSV.
4. Paul Tillich, *Dynamics of Faith* (New York: Harper Torchbooks, Harper & Brothers, 1957), 1.
5. Paul Tillich, *Systematic Theology*, vol. 1 (Chicago: University of Chicago Press, 1951), 11.
6. Deuteronomy 6:4–5, NRSV.
7. Mark 9:22b–24, NRSV.
8. Rudolf Otto, *The Idea of the Holy*, trans. John W. Harvey (London: Oxford University Press, 1957), 60.
9. Tillich, *Dynamics*, 13.
10. Theodore Ziolkowski, *Hermann Hesse* (New York: Columbia University Press, 1966), 14.
11. Wallace B. Clift, *Jung and Christianity* (New York: Crossroad, 1986), 6.
12. Ibid., 43.
13. Hermann Hesse, "A Bit of Theology," in *My Belief*, ed. Theodore Ziolkowski, trans. Denver Lindley (New York: Farrar, Straus & Giroux, 1974), 195, 197.
14. Ibid., 189.
15. Walter Sorell, *Hermann Hesse* (London: Oswald Wolff, 1974), 136.

16. Edwin F. Casebeer, *Hermann Hesse* (New York: Thomas Y. Crowell, 1972), 112.
17. Theodore Ziolkowski, *The Novels of Hermann Hesse* (Princeton, NJ: Princeton University Press, 1974), 248–50.
18. C. G. Jung, *Memories, Dreams, Reflections*, ed. Aniela Jaffe, trans. Richard Winston and Clara Winston (New York: Vintage Books, Random House, 1965), 340.
19. Henry David Thoreau, *Walden*, ed. J. Lyndon Shanley (Princeton, NJ: Princeton University Press, 1971), 216.
20. Harold A. Bosley, *The Philosophical Heritage of the Christian Faith* (Chicago: Willett, Clark & Company, 1944), 33.
21. C. G. Jung, "The Transformation of Libido," *Symbols of Transformation*, in *The Collected Works of C. G. Jung*, ed. Sir Herbert Read, Michael Fordham, and Gerhard Adler, trans. R. F. C. Hull Bollingen Series XX (Princeton, NJ: Princeton University Press, 1953), 5:221:156.
22. Patricia Monk, *The Smaller Infinity* (Toronto: University of Toronto Press, 1982), 80.
23. Thoreau, *Walden*, 95.
24. Robertson Davies, *Fifth Business* (New York: Penguin Books, 1977), 71.
25. Monk, *Smaller Infinity*, 97.
26. I Corinthians 11:28, NRSV.

N i n e

A FINAL FAITH FOR THE FORSAKEN

But the world is sleeping in ignorance and error, sir, and we must be crowing cocks, and singing larks, and a rising sun to awaken her.

—Emily Dickinson

EMILY DICKINSON WROTE THESE words to George Gould, a student at Amherst and editor of its new literary journal, *Indicator*, in which this slightly incoherent valentine to him was published in February 1850.[1] I use this quotation to introduce the person of a poet who informs me in understanding my reliance on my faith in times of plague. Dickinson repeats here the call of Thoreau and other transcendentalists to not only awaken ourselves but also call to others to stir from their sleep. The few decades before and immediately after the Civil War are sparkling in our literary history: the creative and imaginative writings of Melville, Emerson, Thoreau, Hawthorne, Whitman, and Dickinson defy comparison to those of any other period, before or after. Rapid industrialization promoted by the demands of war and the subsequent Gilded Age set aside the thoughtful introspection and sensitivity to matters of the spirit that these authors developed in their work in such a short time. A confident United States turned to the dynamo and the factory for its salvation.

There are certain components of the life and the work of Emily Dickinson

143

that require brief comment before I detail her influence on my developing faith and its derivative ethic. Born in 1830 to an influential family in Amherst, Massachusetts, Dickinson was educated at Amherst Academy and for one year at Mount Holyoke Seminary. Her family background was New England Puritan, although she never joined the church or confessed to its faith. Her life assumed legendary dimensions when she became a recluse in her thirties: she dressed in white, rarely left her house, had a steadily constricting circle of visitors, and devoted her phenomenal creative talents to writing poetry. From letters to friends and family and reminiscences of those who knew her, a shadowy figure emerges of a talented and witty recluse who will not be known by us. All we have is poetry to define for us what this fabulous—fabled—woman thought, felt, hoped, and believed. At her death in 1886, nearly two thousand poems were found in her desk, of which seven had been published in her lifetime. Her styles—personal, social, and literary—continue to confound us. She remains a mystery despite biographers' efforts to create a private life for her.

Her poetry is difficult to read: punctuation, occasional eccentric use of words, and syntax confused early readers and continue to make understanding of the poems a labor, albeit of love. But it is her poetry that offers the reader a sublime documentary of one-half of a bisected life: the creation of an artist obsessed with finding meaning for life in a world left desolate by its fashioner. Like Thoreau, she means every word she writes.

This poetry was collated, dated, and published in the early 1950s, offering readers an astounding collection of intense personal reflections of a profoundly spiritual and intellectual questioner. Her collected poems give scholars and critics the opportunity to study her poetry in its development over time, interpret her style, search out her sources for allusion, and be quite overwhelmed by her creative talents. For me, her consciously divided life, her commitment to her art, her resistance to accepted religious doctrines of her time, and the assurances in her own mind and spirit are bases for a developed faith that ensures courage when we are beset.

A pervasive feeling that life has no essential significance or meaning that transcends our daily transactions has been abroad in Western thought for a century or so, and I have considered it as a form of plague that infects and can paralyze our highest hopes and compromise our finest accomplishments. A terrifying extension of this pestilence is one that Dickinson struggled with: the conviction that God had abandoned His world. Although she acknowledged the existence of God, she saw no evidence of divine intervention. As she observed her world, Dickinson saw only a creation forsaken by its creator. This is a plague of the spirit that can overwhelm us.

A DIVIDED LIFE

Biographers of Dickinson have accrued a mass of evidence, much of it suppositional, to explain her work. Whatever that personal life was—be it defined by thwarted love affairs, Freudian issues around her father, or intense fears of death—we will probably never know. For my purposes as a reader of her poetry, I simplify the scenario and place Emily Dickinson in two roles: (1) a daytime housekeeper, a dutiful daughter attentive to the mundane and consuming needs and demands of her parents and family, and an available friend to others in their hours of sorrow and happiness; and (2) an artist who, over time, committed herself to being a poet as the final expression of that self and of her painful search for meaning in her life and in the universe. At the risk of seeming romantic and simplistic, I divide her life into the compartments of night and day for my own use of her work in deciphering questions of meaning for my life. Her days were taken up in family life; it was the night that provided the hours for her creativity. It was then that she made her legendary retreat up the stairs to her room, locked the door, and established her divorce from house and town so that fancy and imagination might run free to produce the phenomenal inheritance we have in her art: an intense and searching study of her encounter with the universe.

In *Lunacy of Light*, Wendy Barker presents an exquisitely developed study of the metaphoric functions that day/sun and night/moon are assigned in the poetry of Dickinson and other women poets, particularly those of the nineteenth century. In our ancient traditions—secular and religious—the sun is an image of the masculine, the moon of the feminine. A basic assumption would be that creativity and the sustenance needed for flowering are found in sunlight, and this assumption pervades our history of art and culture. For women, this traditional understanding may well be wrong. Barker, in discussing women writers of the nineteenth century, writes:

> Rather than serving as agent for growth and rather than allowing possibilities for development, the light of day for all these women writers seems to order prescriptions: sew, bend your head, bear children, be chaste, be quiet, be humble, be married, be good. A light whose rays carried such constraining admonitions seemed, especially for Dickinson, to cast a stain over one's possibilities, infecting everything.[2]

As I attend to the anima, the feminine component of my self, I am gifted with understanding of another powerful tradition of creativity: the art of those for whom the night offers another source of illumination—not the "alien light" of noon, but the inspired and innovative one of the night. Dickinson lived her generative life within the boundaries defined by her gender and her male-dominated society: she went to her room at night and delivered her gift to us in the light she created for herself. I must know the part of me that belongs to the dark, that must and will be urged to grow by a different light, in a mind and through a spirit held and nourished by another spirit, the ultimate creator and deliverer of art and life. Dickinson is alert, also, to the negative connotations of the night. Darkness is equated with death, with the ultimate and final nightfall of the tomb, with the presence of evil among us. But again, this other side of my self must be known and held as mine. My maturation and my developing faith, an ethic of behavior that I would claim as mine—these must acclaim and yet be informed by the dark, even the "dark night of the soul."

Emily Dickinson, a person who made a conscious, defining choice for her life, is a model for examining mine. Suzanne Juhasz writes:

> Emily Dickinson, a woman who wanted to be a poet, chose to withdraw from the external world and to live her most significant life in the world of her mind. This decision was surely what enabled her to be the poet she became. It gave her control over her own experience: she could select, apportion, focus, examine, explore, satiate herself exactly as she wished and needed to do, such that poetry could result. . . . She did not choose to live where men live, in the public world, or where women live, in the domestic world. She found another place, at once more private and expansive than either of those others: the mind.[3]

The division of living into the working day and the creative night—the persona and the shadow—instructs me in understanding my self and the life that is mine in its parts. I know who I am—and you know who I am—by my work in the day: physician, pastor, husband, father, citizen, friend, and the other components of daily living. Who I am to others is important to me, defining of me. But there is a hidden, submerged aspect that appears as a surprise: the shadow, the nightlife of Emily Dickinson, whose existence must be learned and appreciated if my life is to have any fullness. Recognition of these two distinct parts is crucial to a developed life of the spirit, to that opening of the heart and mind to the creative and redeeming functions of God in my life. Dickinson represents my need to understand my place in the universe, the deep and restless urge to grasp—and to be grasped by—an assurance of faith. Her creative talents, her ways of living and engaging her world, and her relationships with others are certainly not mine. But recognition and acceptance of that division of my life that demands the time and the concentration of effort to know who I am and where I am going—this gift from Dickinson to me is beyond valuing.

As my shadow, Dickinson permits, even encourages, persistent efforts to transcend my education and my training and find learning elsewhere. Her divorce from those parts of life that are routine and accepted by me, her relentless drive to document her developing self-knowledge and revelation, and her unswerving commitment to art as she knew it for herself: these are her shadow gifts that lead me to pursue the eternal voyage of self-discovery and acceptance.

To Know Myself

The life of Emily Dickinson is a prime example of the examined self and the use of that examination to produce an art perhaps unequaled in U.S. literary history. To know the self is a difficult task; the question of ultimate honesty, the capacity for self-delusion, motives that might well be questioned: these doubts distort self-understanding, "slant" our vision, as Dickinson would say, and make personal truths open to question. However, the compulsion to continue the journey of knowledge of the self persists.

The origin of the phrase "know thyself" is lost somewhere in Greek antiquity. According to Juvenal, it was delivered to men from the gods in heaven. Plutarch credits Plato for this injunction, and others are confident that it was one of two inscriptions on the oracle at Delphi. I use the phrase to encapsulate the grand inheritance from Hellenic Greece, particularly from Socrates and Plato, that places knowledge within us, especially our knowledge of truth, beauty, and goodness. Kierkegaard, writing about Socrates, says:

> All learning and inquiry is interpreted as a kind of remembering; one who is ignorant needs only a reminder to help him come to himself in the consciousness of what he knows. Thus the Truth is not introduced into the individual from without, but was within him.... [Socrates] entered into the role of midwife and sustained it throughout; not because his thought had "no positive content," but because he perceived that this relation is the highest that one human being can sustain to another.[4]

This knowledge, within us from before time, can be raised to our consciousness by a teacher. Consciousness is polar in its parts, enhancing the challenge to awareness of ourselves. Am I one with all that is, or am I alone? What roles do reason and understanding play in my definition of my self? Is there a unity in creation, or is all diverse? What does life mean in the certainty of death? The opposites that I must recognize and engage—self-other, inner-outer, heaven-hell, I–not I—must be comprehended by me. My tutor, in this case, Dickinson, brings no wisdom or truth, but through prior and personal experience with truth, she delivers me of it, bringing to consciousness what is there but unrecognized. There is a grand inheritance here as I persist in my search for knowing who I am, have been, may become. Knowledge of myself derived from critical evaluation, from clarity of vision of what I see in the mirror, and the precarious expedition to know matters of my heart are necessary prerequisites for spiritual growth. How do I learn about myself? One way to begin the education is to explore that self.

The injunction to explore thyself is central to attempts to know that self. An advocate for this venture is Sir Thomas Browne, a seventeenth-century English physician and self-explorer and an idol of Sir William Osler, the renowned physician-teacher who revolutionized American medicine and is an idol of mine. In *Religio Medici*, Browne describes the many wonders of nature that he observes and appreciates; he proposes no further travel but rather a search of "the Cosmography of myself. We carry with us the wonders we seek without us; there is all Africa and her prodigies in us; we are that bold and adventurous piece of Nature, which he that studies wisely learns in a compendium what others labour at in a divided piece and endless volume."[5] Henry David Thoreau copied this passage while a student at Harvard College, only to place its meaning in the final chapter of *Walden* as he urges us to learn of ourselves:

> What does Africa,—what does the West stand for? Is not our own interior white on the chart? black though it may prove, like the coast, when discovered. Is it the source of the Nile, or the Niger, or the Mississippi, or a North-West passage around this continent that we would find? Are these the problems which most concern mankind? . . . be a Columbus to whole new continents and worlds within you, opening new channels, not of trade, but of thought.[6]

The search for meaning in my life takes many routes; the map is large, occasionally confusing, always beckoning. There are several roads that I follow; actually, they are well-worn paths. As is obvious from this study, the creative efforts of others inform, challenge, and encourage me. Religious, psychological, and philosophical studies, autobiographical accounts of inner adventures, music, and prayer are strong guides to mapping my interior cosmography. My experience is that a developed and intelligible faith requires sharply tuned attention, experience in the workings of this world, devotion to the object of the beliefs I affirm, willingness to spend barren hours waiting, and confidence that, in many and varied ways, I will know the course I am to follow. There is little that is new in this curriculum of faith, but it is important that I know what I am doing and being. As is so apparent in the literary accomplishments of various authors, time and concentrated effort are essential. *Walden* is the result of ten years of writing and rewriting. Hesse's life is found in his novels. Dickinson is one of the most sharply fixed artists we will ever encounter.

The works of Sir Thomas Browne were in the Dickinson family library, and she was acquainted, to some degree, with the works of Thoreau, who died in 1862 when Dickinson was thirty-two. The concerns of these two men were hers also, as she thought about our need to explore ourselves. Dickinson's fascination with the concepts of "circumference" and her ongoing exploration of her own self come together in two poems that are close partners to Thoreau. The first, a quatrain dated 1864, reads:

> Soto! Explore thyself!
> Therin thyself shalt find
> The "Undiscovered Continent"—
> No Settler had the Mind. [no. 832]

Thoreau, again in the conclusion to *Walden*, asks us to pursue the exploring of the continent and beyond, searching for the circumference that is everywhere. He writes that we are to

> obey the precept of the old philosopher and explore thyself. Herin are demanded the eye and the nerve. . . . Start now on that farthest western way, which does not pause at the Mississippi or the Pacific, nor conduct toward a worn-out China or Japan, but leads on direct a tangent to this sphere, summer and winter, day and night, sun down, moon down, and at last earth down too.[7]

Grasping the totality of our being, the completeness of the self, the infinite possibilities of the explored person that I am and will become, these are Dickinson's desires for herself and for us, her readers, in this poem of 1876:

> The Heart is the Capital of the Mind—
> The Mind is a single State—
> The Heart and the Mind together make
> A single Continent—
>
> One—is the Population—
> Numerous enough—
> This ecstatic Nation
> See—it is Yourself. [no. 1354]

A precursor to exploration of the self is the imperative to awaken. Thoreau warns us, over and over again, that we may not be awake to nature or to ourselves: we may be sleeping our life away. He uses "morning" as a metaphor for that sense of alertness necessary to any knowledge of the self. "Morning is when I am awake and there is dawn in me. Moral reform is the effort to throw off sleep."[8] Certainly I cannot explore my self, learn the multiple facets of my personality—my persona and my shadow—if I am not awake to that self. As we waken at dawn, we become aware of sounds and sights not knowable while asleep. So, with awakening to the self, we experience a new day with its new questions and revelations, its presentation of the recurring issue of meaning to my life. My mind—responsive in faith—interprets experience and directs my thoughts and my actions. Experience is interpreted in the context of my faith. An essential part of my construct of my self is belief that there is more to me than the body I see in the mirror, miraculous though that is. I am convinced that there is a part of me—call it soul or spirit—that responds to the creative and sustaining spirit of God pervasive in the world I know.

Usually related to belief in immortality, the concept of soul or spirit is pervasive in religions. It is often envisioned as contained or encapsulated within the body, to be freed at death to be with its creator, God. A significant part of the process of self-exploration is thinking through this concept of an immortal spirit at one with God. A metaphor that is commonly used to illustrate the transformations envisioned in the inner self is that of the seeming miracle of change from egg to larva to butterfly, this latter word a common trope for the soul. Sir Thomas Browne was fascinated by his understanding of the stages of our lives. We begin in a microcosm. "In that obscure World and Womb of our Mother, our time is short, computed by the Moon. . . . Entering afterwards upon the scene of the World, we arise and become another creature . . . obscurely manifesting that part of Divinity in us." He notes that scripture "hath taught me a great deal of Divinity, and instructed my belief, how that immortal spirit and incorruptible substance of my Soul may lye [sic] obscure, and sleep while within this house of flesh. Those strange and mystical transmigrations that I have observed in Silkworms, turned my Philosophy into Divinity."[9]

Thoreau, on the final page of *Walden*, tells a fantastic tale of transmigration, of

> a strong and beautiful bug which came out of the dry leaf of an old table of apple tree wood . . . from an egg deposited in the living tree many years earlier . . . which was heard gnawing out for several weeks. . . . Who does not feel his faith in a resurrection and immortality strengthened by hearing of this? Who knows what beautiful and winged life, whose egg has been buried for ages . . . may unexpectedly come forth from society's most trivial and handselled furniture, to enjoy its perfect summer life at last?[10]

Is there a "strong and beautiful bug" within me awaiting release to show that I have awakened to the world of the spirit and will declare it with my life?

The poetry of Emily Dickinson recounts an endless struggle with the religious faith of her Puritan ancestors, a faith that was evaporating in the middle of the nineteenth century, to be replaced in Massachusetts by Boston unitarianism and, briefly, by Concord transcendentalism. The question of immortality, what she called her "Flood subject," was important to her, and she wrote to this puzzling concern repeatedly. In this early poem of 1859, she says:

> Cocoon above! Cocoon below!
> Stealthy Cocoon, why hide you so
> What all the world suspect?
> An hour, and gay on every tree
> Your secret, perched in ecstasy
> Defies imprisonment!
>
> An hour in Chrysalis to pass,
> Then gay above receding grass
> A Butterfly to go!
> A moment to interrogate,
> Then wiser than a "Surrogate,"
> The Universe to know! [no. 129]

The transmigration or transformation that the soul makes from within the cocoon to flying free in the sky and knowing the universe will be the adventure for my spirit. Death brings an end to this earthly existence; only then wisdom beyond judging may be possible. In a poem of 1866, she writes of an imprisoned soul hoping for release from the mortal body, a detail of her unresolved conflicts around immortality. She writes:

> My cocoon tightens—Colors tease—
> I'm feeling for the Air—
> A dim capacity for Wings
> Demeans the Dress I wear—
>
> A power of Butterfly must be—
> The Aptitude to fly
> Meadows of Majesty implies
> And easy Sweeps of Sky—
>
> So I must baffle at the Hint
> And cipher at the Sign
> And make much blunder, if at last
> I take the clue divine—[no. 1099]

Confident in an inner spirit that can and will know God, we are beholden to ourselves and our world to awaken to that inner self. We must explore in depth and width the hidden continents that are ours and become our true selves, witnesses to the truths available to the searching heart and mind.

To Grasp the Infinite

Infinity is a reality in two directions: I look to the stars, aware that I see but the nearest ones in a universe that is boundless; I read about subatomic particles and sense that there will be no final "item" found there, either. Placed as I am, somewhere between these two infinities, a minuscule speck on a grain of sand in a sandbox, I am the more confirmed in my faith through humility, awe and wonder, and the inner confidence that comes from prayer. A persistent concern voiced by Dickinson in her poetry is infinity—that realm of the God she pursued—the outermost reaches of our imagination that she refers to as "circumference." A phrase of hers that attracts much attention from critics is found in her July 1862 letter to Thomas Wentworth Higginson: "My Business is Circumference." Her source for using the word *circumference* has bewitched readers. She appears to use it to refer to varied subjects from love to God, from eternity and infinity to the imagination, from art to the mundane.

In my reading of her poetry, I understand circumference to refer to the breadth and depth of the creation, a vision of the infinite and the intimate combined and knowable to us through scripture, nature, experience, artistic imagination, and love. Two authors whom Dickinson read refer to circumference, although in different terms. Sir Thomas Browne, knowledgeable in Hermetic philosophy, writes in *Christian Morals* that we creatures frequently use hyperbole to describe ourselves and our accomplishments but that "nothing can be said Hyperbolically of God." Commenting, probably, on the Hermetic formula, *Sphaera cujus centrum ubique, circumferentia nullibi,* he points out that "[Hermes] *Trismegistus,* his Circle, whose center is everywhere, and circumference nowhere, was no Hyperbole. Words cannot exceed, where they cannot express enough. Even the most winged Thoughts fall at the setting out, and reach not the portal of Divinity."[11] God and the created order are beyond our comprehension. Dickinson very likely read the first series of essays by Ralph Waldo Emerson published in 1841. In the opening paragraph of "Circles," he writes, "St. Augustine described the nature of God as a circle whose center was everywhere, and its circumference nowhere."[12] In *The Confessions of Saint Augustine,* which Emerson read in 1839, we read Augustine's concept of God: "Life of my life . . . penetrating the whole mass of the universe, and beyond it, every way, through unmeasurable boundless spaces; . . . all things have Thee, and they be bounded in Thee, and Thou bounded nowhere."[13]

There is more. Giordano Bruno, the mathematician burned at the stake in 1600 for his heretical descriptions of the universe, is credited with the "affirmation expressed in *De l'Infinito, Universo e Mondi,* that the center of the universe is everywhere, and its circumference nowhere."[14] Finally, in this very incomplete survey, Blaise Pascal (1623–62) writes in *Pensees*, "The whole visible world is only an imperceptible atom in the ample bosom of nature. . . . It is an infinite sphere, the center of which is everywhere, the circumference nowhere."[15] Dickinson is in good company with her exclamation, "circumference is my business." Surely, her artistic vision and her search for the meaning of her life extend about as far as any author we can know, and her commitment to honest engagement with the universe and the creator of it is clear and instructive to the seeker of today.

WRESTLING WITH GOD

In the rural towns of the Connecticut River Valley in the 1850s, religious revivals were regular occurrences. Emily Dickinson was the only member of her family who declined the conversion experience that was "expected" of adults. Albert J. Gelpi writes:

> Here, then the problem lay: how to live when one could not accept Christ's call. Even if one renounced a heavenly goal that gave direction to the transitory world, one could not resign one's self to a merely physical existence in a world of death; one would have to find something that was neither the life of matter nor the life of heaven, but partook of both.[16]

Dickinson chose a path of independence based on her developing creative genius that granted her freedom to be herself in a world that she knew as painful and read as abandoned by God. She does not seem to have denied the existence of God but had serious doubts about any involvement of the Deity with the creation. Cynthia Griffin Wolff, in her superb critical literary biography, writes of Dickinson:

> She had been given years of instruction in the correct way to adjust her vision of the Being Who had created man and Who continued to spell man's fate: teachers had directed her to see signs that would sustain hope in this concealed Divinity; ministers had commanded her to recognize the evidences of a new birth in Christ scattered throughout the natural world. Yet she had refused faith and the promises held out by conversion. Instead, she had clung to independence and the inviolate integrity of an isolated self. When Emily Dickinson looked into the void just behind life's veil, she apprehended a terrible Force of desertion, destruction, and death.[17]

By her late twenties, Dickinson was committed to the task of finding meaning for herself in a world forsaken by God long ago.

Dickinson took a biblical theme that was common in the preaching and religious exhortation of her day—the wrestling of Jacob with God at Peniel—as determinative of her understanding of the relationship between God and humankind. God won the match unfairly by injuring his adversary; He gave Jacob a new name, Israel, and returned to heaven, to be seen and known no more on earth. This first abandonment by God seemed obvious to Dickinson as she surveyed her world. Death and suffering, without any apparent connection to what is due us, were everywhere around her in family and friends. If one needed confirmation of this abandonment, one need look no further than the crucifixion of Jesus. It is not only that this man was killed by such a horrible method; his announcement that he was forsaken by his God closes the argument about a God for us. The God who walked away from Jacob did not even say a word of comfort to one who had given his life in healing the sick, feeding the hungry, clothing the naked, and visiting the prisoner. We witness universal tragedy in these two events. A third view of God's abandonment is noted by Jack Miles in his book *God: A Biography*. Differing from the Christian Old Testament, the Hebrew Bible places Chronicles, not the prophets, at the end. God, known in Genesis as active in human affairs and present to us, retreats steadily as the biblical account proceeds. Finally, God is silent, the work assumed by the people of Israel. "As the Tanakh ends, the mind of God has been objectified in law, the action of God incarnated in leadership, and now, finally, the voice of God transferred to prayer. David's last prayer is the Lord God's farewell speech."[18]

Dickinson saw little evidence that faith—the gift God grants in our struggle with adversity in life and belief—was available to her. In an audacious and powerful move, she assumed for herself the role of creator, or, perhaps better, re-creator; she saw the physical world and its abundant gratuitous suffering as obvious proof of abandonment by God. As her solitary creative spirit developed, she called a new work into being: her poetry, which will examine all that we know of life and of death.

One of her more enigmatic poems describes her choice of writing as her commitment over that of conversion to the orthodox Christian faith of Amherst:

> Two swimmers wrestled on the spar—
> Until the morning sun—
> When One—turned and smiled to the land—
> Oh God! the Other One!
>
> The stray ships—passing—
> Spied a face—
> Upon the waters borne—
> With eyes in death—still begging raised—
> And hands—beseeching—thrown! [no. 201]

Dickinson turns to the world, to the land, for evidence of life and hope for that brief time we know, a life lived in a world of sorrow, abandoned to our fate by an indifferent God. The suggestion of a divided self in the poem is resolved by the decision to pursue the art and leave the religion to others. In this poem, as in much of her writing, death is the opponent, the final victor, an actor in the drama of our lives that she writes about with precision, with curiosity and anxiety, and, finally, with acceptance. The power of the poetry for my developing faith lies in the intensity and the persistence of her quest to understand her world in terms that were comprehensible to her at the time. Her refusal to accept doctrine and creed, the intensity of her combat with "God," however understood, and the distinct feeling of her "presence" in the poetry combine to challenge me to be sure that I understand what I am thinking, believing, and saying. Archibald MacLeish notes the "hot and fearless and wholly human anger" in her poems that confront God. Dickinson speaks with a voice

> in the live locutions of dramatic speech, words born living on the tongue, written as though spoken. . . . The voice is never a voice overheard. It is a voice that speaks to us almost a hundred years later with such urgency, such an immediacy, that most of us are half in love with this girl we all call by her first name. . . . Emily locked away in a chest a voice which cries to all of us of our common life and love and death and fear and wonder.[19]

For one who understands religious faith to be a lifetime work of definition, study, application, and listening, a wonderful aside is offered by the use Dickinson made of what she called her "Lexicon." This book was the family dictionary, *An American Dictionary of the English Language* by Noah Webster, published in 1828 and 1847. Webster lived in Amherst from 1812 to 1824, was a friend of the Dickinsons, and was influential in academic affairs. Careful use of language is essential not only to the poet but also to the person of faith. Dickinson pruned her language down to the point where she meant every word she wrote. Her style is dramatic, definitive, and concise, often to the point of obscurity. Her search for the word that was exactly correct by combing through the synonyms with care is a lesson for all writers. As Charles R. Anderson writes:

> In striking contrast with the practice of her contemporaries is the brevity of her own forms, which she celebrated in an aphorism:
>
> > Capacity to Terminate
> > Is a Specific Grace—
>
> This gift she developed into a highly elliptical style, pruning away all excess in her passion to get down to the clean bones of language. In a poem about writing a love letter the urgency of the message makes her impatient of verbosity and even the standard rules of construction:

> Tell Him—I only said the Syntax—
> And left the Verb and the pronoun out—

The lines also describe her own poetic way.[20]

For those who read theology and deliver and hear sermons, these words are an offering of hope for all. To know what we mean and to express that clearly, simply, and with finesse and beauty are goals that most of us find elusive but that Dickinson reached, with benefit for us.

THE GREAT LEVELER

Death is a prominent subject in her poetry, the event in our brief journey that raises deep questions: How do we live in the knowledge of death? How do we interpret divine justice in the death of children? What is the significance of pain and suffering? Is there meaning in the theological and religious answers posed by the Christian claim of heaven and immortality? Dickinson lays out the issues with chilling clarity. Death comes to us in varied guises, and she varies its significance with the purpose of her poem. Rarely does she stray from the path of detailed description of the event. In perhaps her finest poem on death, she uses the funeral ceremony in the first stanza to suggest the beginning of a spiritual journey on which her soul—Immortality—is her companion.

> Because I could not stop for Death—
> He kindly stopped for me—
> The Carriage held but just Ourselves—
> And Immortality.

In the concluding stanzas, burial is described in the language of the graveyard; then, with her immortal cotraveler, she "surmises" that she is on her way to Eternity.

> We paused before a House that seemed
> A Swelling of the Ground—
> The Roof was scarcely visible—
> The Cornice—in the Ground—
> Since then—'tis Centuries—and yet
> Feels shorter than the Day
> I first surmised the Horses Heads
> Were toward Eternity—[no. 712]

Death is also portrayed as a lover come for his virginal bride-to-be:

> Death is the supple Suitor
> That wins at last—

It is a stealthy Wooing
Conducted first
By pallid innuendoes
And dim approach
But brave at last with Bugles
And a bisected Coach
It bears away in triumph
To Troth unknown
And Kinsmen as divulgeless
As Clans of Down—[no. 1445]

We read here that, as Anderson notes:

The three stages of the poem ... correspond to the awareness of death, the act of death, and the state after death. The last, in relation to the Christian concept of entering heaven as the bride of Christ, is rendered with typical Dickinsonian obliqueness.[21]

Dickinson is a model for the seeker after faith. Her relentless, yet deeply thoughtful, pursuit of understanding at least the questions of our existence is exemplary for me. Of course, there are no answers to the questions we pose; what happens at our death can hardly be imagined. It remains a mystery we must accept. Paul, in his first letter to the church at Corinth, wrote:

But someone will ask, "How are the dead raised? With what kind of body do they come?" Fool! What you sow does not come to life unless it dies. And as for what you sow, you do not sow the body that is to be, but a bare seed, perhaps of wheat or some other grain. But God gives it a body as he has chosen. . . . So it is with the resurrection of the dead. What is sown is perishable, what is raised is imperishable. . . . It is sown a physical body, it is raised a spiritual body. . . . What I am saying, brothers and sisters, is this: flesh and blood cannot inherit the kingdom of God. . . . Listen, I will tell you a mystery! We will not all die, but we will be changed, in a moment, in the twinkling of an eye, at the last trumpet.[22]

This concept of the old self dying so that a new one may be born applies, of course, to each day of life, not just to the end of it.

A FOUNDATION FOR FAITH

Dickinson and the apostle Paul confront the fact of death. Each, according to experience and faith, constructs images, possible scenarios for what happens at the moment and thereafter. Each admits that mystery shrouds the finale of knowable life, that there is a veil that we shall not lift here. But there is a difference between them that is helpful to me as I seek to understand my faith, that foundation of belief and hope. Accepting the obvious risk of oversimplification, I understand Dickinson to ground her faith in God in the incarnation of God in the man Jesus; Paul bases his on the resurrection of Jesus as the Christ. In his early letters, Paul writes of his expectation that Jesus Christ will return in the immediate future to usher in a new age, perhaps as an apocalypse that will change the world. Over time, ending with his letter to the church at Rome, there is a softening of this expectation, a realization that our life here must continue, informed as it is by the presence of a Holy Spirit that was manifest to us in the life, the death, and the resurrection of Jesus. Eternal events are not determined by human will or desire, but by the will of God, and we are to live out our lives in hope and in confidence that salvation has already been revealed for us in Jesus. Paul sees Jesus' life and his teachings as our directives in this new faith, now establishing itself as an organization, as a church that will become, in its own way, a powerful secular force in a corrupt world.

Dickinson, responsive in her own way to the radical shifts in U.S. social culture and the disintegration of Puritan religious thought and theology, seems to maintain a belief in God as existent, as creative, but as absent from the affairs of the world. There is a wide ambiguity in her poetry about God, telling me of her persistent attempts to hold to a faith, to feel assured of the existence and nature of God in light of her challenging and brilliant mind. The collapse of a severe Puritan theology, replaced by a Victorian faith sentimentalized in Jesus as a man of love, placed an emphasis on the hope of heaven, where we would rejoin members of our family, see old friends, and know eternal love, light, and peace. Dickinson had difficulties with this concept:

> I know that He exists
> Somewhere—in Silence—
> He has hid his rare life
> From our gross eyes.
>
> 'Tis an instant's play,
> 'Tis a fond Ambush—
> Just to make Bliss
> Earn her own surprise!
>
> But—should the play
> Prove piercing earnest—
> Should the glee—glaze—
> In Death's—stiff—stare—
>
> Would not the Joke
> Look too expensive!
> Would not the jest—
> Have crawled too far! [no. 338]

In contrast to Paul, for Dickinson, the reality of God was known in the incarnation. That God became one of us, shared the hazards of this life, and suffered at the hands of others to die a horrible death—this event linked God to human experience. Despite her anxieties about death, the loss of family and friends, and the virtual absence of a personal life as most of us know it, Dickinson accepted "God with us" as a reality for her own life. She presents, finally, a story of a developed faith. Her decline of the accepted tradition of conversion and her commitment to a life of separation from the usual womanly activities to devote her energies to art are unusual for her time. More astounding is the pathway of developing faith we see in her poetry. Because of her anger and fear before the God of her fathers, she came close to unbelief: mere acknowledgment of a God who abandoned us long ago. In time came her acceptance of a God of love and caring that was made known to us in the person of Jesus, who underwent our trials, was abandoned by God, but showed forth, in his life, how we are to love and live.

Dickinson, like Jacob, certainly wrestled with God for all of her creative life. As Wolff tells us, "Dickinson had refused faith in her youth, but when at length she began to believe, God was there, unchanged and ready to accept her." She had made her choice to be a poet rather than any of the other options—limited though they were—open to her. Her faith is in her final communiqué:

[T]he very last letter she wrote was addressed to the Norcross cousins, and its meaning is entirely clear. Dickinson had read Hugh Conway's sentimental, spiritual novel, *Called Back*, and this note was an expression of confidence about the realm that awaited her.

May 1886

Little Cousins,
Called back.
Emily.[23]

HOLDING TO THE FAITH

Faced, as we are and probably always will be, by plagues of such profound and powerful dimensions, how can we hold to a faith that will sustain us, encourage us, confirm us in our humanity? The most powerful antagonist of faith in a God of love, justice, and mercy is the world as we see it. Even the most superficial experience confirms an apparent abandonment by God of the created world we affirm. The suffering of children, hunger in a world replete with food, strife based on differing faiths in the same deity, and the striking maldistribution of goods and services—test any faith in a God active in our affairs. Intelligent, faithful, and unbiased theologians; humble confessors of a simple belief; and untold millions of us who doubt and believe at the same time struggle with the question of a God absent from our lives. There is no ready cure for this pestilence of forsakenness we fear, nor is there a vaccination against it. It is the final test of faith that, in our unbelief, we can believe.

The poetry of Dickinson is important to me in its persistent questioning with intelligence and daring. Knowing little of her life, knowing nothing of her thoughts aside from her art, and reading her poems with a sympathetic but not critical eye, I can nevertheless, follow her struggle for faith. She presents a most serious and lively challenge to my faith. Her role for me as my shadow, the isolated and driven searcher for understanding of my self and my relationship to others and the world, remains quite central. I take her fully at her word: life is a constant pursuit of whatever truth we can ascertain. Experience is essential but often misleading. I am finally driven within my self to find my relationship to God, to others, and to this vast and unknown universe, within and without. My faith receives its strength, and I my courage, in prayer and supplication, in my ongoing confrontation of unbelief by belief, in that cloud of witnesses in the here and now, and in that long past of encounters with the plague of the fear of abandonment by the very source of life and faith.

In the closing pages of his biography of Dickinson, Richard B. Sewall writes, "She mediated truths of nature and human nature, sights and sounds and meanings; she lit the poet's 'vital lamp'; she did the poet's (and God's) primal work of creation." She found joy in her life and in her art; she knew an ecstasy that seemed to satisfy; she was enriched beyond all counting. "This was her pilgrimage: to 'regulate' (her word) a faith that 'doubts as fervently as it believes'—a faith that was everywhere tried, not only by personal sorrow and loss, but paradoxically by the very love of this world that 'holds—so—'."[24] As she learned, God was there for her, unchanging, patient, knowing the suffering she knew. In the astounding miracle of God becoming one of us, Dickinson recognized not her abandonment by God but her acceptance within the circumference of creation.

NOTES

All citations from the poems of Emily Dickinson are from *The Complete Poems of Emily Dickinson*, ed. Thomas H. Johnson (Boston: Little, Brown, 1960).

1. Richard B. Sewall, *The Life of Emily Dickinson* (Cambridge: Harvard University Press, 1974), 420.
2. Wendy Barker, *Lunacy of Light* (Carbondale: Southern Illinois University Press, 1987), 25.

3. Suzanne Juhasz, *The Undiscovered Continent* (Bloomington: Indiana University Press, 1983), 10–1.
4. Søren Kierkegaard, *Philosophical Fragments*, trans. Howard V. Hong (Princeton, NJ: Princeton University Press, 1962), 11–2.
5. Sir Thomas Browne, *Religio Medici and Other Writings* (New York: E. P. Hutton, 1951), 16.
6. Henry David Thoreau, *Walden*, ed. J. Lyndon Shanley (Princeton, NJ: Princeton University Press, 1971), 321.
7. Ibid., 322.
8. Ibid., 90.
9. Browne, *Religio Medici*, 45–6.
10. Thoreau, *Walden*, 333.
11. Browne, *Religio Medici*, 294.
12. Ralph Waldo Emerson, "Circles," in *The Essays of Ralph Waldo Emerson* (New York: Random House, 1944), 175.
13. Saint Augustine, *The Confessions of Saint Augustine*, trans. Edward B. Pusey (New York: Pocket Books, 1951), 105.
14. Ksenija Atanasijevic, *The Metaphysical and Geometrical Doctrine of Bruno*, trans. from French by George Vid Tomashevich (St. Louis: Warren H. Green, 1972), 29.
15. Blaise Pascal, *Pensees* (New York: Random House, Modern Library, 1941), 22.
16. Albert J. Gelpi, *Emily Dickinson* (Cambridge: Harvard University Press, 1965), 33.
17. Cynthia Griffin Wolff, *Emily Dickinson* (Reading, MA: Addison-Wesley, 1988), 134–5.
18. Jack Miles, *God: A Biography* (New York: Alfred A. Knopf, 1995), 396.
19. Archibald MacLeish, "The Private World," in *Emily Dickinson: Three Views* (Amherst, MA: Amherst College Press, 1960), 25, 19–21.
20. Charles R. Anderson, *Emily Dickinson's Poetry* (New York: Holt, Rinehart & Winston, 1960), 35.
21. Ibid., 248.
22. I Corinthians 15:35–38b, 42, 50a, 51–2, NRSV.
23. Wolff, *Emily Dickinson*, 533–4.
24. Sewall, *Life of Emily Dickinson*, 724.

T e n

NO REMEMBRANCE OF THINGS PAST

For who to dumb forgetfulness a prey,
This pleasing anxious being e'er resigned,
Left the warm precincts of the cheerful day,
Nor cast one longing ling'ring look behind?

—Thomas Gray, "Elegy Written in a Country Church-Yard"

FOR MANY, *DEMENTIA* IS a terrifying word that signals a new plague of our century, challenging cancer as the most feared diagnosis we may hear. As the number of elderly persons increases, so does the number of us losing our minds. In this chapter of my study of the role of faith in determining behavior in the time of plague, loss of memory and the inexorable disintegration of personality associated with dementia are chilling examples of the ultimate testing of the very nature of the self. To die to the self while still living may be the ultimate degradation, the final insult to our concept of what it means to be a person. From a moral and ethical viewpoint, dementia is an exquisitely trying and painful test of our understanding of the meaning of *imago Dei* and our commitment to caring for one another on this brief journey.

Memory is a precious possession. Not only is it critical for my day-to-day functions as citizen, worker, participant in a culture, family member, and committed partner in a variety of relationships; memory also serves to de-

162

fine me to myself as a unique entity that develops over time. Memory is essential for knowing who I am today in relation to who I was yesterday and will be tomorrow. Plutarch (46–120 C.E.), noting that foolish people ignore the good things of their lives, living only in the present, writes that "intelligent people, on the other hand, use their memories to keep them vivid for themselves even when they are no longer present." He notes, further, that the oblivion experienced by the foolish "prevents life from being a unity of past events woven with present ones: it divides yesterday from today, as if they were distinct, and likewise treats tomorrow as different from today, and it immediately consigns every occurrence to non-existence by never making use of memory."[1]

Much of our understanding of who and what we are comes from reminiscences about the past. We search that past to recall conversations, interpret events, remember relationships, and understand callings. Only thus can we be fully human beings, fit in mind and emotion, if not in body, to fulfill our hopes and expectations for who we are becoming. Reminiscences can be essential for defining ourselves, the forces that shaped us, the influences— negative and positive—on our choices and promises, and the sources of our morality. It is remembering that provides continuity with our past. Philosopher Hans Jonas notes:

> Old age in humans, means a long past, which the *mind* must accommodate in its present as the substratum of personal identity. The past grows in us all the time, with its load of knowledge and opinion and emotions and choices and acquired aptitudes and habits and, of course, things upon things remembered or somehow recorded even if forgotten.[2]

If we are to make appropriate appraisals, execute proper decisions, and plan properly for the future, we need accurate memory of the past. For many of us, memories will be those of contentment, pleasure, and confirmation. Old age should be a time of assessment, of consideration of wisdom and experience, a life review that provides a warrant for the decisions, the actions, and the promises we made. Martial (circa 40–104 C.E.) writes about the enviable old age of Antonius Primus:

> Looking back on the past, on his panorama of decades,
>   Calm and serene he smiles, while the current of Lethe
>   nears.
> Not one day of the past, he reflects, was hateful or gloomy.
>   Never a bygone time he is not glad to recall.
> So, a good man's years are prolonged, and he has them twice
>   over
> When he can summon them back, doubly enjoying them
>   all.[3]

In the normal course of events, even without pathological interruptions in the process of remembrance, our memories may not be as accurate as we would wish or as we think them to be. Why, then, do some of us recall in detail the myriad events of childhood, while others have only dim recall and focus almost entirely on the present? Many factors operate to distort memory: difficult relationships with parents, siblings, teachers, peers; medical and psychological mishaps that sharply alter perception and interpretation; the quality and the amount of education and pedagogical methods; painful and definitive events that are forgotten with intent. Intentional forgetting, for some of us, is a way to protect ourselves from pain, humiliation, and sorrow. Whether events are ever truly forgotten in the psyche is an unanswerable question; although we may seem to set them aside, relationships and actions may well mold us forever. All these can so influence memory that it may become false. Hope and fantasy color reality, and the dreams we had are not translatable in today's words. In an 1841 journal entry, Thoreau wrote, "We seem to linger in manhood to tell the dreams of our childhood, and they vanish out of memory ere we learn the language."[4] We cannot recall truly the dreams we had for ourselves; by the time we try to tell our hopes, we may have forgotten them.

Not only do we forget; we will be forgotten. Some people are remembered for public actions, noble or nefarious. Most of us will be lost to recall by anyone after two generations of our descendants have died. This certain knowledge could well be a powerful stimulus to a moral and ethical stance before the world that defines us now. In my daily development of the person I am becoming, that immediate goal of a realized self committed today to the good and the truth might well be a more precious treasure than any hope of remembrance, since I know that I will be forgotten. Who I am becoming—my goals, defining standards, and relationships—will be who I am at the close of this life.

When we sustain serious memory loss, our understanding of self, others, and world is damaged, and the person we were is altered to another state, often unknowable to ourselves and to others. When this loss is progressive and severe and is associated with a variety of altered intellectual and behavioral states, we call it dementia. To develop the ethical and moral problems that dementia presents, I give a brief summary of our current knowledge of Alzheimer's dementia, aware that the rapidly evolving research of neurophysiologists, geneticists, and molecular biologists will alter current prognostic and therapeutic standards. Some implications of memory loss for knowing who we are and what history means for our cultures are presented in a study of the novel *The Forgotten*, by Elie Wiesel. This novel offers an opportunity to think about the experiences of individuals who are aware of the beginning of dementia, their expectations for the future, and the impact of this epidemic on those who care for the demented, on the general society, and on the health care systems we employ.

A final section discusses the ethical issues involved by examining the concept of personhood for one who is no longer knowable to self or to others as a person. This central issue—understanding the implications for all of us of the loss of another's selfhood—is the burden of the plague of dementia we all face.

The process of aging offers varied opportunities to learn and to reflect. A. L. Vischer writes:

> Old age is capable of positive organization only if the mental powers of the individual concerned remain sufficiently alert. The last phase of life will either take the form of a synthesis, a summing up, or it will be a period of disintegration and decay. And so old age is seen to possess a polar character and to develop between two extremes.[5]

When the past—experiences, emotions, joys and sorrows, accomplishments and failures—cannot be integrated into a construct of a life, is there a person still there, or has that reality disappeared? Reminiscences of the past define our lives. We see a combination of destiny and fate that brought us to where we are. An ordering and an acceptance of a realized life become possible. Edmund Sherman notes:

> There is the creative pleasure and fascination of recreating the story of one's destiny and one's self through reminiscence, which we can look forward to in old age. There is also the possibility of a change of consciousness to a more accepting and contemplative state of being. In that state memories can take on a richness never experienced before in life.[6]

What happens to us when memory no longer functions, when reminiscence is not possible? Does what has been known as a person no longer exist? Classical philosophy has always maintained a firm commitment to self-knowledge as defining of a realized person. The search of the self for that elusive quality of being a human being with a mind, with reason, with a love of beauty and a commitment to the good or to God: this pursuit determines who I am to myself as well as to you. In his intriguing study *The Heart of Philosophy*, Jacob Needleman places great emphasis on memory. He writes, "The function of philosophy in human life is to help man remember. *It has no other task.*" He continues, "The magic of real philosophy is the magic of the specifically human act of self-questioning—of being in front of the question of oneself."[7] We have a long history of remembering, of driving our minds back to the past to fill out the meaning of our lives. We meet ourselves in this journey into our remembered history, and this defines us. Needleman comments, "The idea of *remembering* has been used not only by Socrates and Pythagoras, but by all the great teachers of truth of all epochs."[8] But what if we do not remember?

Memory loss is an accepted part of old age, acknowledged with humor by many of us as we try to locate our glasses, remember the name of an old friend, or try to recall a telephone number. But memory loss can be the herald of a terrifying symptom complex—a diminishing mind—known as dementia. Senility has a long history: loss of mental capabilities and destruction of psychological, intellectual, and behavioral abilities are frightening additions to forgetfulness. William Shakespeare, in *As You Like It*, places us on the world's stage, players in a drama that we little understand, acting prescribed roles dictated by time. The final act, the "Last scene of all, / That ends this strange eventful history, / Is second childishness, and mere oblivion, / Sans teeth, sans eyes, sans taste, sans everything."[9]

G. E. Berrios and H. L. Freeman, in their historical study *Alzheimer and the Dementias*, write:

> At the end of the nineteenth century, the term "dementia" was used to name any state of psychological dilapidation associated with chronic brain disease. Since deficit states from the functional psychoses were included under this term, irreversibility was not then considered a requirement of dementia, though efforts had been made since the 1820s to relate the two. When states of dementia occurred in the elderly, they were called "senile dementia"; even as late as 1900, "dementia" did not necessarily evoke an association with old age, as it mostly does now.[10]

Dementia praecox was an accepted diagnosis for psychotic behavior in young persons. By the middle of the nineteenth century, the diagnosis of dementia referred mostly to senile (arteriosclerotic) dementia. Reasons for this were the emphasis in psychology on the intellect and the association of dementia with old age—senility. Berrios and Freeman note:

> Intellect was still considered the defining feature of the human species; not only was madness defined in "intellectualistic" terms, but after the 1860s, the view had become popular that psychosocial incompetence, whether in the mentally ill, the elderly, idiots, or members of non-European races, specifically resulted from intellectual failure. . . . Cognition, however, proved too broad a function to measure. Those interested in the assessment of severity resorted to memory, the only intellectual function whose measurement had reached adequate development during the 1880s. Thus, deficits in memory became, *de facto*, if not *de jure*, the central feature of the state of dementia.[11]

In the early years of the twentieth century, considerable differences of opinion were voiced by neurologists, psychiatrists, and pathologists concerning dementias. Only gradually did behavioral dysfunction, psychosocial disorders, and irreversibility become defining characteristics of dementia. Many causes were suggested in that era, when staining and microscopic techniques were burgeoning. Arteriosclerotic disease accounted for many cases, but over succeeding decades, the anatomy of neurons and glia was gradually clarified, and pathologic changes in structure became more closely related to clinical findings.

In 1906, Alois Alzheimer reported to his colleagues the case of Frau Auguste D., who died that year. She had been admitted to a mental asylum in Frankfurt in 1901 at the age of fifty-one with disorientation, aphasia, paranoia, odd behavior and psychosocial incompetence. The pathological findings in the cerebral cortex were the focus of Alzheimer's paper. His mentor, Kraepelin, named this "new" syndrome of presenile dementia Alzheimer's disease, or Morbus Alzheimer, in his 1910 textbook. In succeeding years, this *senium praecox* has become more prevalent and is now a plague in our midst, one that will increase. Interpreting the pathological findings and proposed etiological causes and detailing the developing relevance of inheritance are not attempted here. General remarks on these topics are made where relevant to our responses to this pestilence.

ALZHEIMER'S DEMENTIA

Alzheimer's disease is a progressive dementia, a condition in which there is a primary degenerative process occurring in the brain. This pathologic process, which is still not absolutely clear, destroys mental function: memory, language use, and what we call cognitive skills (judgment, calculation, abstract thought) disintegrate. There are also serious noncognitive symptoms of great concern for caregivers. Delusions and hallucinations, confusion about time and place, foul language, violent behavior, and other distressing behaviors are common. Depression is very common and may confound the diagnosis. Death usually occurs some seven to ten years after onset.

In the past two decades, Alzheimer's disease has become a prominent medical and social concern. I make no serious differentiation here between senile dementia and Alzheimer's disease, which is usually associated with an earlier onset of dementia. Since the eponym was established early in this century, I call our current plague Alzheimer's dementia. The rise in the incidence of this devastating disease is closely tied to remarkable changes in population statistics. Both the total number of persons (the ratio between birth and death rates) and the age at death have risen steadily. Olshansky and colleagues, in their study on aging, note that "during the 20th century, the disparity between high birth rates and low death rates led to population growth rates that approached 2 to 3 percent and a population doubling time of only about 25 years."[12] Associated with this increase is a radical change in the age distribution of that population. Their study found that, in 1900, less than 1 percent of the world population was sixty-five years of age or older. This number rose to over 6 percent by 1992 and might well reach 20 percent by 2050—an alarming look into the future.

Although numbers such as these do not have any direct bearing on the individual, they imply distinct and serious issues for us as a society. The dramatic rise in the incidence of dementia with increasing age is cause for concern: the prevalence of Alzheimer's disease rises between the ages of sixty-five and eighty-five, doubling every five years. By the age of eighty-five, as many as 40 percent of persons may have Alzheimer's disease. Although estimates of the number of cases are always questionable, Khachaturian and associates write, "At present the number of individuals affected by AD in the United States is estimated to be nearly 4 million, but the projections are that during the next 50 years the number will increase to nearly 14 million."[13] Age-specific rates are similar in diverse nations. Women are at greater risk than men; the Lundy study in Sweden (1947–72) showed that the lifetime risk for men was one-fourth, and for women nearly one-third. A family history of dementia is a definite risk factor and highlights the importance of research in population and molecular genetics. There is also a clear relationship between the level of education and dementia: the less education, the greater the risk. Head trauma, especially that sustained by boxers, is a factor in various studies.[14] Alzheimer's disease is a strong determinant of mortality. Life expectancy at the onset of presenile dementia is approximately seven years, compared with twenty-one years for unaffected individuals; comparable survival figures for those with and without senile dementia are five and ten years, respectively.[15] The appearance of the pathophysiological findings of Alzheimer's disease in persons with Down's syndrome in their thirties, and the high rate of dementia in their sixties, support current evidence that genetic factors are important.

FORGETTING

There are two components to memory loss, each definitive of us as persons: what it means to forget, and what it means to be forgotten. In the closing pages of his 1992 novel *The Forgotten*, Elie Wiesel has the protagonist, Elhanan Rosenbaum, ask the question, "But what is man deprived of memory?"[16] Elhanan (El-hanan, "God is gracious") is a revered teacher and psychotherapist in New York who is knowingly experiencing dementia. His disintegration and his son's efforts to help him record the events of a faithful life form the novel. A survivor of the Holocaust who is active in the drive to establish the state of Israel, Elhanan observes his own descent into oblivion—what his son, Malkiel (Malki-El, "God is my King"), calls "the most inhuman of evils."[17] To forget the past has two profound effects: we do not remember our own lives, and we abandon those who preceded us, taught us, protected and loved us. The traditions that we revere, the long history of defining the meanings of texts, the certainty of God in the face of our unbelief and our straying from the paths of righteousness can be lost: we become nothing to ourselves, perhaps also to others. We cannot live only in the present, with no knowledge of the past, no hopes and expectations for a future. How we understand the significance of oblivion of the self while the body remains alive will determine future planning for the care of demented persons. Our response to dementia reveals the moral and ethical commitments of society in the time of plague.

Questions about dementia are not only those about personal loss. They call us to question the role of God in our affairs. When Malkiel was an adolescent, he and Elhanan debated notions of Providence. "If God is everywhere, how do we explain evil? If God is good, how do we explain suffering? If God is God, how are we to conceive man's role in creation?" God likes an argument, "an admission of conflict and separation; these God creates and destroys, by His presence as much as by His absence. All is possible with Him; nothing is possible without Him. . . . He is the limit of all things, and He is what extends the limit."[18] Is this the perennial affirmation of a God whose center is everywhere and circumference nowhere? The dilemma of the coexistence of evil and a God of justice and mercy persists. Wiesel presents his case again in this novel: we believe in God, we trust in God, we cannot explain God. We do not know the meaning of events of our lives, yet we believe in our God.

With loss of memory comes the possibility that we will forget God and be alone in the universe. In the prayer at the beginning of the novel, Elhanan calls upon God:

> God of Abraham, Isaac, and Jacob, forget not their son who calls upon them now.
>
> You well know, You, source of all memory, that to forget is to repudiate. Do not abandon me, God of my fathers, for I have never repudiated You. . . .
>
> God of truth, remember that without memory truth becomes only the mask of truth. Remember that only memory leads man back to the source of his longing for you. . . . Remember, God of history, that You created man to remember. . . . What sort of witness would I be without my memory? . . .
>
> Even if you forget me, O Lord, I refuse to forget You.[19]

And yet, it will happen to many of us. We will forget God, the ones we love, the earth we cherish, the created arts we know—all will be forgotten. We will not know ourselves.

Thus did Elhanan helplessly witness his own destruction. Forgetfulness was for him the death not only of knowledge but also of imagination, hence of expectation. . . . His reason, still clear, watched over a shrinking, progressively impoverished memory. . . . Time no longer flowed, but toppled over the edge of a yawning precipice. . . . Forgetfulness was a worse scourge than madness: the sick man is not somewhere else; he is nowhere. He is not another, he is no one.[20]

When we lose our memory, we lose the self, that unique entity that is a bundle of loves, desires, hopes, promises, fears, anxieties, and creativity. We also lose the faith that informs, directs, critiques, and forgives that self. Prayer, that searching and critical laying out of the self before God, is also lost when memory is lost. The offering of thanks, the hope that the will can be bent to the will of God, the bald need of forgiveness for sins acknowledged or not, and the express need for direction and strength to live a full life are lost when memory is lost. Inherent in the need for memory is to know and remember our religious heritage and faith. Only when we understand and accept our own tradition are we bold enough to support others in theirs. Only as I acknowledge the faith that I have chosen can I promise to support others in their faiths. In my professional life, as in my faith, I chose models for my behavior, examples for my level of commitment, and guidelines to define my loves and my promises.

The inherent horror in forgetting is the likelihood that the past will be repeated endlessly. George Santayana's famous comment, "Those who cannot remember the past are condemned to repeat it,"[21] has been confirmed many times in our history, to the sorrow of many. We are impoverished if we cannot keep steadily before us the history of this century. There are those who deny, excuse, or diminish the significance of the Holocaust and the other massive killings and destruction of the twentieth century. Wiesel, in his writing, will not let us forget. The message is clear: we must remember, with all passion and resolve, what has happened in our time. The poignancy of dementia as the fading of memory, the very quality of being human that we must never lose, highlights his insistent plea that we not forget.

FORGOTTEN

Dementia, with its loss of cognition, also presents the other side of the meaning of memory: what it means to be forgotten. That we will forget the past has implications for the forgotten: the persons, the events, and the values of our time. We, as individuals, will fade into nothingness in history, but that history must not be forgotten. The testimonies of witnesses to glorious occasions, to the horrors of tragedy, and to the life of the mundane must be written down and kept for the future to know. Certainly that motive lies behind the absolute necessity to document the Holocaust. Although individuals are finally forgotten as individuals, the fact of the suffering and death visited upon them must be remembered always. By memorial, museum, book, and film, the havoc must not be forgotten.

Although we will be forgotten by other persons, it is our faithful hope that we will not be forgotten by God. Our biblical traditions, Jewish and Christian, assert that God will not forget; yet there are observations that events in the life of Israel point to God forgetting the Chosen. But the prophetic voice is stronger in affirming the presence of God with His people. Isaiah recounts, "But Zion said, 'The Lord has forsaken me, my Lord has forgotten me.' Can a woman forget her nursing child, or show compassion for the child of her womb? Even these may forget, yet I will not forget you."[22] We live in the hope, the promise, that God will not forget. Our history does not reveal a special concern for those who confess to faith in God, but it is that faith, spoken to by Elhanan, that upholds us: a developed faith, one that is nourished by years of study and observance. The years of our lives that precede those of disintegration and decay are the ones we use to learn our faith. We must learn the meaning of our religious community of believers, the precepts and the laws that bind us to one another and to our God, and the expressions of our faith in the larger community. This requires preparation. Robert Southey closes his famous 1799 poem, "The Old Man's Comforts," with these lines: "In the days of my youth I remember'd my God! / And He hath not forgotten my age."[23] We must prepare for the possibility that we will forget, but remain confident that God will not.

How Will I Die?

We know that we constantly define ourselves, molding the persons we will become, creating those portraits. Concerns about commitments, failed promises, sins of commission and omission, and anticipated joys persist. Who will that be, the "I" who comes to the final act of my life: my death? Gilbert Meilaender writes:

> Caught as we are within the midst of our own life stories, and unable as we are to grasp anyone else's story as a single whole, we have to admit that only God can see us as the persons we are—can catch the self and hold it still. What exactly we will be like when we are with God is, therefore, always beyond our capacity to say. But it will be the completion of the someone who we were and are.[24]

Alzheimer's dementia is a severe test of knowing how we will die. The nightmare that I will not know who I am as I approach the end of my life is a threat that focuses with exquisite and painful clarity the whole concept of what it means to be a person. The possibility of loss of cognition—not knowing who, what, why—is one that I imagine with difficulty. The scenario around dying is sobering enough in itself; to act out the part that I will play in it without my mind is beyond my conceiving. The function of faith in my thought and actions as I die is central to this study; the way I die will—or should—be the logical finale to the role I played in the drama. Obviously, dememtia will radically alter the plot, the cast, the costumes, the final scene. Before considering the powerful consequences of dementia on our dying, I survey some significant current thoughts about death.

In his 1993 book *Life's Dominion: An Argument About Abortion, Euthanasia, and Individual Freedom*, Ronald Dworkin writes:

> It is a platitude that we live our whole lives in the shadow of death; it is also true that we die in the shadow of our whole lives. Death's central horror is oblivion—the terrifying, absolute dying of the light. But oblivion is not all there is to death; if it were, people would not worry so much about whether their technical, biological lives continue after they have become unconscious and the void has begun, after the light is already dead forever. Death has dominion because it is not only the start of nothing but the end of everything, and how we think and talk about dying—the emphasis we put on dying with "dignity"—shows how important it is that life ends *appropriately*, that death keeps faith with the way we want to have lived.[25]

Faith can be the unifying power in life. Our decisions concerning what makes us whole persons, what draws us to community, what inspires our loyalties, and what empowers us to give ourselves away are confirmed by our convictions, by our faith in what holds us in this life and at death. Faith is a final confidence, an assurance of purpose and of means, and a certainty of support that, although shaken by events, remains. Finding the foundation, living in the assurance that that foundation will not fail, is our task. A weak faith, one based upon the self and the things that rust and are so easily corrupted, may not be able to carry us along when the journey is frightening and the road narrow. In my limited and partial experiences in this world, faith and confidence in the God known to me through my Judeo-Christian heritage is the rock on which I build my life. Obviously, for others, there are different final and definitive sources of inspiration and revelation that are attended to in clarifying the goals and purposes of living. But it is faith that carries us along. It is of central importance, then, that that faith be capable of meeting the expectations we have for it. Faith is not something that we know only in ourselves; it is a reality known to a community, that group of others that will know us and hold us to itself as we proceed through this life to our death.

As I define my faith, so it defines me and will be a major factor in this construct I know as my self. This self is in a constant process of development. This self is also the one that will die, that has to die. How do I make this death an honorable one, a conclusion to a life that will be seen and known as fitting, qualifying that life and expressing it as one that would be esteemed and appreciated, perhaps admired? At issue here is the concept of character, the person I have been in the process of creating. My hope is that my death will be consistent with my life, that I will have lived in preparation for that death, fully aware of its inevitability and its finality. Ronald Dworkin asks:

> How does it matter to the critical success of our whole life how we die? We should distinguish between two different ways that it might matter: because death is the far boundary of life, and every part of our life, including the very last, is important; and because death is special, a peculiarly significant event in the narrative of our lives, like the final scene of a play, with everything about it intensified, under a special spotlight.[26]

How do I decide what will define me now and at the hour of my departure? The need to prepare is paramount. Not doing anything at all is still a decision lived out and with results that will be known. For most of us, the process is multilayered: we must study and learn from others: biography, history, science, and philosophy; most of us engage our hearts and minds in introspection and critique of the ego: analysis of motive and action, prayer, the search for a center to one's life; dialogue is important: openness to friends, intimate members of family, colleagues who know our deepest secrets; and finally, there is the source of life, inspiration, and courage that carries us through this life to its end: God, Ultimate Being, or whatever we acknowledge as asking our final allegiance, our paramount trust and last hope.

Our dying should be a realized confirmation of our living. The way we die, the circumstances around that awesome event, should reflect most clearly the life that was lived up to that moment. Daniel Callahan writes, "we must find our own meaning for death and die our own deaths." He notes that preparation for death is a living process: we cannot find this on our own. "We need the help of others, of a community whose meaning we can share, making it our own with the same strength as if we had discovered it for ourselves."[27] This is, of course, our central question: how to live so that a good death is the crown on a good life. We can all imagine the good death in a previous time: the elderly matriarch lying in what had been her wedding bed, the place where she bore her children; the room filled with family, neighbors, and friends, all come to bid her a fond farewell; kisses, blessings, forgiveness, and encouragement palpable as she prepares to join her Maker. This touching and realistic scene was a likely occurrence in a time

when physicians had little to offer besides surgery and opiates for pain relief. Now, in an age of technology that can maintain physiological functions
for protracted periods, we are often unsure whether a person is dead or
alive, or what those words mean.

This possibility—months or years of living death—is one that enlivens
public and private interest in living wills, advanced directives, and the Patient Self-Determination Act of 1990, which applies to persons admitted to
hospitals; it brings propositions before state voters to permit active euthanasia or physician-assisted suicide; it raises questions that can encourage us to
examine the very core of our religious faith, our private morality, and our
public conscience. This possibility offers the opportunity to ensure now, in
these days when we still possess reason and sensibility to think through
what defines us, that our deaths will be fully commensurate with our lives.

When I Am No Longer Me

Although we may hope to die as did the matriarch, for many of us, this is
unlikely. Violence and accidents, premature birth, congenital and genetic
defects, cancer in children and young adults, infectious diseases and malnu-
trition, hate and greed—all these take a terrible toll on us, making a calm
and reasoned death a sham of personhood for many. These natural and moral
evils that we know do not remove the burden of how we are to die: rather,
they put a different face on the question and call for consideration of different answers. To start my discussion of a good death, I ask the question, Is
it ever better to be dead than alive? This may seem easily answered when
we think of suffering, pain, isolation, and depleted resources—financial and
emotional. But it is not always so. As a pediatrician helping parents face
shattering situations, I often ask myself that question: is death ever better
than life? Even for a severely damaged infant, is death preferable to being
fed, held, sensing the beat of country music, the warmth of the bath? Certainly for me, as an adult who has lived out a life, the answer is yes. But
for that infant, for the severely retarded adult, for the quadriplegic, for the
demented, I cannot say. And here lies the dilemma for the faithful. Does
faith inform us, and how does it do so? I have been cheered in my heart for
many years by a medieval legend told to me by a chaplain at a residential
facility for seriously retarded adults. The legend tells us that before each
person, regardless of status, there proceeds a host of heavenly angels pro-
claiming, "Behold, the image of God!" I hold this closely when I am tempted
to make judgments and establish gradations of my fellow travelers.

Alzheimer's dementia presents a special case for consideration of our moral
stance, our ethical base for behavior in the time of plague. It does this because it offers a view of lives that undergo protracted dissolution before

death ends the tragedy. Dementia is a model for the worst that can happen to us: living as a body without the mind that we previously used for making decisions, for knowing the emotional components of relationships, for comprehending a Mozart piano concerto or his *Ave Verum*. Dementia is a test of our willingness to decide now who we are and will be in the future, what values we hope to hold to the end when we no longer know who we are, and what our relations to our communities will be: to persons, to political structures, to the earth, and to our God. We are each, willy-nilly, building a character, that soul-deep person that will respond intuitively and instinctively to the difficult questions when they arise, based on the faith chosen. For those who see themselves creating the persons they are becoming, day by day, it is important to make decisions that confirm that creation, not deny it or ignore it. It is here that advance directives, or whatever label one applies to careful delineation of future care when cognition is no longer present, are so important. These decisions will depend precisely on who one is now. Is my life determined by the observation that I am breathing? I do not think so. There is much more that I am, and when that is not known to me, I am not a person.

This is a difficult and contentious position. There is a sanctity to life that we acknowledge in our long and tortured history, regardless of religious conviction or denial. We struggle with the possibility, the necessity, the horror of killing another person, although this century might well dispute that notion. I do not know why we are distraught when deciding to allow one person to die yet quite indifferent to mass murder that plagues us forever. But we hold to the belief that the life of another is precious and not to be destroyed needlessly. Deliberately killing a patient, regardless of the state of deterioration, is a questionable act, especially for a physician committed to caring for others. Leon Kass writes:

> I continue to applaud those courageous patients and family members and those conscientious physicians who try prudently to discern, in each case, just what form of treatment or nontreatment is truly good for the patient, even if it embraces an increased likelihood of death. But I continue to insist that we cannot serve the patient's good by deliberately eliminating the patient.[28]

Each of us is an entity, a whole being. I am a person determined by thousands of decisions and actions, many instigated by conviction of my purpose of being a person, a created part of a universe of beauty and grace. I do not think that this life is all there is to my life; I do not know of another, but I believe in it. I am defined by my beliefs and by my actions, all of which are, if not completely controlled by my mind, powerfully influenced by it. When that mind no longer functions as defining and determining of me, I am not me any longer. The hour has come for recycling. It is in the best interests of the world to do just that: recycle ourselves through organ donation, through offering the body for dissection by medical students, and, finally, through a return to the earth from which we came, "dust to dust." The epitome of denial of the need to recycle ourselves is the image I still have of the wake of a friend: in a steel coffin, fully dressed in tie and jacket, wearing glasses and holding a book, was a body destined to be there forever. Marcus Aurelius has something to tell me:

> Reflect that, in a little while, thou shalt be nothingness and no place shall know thee, nor shall anything be of all that thou now seest, nor any man of those who are now in life. For all things are by nature framed to change, transmute, and decay, that others may rise to fill their places.... [T]o man, the end of life is not an evil; ... it is a good, inasmuch as it is opportune, advantageous, and congruent to the universe.[29]

I hope that, when the hour comes when I no longer know who I am and others do not know either, I will be allowed to die of whatever natural cause appears. In a real sense, severe dementia will change me into someone else. I will not be me any longer. The man I was, with the beliefs, the convictions, the prejudices, the loves, and the joys, will be gone—will be, in fact, already dead to himself and to others. As my thought develops over time, I may consider assisted suicide. The Greek and Roman concept of rational suicide is a real option, a final commitment to the wish to be oneself, not some other unknown and unknowable person who is a body without a mind. Here, of course, is a point on which disagreement will persist, because beliefs are so different. They must be honored, and the arguments must continue: discussions around the definition of what it is to be a person, how that is manifested and known to others, and what are the final characteristics of the self. Herbert Hendin writes:

> How we deal with illness, age, and decline says a great deal about who and what we are, both as individuals and as a society. We should not buy into the view of those who are engulfed by fear of death or by suicical despair that death is the preferred solution to the problems of illness, age, and depression.... Death ought to be hard to sell.[30]

The issue is that of choice, of who I follow in my life. Upon what foundation of faith will I rest my life and my death? I choose to live in the hope of the promise of a kingdom of God, a reign of justice and love and mercy that I will know at my death, that point of transition from one life to another life. I choose this, fully recognizing the particularity of my choice, the serious limits of my experiences, and the narrowness of my vision; yet I am called to this path of the life and the teaching of Jesus, whom I am bold enough to call the Christ. William Sloane Coffin tells us:

Just as the call of God is embedded in a cry of pain, so the acceptance of God's call is at one with our self-fulfillment. We give, true, but in return we receive so much—our whole identity. "Cogito, ergo sum," said Descartes: "I think, therefore I am." Nonsense! *Amo*, ergo sum—I love, therefore I am.[31]

I choose this course, also, as the alternative to an ultimate despair—the utter loss of hope. I decline the despair that Kierkegaard called "the sickness unto death." He writes that we speak of a mortal sickness being one that ends in death.

> In this sense despair cannot be called the sickness unto death. But in the Christian understanding of it death itself is a transition unto life. In view of this, there is from the Christian standpoint no earthly, bodily sickness unto death. For death is doubtless the last phase of the sickness, but death is not the last thing. If in the strictest sense we are to speak of a sickness unto death, it must be one in which the last thing is death, and death the last thing. And this is precisely despair.[32]

The choosing of who I will be is difficult, as it has always been. But choose I must, each day. I choose to live in hope of a final redemption into a new life, of which my death will be but a point of departure. With Paul, I can say, "For in hope we are saved. Now hope that is seen is not hope. For who hopes for what is seen? But if we hope for what we do not see, we wait for it with patience."[33] I attend to the offer of Joshua: "choose this day whom you will serve, whether the gods of your ancestors served in the region beyond the River or the gods of the Amorites in whose land you are living; but as for me and my household, we will serve the LORD."[34]

NOTES

1. Plutarch, "Contentment," in *Essays* (London: Penguin Books, 1992), 229.
2. Hans Jonas, "The Burden and Blessing of Mortality," *Hastings Center Report* 22, no. 1 (1992): 40.
3. Martial, *Selected Epigrams*, trans. Rolfe Humphries (Bloomington: Indiana University Press, 1963), 92.
4. Henry David Thoreau, *The Journal of Henry D. Thoreau*, vol. 1 (Boston: Houghton Mifflin, 1906), 217.
5. A. L. Vischer, *On Growing Old*, trans. Gerald Onn (London: George Allen & Unwin, 1966), 18.
6. Edmund, Sherman, *Reminiscence and the Self in Old Age* (New York: Springer, 1991), 245.
7. Jacob Needleman, *The Heart of Philosophy* (New York: Alfred A. Knopf, 1982), 4, 13.
8. Ibid., 140–1.
9. William Shakespeare, *As You Like It*, in *The Complete Works of William Shakespeare*, ed. W. J. Craig (London: Henry Pordes, 1973), 2.7. 163–6.

10. G. E. Berrios and H. L. Freeman, *Alzheimer and the Dementias* (London: Royal Society of Medicine Services, 1991), 2.
11. Ibid., 26–7.
12. S. Jay Olshansky, Bruce A. Carnes, and Christine K. Cassel, "The Aging of the Human Species," *Scientific American* (April 1993): 47, 46.
13. Zaven S. Khachaturian, Creighton H. Phelps, and Neil S. Buckholtz, "The Prospects of Developing Treatments for Alzheimer Disease," in *Alzheimer Disease*, ed. Robert D. Terry, Robert Katzman, and Katherine Bick (New York: Raven Press, 1994), 445.
14. Robert Katzman and Claudia Kawas, "The Epidemiology of Dementia and Alzheimer Disease," in *Alzheimer Disease*, 114, 116.
15. Ibid., 115.
16. Elie Wiesel, *The Forgotten*, trans. Stephen Becker (New York: Summit Books, 1992), 235.
17. Ibid., 230.
18. Ibid., 211.
19. Ibid., 11, 12.
20. Ibid., 197.
21. George Santayana, *The Life of Reason: Introduction and Reason in Common Sense* (New York: Charles Scribner's Sons, 1905), 284.
22. Isaiah 49:14, NRSV.
23. Robert Southey, *Poetical Works of Robert Southey* (New York: D. Appleton & Co., 1842), 135.
24. Gilbert Meilaender, "*Terra es animata*: On Having a Life," *Hastings Center Report* 23, no. 4 (1993): 32.
25. Ronald Dworkin, *Life's Dominion: An Argument About Abortion, Euthanasia, and Individual Freedom* (New York: Vintage Books, 1993), 199.
26. Ibid., 209.
27. Daniel Callahan, *The Troubled Dream of Life: Living with Mortality* (New York: Simon & Schuster, 1993), 222–3.
28. Leon Kass, "Is There a Right to Die?" *Hastings Center Report* 23, no. 1 (1993): 42.
29. Marcus Aurelius, *The Meditations of Marcus Aurelius Antoninus*, trans. John Jackson (Oxford: Clarendon Press, 1906), 207, 208.
30. Herbert Hendin, "Selling Death and Dignity," *Hastings Center Report* 25, no. 3 (1995): 23.
31. William Sloane Coffin, "Being Called," in *The Courage to Love* (San Francisco: Harper & Row, 1982), 35.
32. Søren Kierkegaard, "The Sickness unto Death," in *Fear and Trembling and the Sickness unto Death*, trans. Walter Lowrie (Princeton, NJ: Princeton University Press, 1941), 150.
33. Romans 8:24–5, NRSV.
34. Joshua 24:15, NRSV.

Chapter 11
E l e v e n

A PRESENT DANGER, A CLEAR WARNING

Those who have crossed
With direct eyes, to death's other Kingdom
Remember us—if at all—not as lost
Violent souls, but only
As the hollow men
The stuffed men.

—T. S. Eliot, "The Hollow Men"

A YOUNG MAN, A member of the faculty in the department of English literature at a university, was admitted to the medical center with pneumonia. After his evaluation was completed and his treatment started, the resident physician came into his room and said, "I have three things to tell you: you have AIDS; you are going to die; you should use a condom." This personal and professional response to a man with AIDS was not rare in the middle 1980s: the disease was initially seen in homosexual men, and this new and apparently fatal disease was interpreted by many as a judgment— divine or otherwise— upon a socially unacceptable segment of our society. In the next few years, the international ramifications of this plague became clear. AIDS is a new disease caused by a virus that is a design model for becoming the final survivor in our world. Through the evolutionary process of mutation appeared a complex of amino acids that invades and destroys the very cells in our immune system that should protect us, our helper T-cell lymphocytes. Thus immunosuppressed, we can become fatally infected by bacteria, fungi, and viruses that ordinarily do not produce diseases in human beings. I recall the closing lines of "The Hollow Men": "This is the way the world ends / Not with a bang but a whimper."[1]

Another characteristic of this virus is its apparent permanence; HIV does not go away in most persons but remains an integral part of the molecular structure of the lymphocytes in the immune system. HIV also invades the human brain, where it is shielded from many antibiotic and antiviral agents by the blood-brain barrier. A final twist to the vagaries of this infecting agent is the known capacity for retroviruses to continue the process of mutation so that their biochemical characteristics, often essential to the production of effective vaccines, can vary over time—a talented combination of survival attributes for an invisible destroyer. The sporadic appearance of deadly viruses during the past few decades is alarming. The destruction of tropical rain forests, the movement of pastoral and tribal persons into cities from locations distant and isolated, and the availability of transportation around the world have opened the way for rapid spread of diseases previously unknown—diseases to which native populations are often immune or resistant but that can be fatal to those previously unexposed. These facts of our times that influence the methods and modes of transmission of viruses create the plague image of this epidemic.

A BRIEF HISTORY OF AIDS

In June 1981, a short article in the *Morbidity and Mortality Report* of the Centers for Disease Control described five cases of pneumonia in homosexual men in Los Angeles caused by a microorganism, *Pneumocystis carinii*, not usually pathogenic for humans. Within months, the number of reported cases—all in homosexual men—increased rapidly, and a disease was described that showed the characteristics of severe deficiency of the immune system. What would become known as AIDS was reported soon thereafter in New York City and San Francisco, and then in many other cities. In addition to pneumonia, symptoms of serious weight loss, fungal infections, a previously rare skin cancer—Kaposi's sarcoma—and serious viral infections of the eye and brain combined to produce a disease complex that seemed incurable. Within the year, cases were reported in Europe, Africa, and Latin America that showed the same picture of suppressed immunity and lymph node involvement, strongly suggesting infection with a virus. In 1983 at the Pasteur Institute in Paris, and in 1984 at the National Institutes of Health in Washington, the virus was isolated: a retrovirus named human immunodeficiency virus, or HIV. It is in the family of lentiviruses (in Latin, *lenti* means "slow"), known for a century to cause serious diseases in monkeys, sheep, horses, and other animals.

AIDS is an international plague, a pandemic. During the past decade, as reporting of cases improved, AIDS became a top runner on the list of causes of death worldwide. With knowledge of the means of spread, the disease has moved from being a problem for homosexual men and intravenous drug users to being a social disease transmitted from person to person by well-understood methods. Sexual intercourse—one of the most powerful human desires and drives—is the main route for transmission of the virus. It is this aspect of AIDS that makes *plague* a common noun for the disease. As Susan Sontag writes:

> The emergence of a new catastrophic epidemic, when for several decades it has been confidently assumed that such calamities belonged to the past, would not be enough to revive the moralistic inflation of an epidemic into a "plague." It was necessary that the epidemic be one whose most common means of transmission is sexual.[2]

It is the means of transmission—sexual and/or drug use—that has led so many to use the word *plague* as a judgmental label for AIDS. We learned that contaminated blood conveyed by transfusion, accidental needle puncture, and surgical mishap is a potential source of infection, but the original caption was *gay plague*.

It is of interest that the word *plague* was not used to define the influenza pandemic of 1918–19, although the death toll was phenomenally high; the key lies in the different method of transmission. In developed countries, the hope is that medical and public health facilities will be capable of converting this plague into a "chronic disease." This term—a euphemism for a disease that is currently neither curable nor preventable by vaccination—undervalues a potential catastrophe. In African countries, however, where the cost of the test for AIDS exceeds the budget allocation for public health, death from the "slim diseae" will be a constant companion.

The detective work involved in tracing the origins and the path of spread of this disease is fascinating. The virus probably had its start in central Africa, perhaps in a disease of monkeys that are a source of food. This probable origin of the virus also fits well with the ancient concept of plague as a visitation from a foreign— usually barbaric—place, usually read as a judgment on the people. When this occurred is not known, but educated guesses put it sometime in the middle of the twentieth century. The spread of the virus, or its mutations, was slow, and patients with symptoms suggestive of AIDS did not appear until the 1970s. There were a few cases with pathological findings suspiciously like AIDS reported before this in Scandinavia and England, with infection probably occurring in Africa. For the purposes of this study, the U.S. experience is the center, because the patient population brought such sharp focus on the moral and ethical questions raised across the country. The early and obvious association of AIDS with male homosexuality and intravenous drug use placed this disease outside the usual concerns of the general public, health professionals, religious organizations, and governments. The struggle to correct this deficit is the subject of this chapter, because it so clearly presents a challenge to any ethical understanding of our relations with one another when plague appears. Another ethical question raised by AIDS is the limit of privacy when a deadly infectious disease appears in our community. In the early years of the epidemic, this was a major concern; it is interesting that as the disease has decreased in the homosexual population, this concern has lessened, and the more common public health procedures of reporting cases and notifying contacts have reappeared as public policies.

The Sexual Revolution

Following upon the civil rights movement and resistance to the expanding war in Southeast Asia was a sexual revolution. The introduction and rapid acceptance of oral contraception in a time of rebellion against established authority changed heterosexual behavior; promiscuity became a distressing aspect of social life. There were probably also some effects from the growing and vocal feminist movement that was finding its place in social and political milieus. Certainly one of the more obvious and startling movements of the time was gay liberation. Randy Shilts writes that the Gay Freedom Day parade in San Francisco in 1980

> commemorated the riot in which Greenwich Village drag queens attacked police engaged in the routine harassment of a gay bar called the Stonewall Inn. From the Stonewall riot, on the last weekend of June 1969, the gay liberation movement was born, peopled by angry women and men who realized that their fights against war and injustice had a more personal side. This was the gay liberation movement—named after the then-voguish liberation groups sweeping the country—that had taken such delight in frightening staid America in the early 1970s.[3]

The "liberation" of homosexual men had a deadly future immediately ahead. The sexual practices of gay men were such that sexually transmitted diseases and intestinal infections and parasites were common and of growing concern to physicians. An astounding promiscuity was a secondary effect of the new freedom of expression. Bathhouses, gay bookstores and bars, and parks became locations for indiscriminate sexual encounters, often without any personal relationships evident. Descriptions of homosexual acts horrified much of mainstream America and produced fear and revulsion toward homosexuals. The new freedom brought many gay men to New York City and to San Francisco, where expression of their sexuality was permitted, even tacitly encouraged. The combination of promiscuity, methods of sexual intercourse, and prevalence of debilitating transmissible diseases was the perfect setting for the beginning of the plague of AIDS. Whether it was brought to San Francisco by an Air Canada steward, to New York City and Miami by Haitians recently employed in Africa, or by unknown sailors at the bicentennial celebration in New York Harbor in 1976 matters little; the physical signs and symptoms of AIDS became known on both coasts by the early 1980s, and a dividing line was drawn in the United States. As Shilts writes:

> Before . . . was to be the word that would define the permanent demarcation in the lives of millions of Americans, particularly those citizens of the United States who were gay. . . . The epidemic would cleave lives in two, the way a great war or depression presents a commonly understood point of reference around which an entire society defines itself. Before would encompass thousands of memories laden with nuance and nostalgia. Before meant innocence and excess, idealism and hubris. More than anything, this was the time before death.[4]

RESPONSES TO THE EPIDEMIC

As expected, AIDS stimulated a wide range of responses. The initial understanding that it was a disease of "marginal" persons—gay men and IV drug users—discouraged public sympathy for those with the disease. It seemed to many that this was a judgment upon men with deviant behavior who performed "unnatural acts," untouchables who were getting their just desserts. Conservative Protestant religious leaders saw the disease as a God-given punishment upon a segment of the population justly deserving a fatal disease. Homosexuality is condemned by many as immoral and an act defined as a sin in the Bible. The Roman Catholic Church persisted in its opposition to the use of condoms, even though there was evidence that condoms decreased the chances of infection. This populist response to AIDS included banning children from school, keeping workers from their jobs, and limiting access to health care facilities such as hospices. Government responses were in keeping with the need for care and assistance, but the government was slow in organizing its response to the near despair of the sick.

Deeply disturbing were the changes in public understanding of medicine and of sexual mores. Sontag notes:

AIDS marks a turning point in current attitudes toward illness and medicine, as well as toward sexuality and catastrophe. . . . The advent of AIDS has made it clear that the infectious diseases are far from conquered. . . . Contraception and the assurance by medicine of the easy curability of sexually transmitted diseases (as of almost all infectious diseases) made it possible to regard sex as an adventure without consequences. Now AIDS obliges people to think of sex as having, possibly, the direst consequences: suicide. Or murder.[5]

Although research looking for the infectious agent started early, funding was meager, and political figures were reluctant to appear sympathetic to persons with AIDS.

The gay community had been successful in building political power. San Francisco, a city to which tens of thousands of homosexual women and men had migrated from hostile and unwelcoming towns and cities across the United States, was noteworthy in its open political climate. From the viewpoint of early control of social and personal factors that were instrumental in the spread of AIDS, this was unfortunate. Attempts to close the bathhouses and educational efforts to encourage a radical curtailment of promiscuous sexual behavior were seen as a retreat from hard-won liberation, as new strictures upon a lifestyle that demonstrated that homosexual men, in particular, had the courage to admit who they were and to live their lives openly. Those who saw this struggle as a political one and not as a public health concern delayed efforts to slow the spread of AIDS.

In his prologue to *And the Band Played On*, Shilts writes:

In those early years, the federal government viewed AIDS as a budget problem, local public health officials saw it as a political problem, gay leaders considered AIDS a public relations problem, and the news media regarded it as a homosexual problem that wouldn't interest anybody else. Consequently, few confronted AIDS for what it was, a profoundly threatening medical crisis.[6]

The succeeding decade, 1981–91, saw the rewards of the political skills that the gay community had acquired. New cases of AIDS declined in homosexual men as the numbers rose among IV drug users and their sexual partners. A causally related rise in the number of children with AIDS was equally apparent. This demographic shift, associated with the political and social power of the patient population, is evident in a decline in public concern for the disease and its victims. There is no question about where resources are applied: the squeaky wheel gets the oil. Ronald Bayer and David L. Kirp write:

As the focus of public health concern has shifted from gay men, among whom the incidence of HIV infection has remained low for the past several years, to poor black and Hispanic drug users and their sexual partners, the influence of gay spokespersons has begun to wane. Racial minorities and drug users are less adept at influencing policy, and those who speak on their behalf often lack the commitment to privacy and consent that characterizes gay organizations.[7]

The level of expenditures for AIDS treatment and for investigation of HIV approaches that for cancer research and surpasses that for diabetes research, raising questions about the use of limited resources for expanding demands of many special-interest groups.

A SPECIAL RESPONSE

I noted some of the ways we reacted to the appearance of AIDS in the United States. The disease originally occurred in homosexual men and Haitians. This fact delayed governmental reaction to a potential epidemic; there was a sense that AIDS was a disease limited to a special group of persons—perhaps a judgment on their lifestyle. When we learned that it was a virus transmissible by blood transfusion, use of contaminated needles by drug users, and heterosexual intercourse, there was a distinct increase in public interest in preventing its spread to the rest of the population. Early in the epidemic, gay communities in the large cities mobilized their forces—financial and political—to assist the sick and the dying. The creative arts professions most stricken by AIDS—theater, art, dance, and design—staged large fund-raising events. More important from an ethical and moral stance was the impressive development of groups of persons who began to care for the sick and the dying. Volunteers were trained to join the professional nurses and physicians who were assuming the large task of caring for very ill men whose numbers were increasing daily.

There is a bitter irony in the severity of the test of community that was applied to our gay citizens. The intense social, emotional, and personal strains of "coming out," the delight in full acceptance by many people, the freedom to declare openly one's sexuality—all this was almost immediately thrust into deepest doubt and fear by the irruption of a fatal disease limited initially to homosexual men. For those of us who seek direction and sources of strength for engagement with the plagues of our time, the experiences and emotions of gay and lesbian writers are most informative. In his afterword to Part Two of *Angels in America*, Tony Kushner writes:

> The world howls without, it is at this moment a very terrible world—what the first character you meet in *Perestroika* calls an "inevident welter of fact, event, phenomenon, calamity." I have been blessed with remarkable friends, colleagues, comrades, collaborators: Together we organize the world for ourselves, or at least we organize our understanding of it;

we reflect it, refract it, grieve over its savagery; and we help each other to discern, amidst the gathering dark, paths of resistance, pockets of peace, and places from whence hope may be plausibly expected.[8]

The social and political responses that the gay community made were instrumental in caring for one another and in alerting the rest of us to the severity of the tests we would all face as the disease escalated.

Attempts were made to apply the growing political power of the gay community to government to increase funding for medical care, education in prevention, and research. The Gay Men's Health Crisis (GMHC) and ACTUP struggled to force governmental attention on the epidemic. The desperate need for this was succinctly noted in *The Normal Heart*, a play written by Larry Kramer, founder of GMHC, that opened in New York City on April 21, 1985. On the wall of the set was a quotation from "American Jewry During the Holocaust," which had been prepared in 1984 for the American Jewish Commission on the Holocaust:

> There were two alternative strategies a Jewish organization could adopt to get the American government to initiate action on behalf of the imperiled Jews of Europe. It could cooperate with the government officials, quietly trying to convince them that rescue of Jews should be one of the objectives of the war, or it could try to pressure the government into initiating rescue by using embarrassing public attention and rallying public opinion to that end.[9]

Unfortunately for all of us, the former course was taken. No moves were made to rescue the Jews. Kramer and other activists on both coasts took the latter approach to force attention to the growing AIDS epidemic. In his introduction to *The Normal Heart*, Andrew Holleran writes:

> Millions of our fellow citizens, of course, were sure this illness was nothing more, or less, than what homosexuals deserved: a kind of divine leprosy.... The human capacity to care about the deaths of anyone but ourselves, or those close to us, is not very great—and society at large seemed at best uninterested.[10]

Kramer's play was a success and an early force for mobilizing public concern about the fate of patients with AIDS.

THE RESPONSE OF LOVE

As the momentum of the AIDS epidemic accelerated, so did dedicated, accepting, and loving personal responses of families, friends, lovers, and health care personnel. There is a medieval tone to the writings about shared love and commitment in those years of rapid spread of the disease in the gay community. The concept of passionate love coursing deeply through the soul; the ability, even willingness, to be with the dying, hideous as it can be with AIDS; the definition of the self inherent in caring for one approaching death; the alteration in perspective on living: all these appeared—as in a revival—in plays, essays, and fiction. In *Millennium Approaches*, Part One of *Angels in America*, Louis describes with obvious admiration the exemplary love of Mathilde for her husband, William the Conqueror:

> She waited for him, she stitched [the Bayeux tapestry] for years. And if he had come back broken and defeated from war, she would have loved him even more. And if he had returned mutilated, ugly, full of infection and horror, she would still have loved him; fed by pity, by a sharing of pain, she would have loved him even more, and even more, and she would never, never, have prayed to God, please let him die and if he can't return to me whole and healthy and able to live a normal life. . . . If he had died, she would have buried her heart with him.[11]

In the early years of the AIDS pandemic, many patients expressed shame at their diagnosis. This is one of the negative feelings associated with diseases assumed by others to be self-inflicted by unacceptable behavior. The time lapse between infection and symptoms—delayed in "slow" viral infections—is a cause of anxiety as one looks for the first sign; obviously, there is apt to be a profound overreading of signs and symptoms as one awaits the first hint of a fatal disease. Another part of AIDS that is terrifying is the disintegration of the body. Susan Sontag writes that "the most terrifying illnesses are those perceived not just as lethal, but as dehumanizing, literally so."[12] She continues, "The most feared diseases, those that are not simply fatal but transform the body into something alienating, like leprosy and syphilis and cholera and (in the imagination of many) cancer, are the ones that seem particularly susceptible to promotion to 'plague.'"[13] AIDS is that type of disease, with its wasting of the body, possible dementia and blindness, and eventual death. Not only the fear of contagion but also the progressive loss of the "person" is a source of terror. This makes all the more impressive the mobilization of volunteers and others to be with, and for, those afflicted with AIDS.

The isolation, social and medical, that AIDS forces on many is reminiscent of the responses to leprosy recorded in the Bible. Although it is unlikely that the disease we know as Hansen's disease—leprosy—is the one to which the Bible speaks, the responses of the people, religious leaders, and Jesus are instructive for us today. Lepers were forced out of the community and out of their houses and led isolated lives. One was forbidden to touch lepers, and they were required to notify others of their presence. In the Gospel of Matthew, Jesus cleanses a leper:

> When Jesus had come down from the mountain, great crowds followed
> him; and there was a leper who came to him and knelt before him, say-
> ing, "Lord, if you choose you can make me clean." He stretched out his
> hand and touched him, saying, "I do choose. Be made clean!" Immedi-
> ately his leprosy was cleansed.[14]

Healing skills of a miraculous nature were well known in the days of Greco-
Roman culture, so we cannot judge the medical bases for the many cures
described in the Bible. Here, however, is a profound lesson for us, lived out
in reality by so many who have cared for persons with AIDS. Jesus *touches*
the leper, an action both prohibited and, in light of medical knowledge of
that time, risky. Yet Jesus does touch him, symbolically returning him to
community even as he cures the affliction. The isolation from community
was understood as the cruelest aspect of leprosy. In like manner, various
gay organizations joined earlier ones, such as the Shanti Project in San Francisco, to care for the suffering and the dying. This response of being with,
of *touching*, was significant in its actual demonstration of acceptance, of
care, of unity in the process of living until we die. Is that not what we all
are doing: living until we die?

The often-expressed opinion that AIDS is a judgment of God upon a certain way of life, a sexual orientation, a behavior based on drug dependence,
is a serious religious question. Confidence in a God of justice has been a
perennial belief in Jewish and Christian thought, even though the mind cannot always understand events in terms of justice. Suffering and pain, the
death of infants and the helpless, the apparent randomness of violence in
our times—these realities question belief in a God of justice. Yet it is often
the very sufferers, as in the Nazi death camps, who profess their belief. For
many, the multifaceted issues of sin, grace, redemption, forgiveness, and
grief are beyond our understanding; faith in an all-knowing God supports
those who suffer and are in ultimate distress. The issue of disease—in this
case, AIDS—as a punishment from God is not a question of justice but of
epidemiology. Tony Kushner, in *Millennium Approaches*, differentiates between the verdict and the judgment of a judge. The former is the execution
of the law; the latter is the evaluation of a life. If, as Louis says, God is
justice, then

> it's the judge, sitting in his or her chambers, weighing, books open, pon-
> dering the evidence, ranging freely over categories: good, evil, innocent,
> guilty; the judge in the chamber of circumspection, not the judge on the
> bench with the gavel. The shaping of the law, not its execution. . . . [I]t
> should be the questions and shape of a life, its total complexity gathered,
> arranged and considered, which matters in the end, not some stamp of
> salvation or damnation.[15]

Life, as a construct over years of decisions and acts, is to be considered in its whole before God.

To continue the metaphor from a Christian perspective, it is Jesus, as the Christ, who is our advocate, our attorney and counsel before the God of justice, asking that our sentence of punishment be nulled through the price of our redemption paid by his death. But it is a model other than that of Good Friday and Easter that I hold to in understanding the Christian message for me in these days of powerful pestilences that have the potential to destroy all we hold dear. The image that I see in my mind's eye is a young man walking down a dusty road in a rural town, Galilee. The people are poor and oppressed, sick and fearful. Our young man, quiet and with a somber countenance, seems committed to making his stand with these people, to being with and for them in their resistance to secular and religious authorities that ignore them. He heals the sick with his touch, eats with the despised, feeds the hungry, opens the eyes of those who are blind. This young man, with a quizzical look on his face, asks me if I would join him in his work, come closer to him to learn what he knows of the ways of God in our troubled world. The future is not bright, the challenges seem overwhelming and frightening, the risks are immense when one takes on the established order to be with and for those who suffer. What will my answer be?

For all the talk about a plague, about a pandemic whose magnitude remains unknowable to us, it is the personal and the intimate remembrances of those who become sick and struggle to live that hold us. Love remains the defining determinant in that embrace; we live on, perhaps incomplete and sad, with our memories. Joseph Brodsky, in his memoir of Stephen Spender, writes about the values of a life of creativity and affection:

> People are what we remember about them. What we call life is in the end a patchwork of someone else's recollections. With death, it gets unstitched, and one ends up with random, disjointed fragments. With shards or, if you will, with snapshots. Filled with their unbearable laughter or equally unbearable smiles.[16]

Although it is, and must always be, an individual voyage through life that no other person can really share, it is the relationships, the expressions of love and of care—perhaps even correction—that sustain us. It is the life enriched by love and grace that is worth living. The experiences of the past fifteen years have shown us much to confirm our confidence in love as our only constant, the sole compass, the reliable guide through the wilderness of our lives toward an ultimate and mysterious union.

Be it transfiguration or transformation, there is a lesson for us in the certain knowledge of our death. And that lesson is that this life is to be lived in honesty and in community with all others if there is to be any hope.

Without morbid words or thoughts, the end of this life must be considered, thought through, and planned as best we can. Only after introspection and reflection on the self in a created world can sense be made of it—if any rational sense can be imagined at all. Paul Monette died of AIDS. His long-time partner died earlier, as did other friends and companions. In his essay "Last Watch of the Night," Monette writes:

> I see the difference now between mere baggage and what the heart pos-
> sesses. Not that the latter is any less stolen goods—the brimming of love
> and the joy of a comrade—requiring every bit of a pirate's brazen stealth.
> And no less snatched in the end by the icy clutch of Death. . . .
>   But the heart transformed in the process, no longer just a thing that
> ticks, and no longer simply mortal. . . . Something lasts, firm as the pen
> in my hand. Jackals and buzzards cannot get at it. Its price doesn't trans-
> late into dollars. Saved as it is in the spending, till nothing's left in the
> vault. Invisible in the blinding shine of the setting sun, weightless as a
> mid-ocean breeze. To have greatly loved is to sail without ballast—with
> neither chart nor cargo, not bound for the least of kingdoms. Nothing
> remains, except this being free.[17]

In the time of pestilence, when disaster seems near to us and to those we love, hope is defined by the willingness—often a self-imposed demand—of some to be with and for us, to stay with us when others depart. Perhaps the healing of AIDS is not possible, and patients will live with the virus as an integral part of their bodies if means are found to slow or halt the reproduction of the virus in the lymphocytes. Lifestyle, personal choices, commitments to others, and concern for the common good will dictate how we behave. The epilogue of *Perestroika*, Part Two of *Angels in America*, finds the characters at the Bethesda fountain in Central Park. The statue of the angel recalls the story of the creation of the fountain just north of the Second Temple in Jerusalem, where an angel descended and touched the earth, bringing forth water and creating a pool. In the Gospel of John, this pool by the Sheep Gate, named Bethzatha, is the site of a famous healing by Jesus on the Sabbath of a man who had been ill for thirty-eight years. "Jesus said to him, 'Stand up, take your mat and walk.' At once the man was made well, and he took up his mat and began to walk."[18] Tradition has it that when the millennium comes, the fountain at the Sheep Gate will flow again and the sick will be made well, the unclean will be made clean. A main character in *Angels in America*, Prior, closes the play with these lines:

> This disease will be the end of many of us, but not nearly all, and the
> dead will be commemorated and will struggle on with the living, and we
> are not going away. We won't die secret deaths anymore. The world only
> spins forward. We will be citizens. The time has come. . . .
>   The Great Work Begins.[19]

WHAT MAY LIE AHEAD

In the introduction to his book *History of AIDS*, Mirko Grmek notes that the conclusion drawn by Susan Sontag that "cancer lacked certain elements to qualify it as the ideal metaphor" for our society has been corrected. "We now have that metaphor: with its links to sex, drugs, blood, and informatics, and with the sophistication of its evolution and of its strategy for spreading itself, AIDS expresses our era."[20] This new pandemic may also provide an opportunity for a reassessment of our values and our relations to one another on a shrinking planet. The potential for moral and ethical development and expression is in direct relation, it seems, to the threats that we face from diseases—social as well as medical. It is a distant but real possibility that the community hazards associated with infectious diseases can stimulate the true sense of unity essential to control. Barry R. Bloom and Christopher J. L. Murray write, "In the world of infectious diseases, there is nothing from which we are remote and no one from whom we are disconnected."[21] It is distressing that observations about the possibilities for controlling the new epidemics are still the same as those voiced nearly two decades ago at the onset of AIDS. In a 1996 paper, "Emerging Bacterial Zoonotic and Vector-Borne Diseases," the authors list the very strategies hoped for when AIDS appeared in the early 1980s: (1) development of the capacity to study and document the appearance of new diseases; (2) increased emphasis on ecological and clinical issues in the transmission of insect- and animal-borne infections; (3) improved laboratory methods; and (4) provision of understandable and definitive information about the nature of the diseases and their recognition. The authors close with this comment: "Science has created the contemporary tools and trained scientists to address these problems far more effectively than at any other time in the history of medicine. What is required is a visionary investment of a relatively modest nature."[22] The question is, of course, when will we make that investment?

Tuberculosis, known as the White Plague, is a sharp reminder of pestilence. Among infectious diseases, TB is the leading cause of death in the world, as it has been in Europe and the United States since records have been kept. John Bunyan, in *The Life and Death of Mr. Badman* (1680), notes the cause of one death: "Yet the Captain of all these men of death that came against him to take him away, was the Consumption, for 'twas that that brought him down to the grave."[23] The name consumption became popular in novels and operas in the Romantic Age. It is an ancient disease; the pulmonary type spread by cough and sneeze, the bone type by milk from infected cows. The recent resurgence of tuberculosis in AIDS patients poses public health concerns of considerable consequence. In a way similar to HIV, the microbiology of the tubercle bacillus is poorly understood. Its protective waxy coat makes it impervious to many drugs, its slow reproductive rate makes investigation slow and difficult, and little is known about its genetic structure. The bacillus resists dying, surviving almost indefinitely in the environment. The sudden appearance, in a shelter for the homeless in New York City, of a mutant strain of the tubercle bacillus that is resistant to current drug therapies is another example of biologic variation that becomes lethal for us, a warning for continuing surveillance.

It is fascinating to observe the ways in which physicians and public health officials have approached the treatment and control of tuberculosis. Whereas Canada, Britain, and many European countries have vaccinated children with BCG (bacille Calmette-Guérin), developed by the Pasteur Institute and announced in 1924, U.S. approaches have been to try to alter the socioeconomic factors of poverty and urban crowding that cause its rapid spread. There were stigmata associated with TB: immigrant status, female, nonwhite, poor. As Georgina Feldberg writes in the introduction to her book *Disease and Class*: "Like plague before it and AIDS after it, tuberculosis also summoned up images and myths that gave shape to human experience. The explanations offered for patterns of susceptibility to tuberculosis defined social roles, framed social differences, and betrayed asumptions about deviance." Her study "clarifies the meanings American physicians attached to experiences with TB and reveals the ways in which the control of tuberculosis formed part of a larger material, institutional, and ideological effort to shape the middle-class state."[24] A diagnosis of TB in the century 1860–1960 told a lot about the social standing of the patient. This is also true today; tuberculosis is another plague that is a model for testing our moral and ethical stance toward the afflicted.

The list of other plagues we know in our time is long: our children die of hunger, malaria, diarrhea, and many other endemic medical and social problems. The toll on life of the pestilences we bring down upon one another is another story. William H. McNeill closes his 1977 book *Plagues and Peoples* with this observation:

In any effort to understand what lies ahead, as much as what lies behind, the role of infectious disease cannot properly be left out of consideration. Ingenuity, knowledge, and organization alter but cannot cancel humanity's vulnerability to invasion by parasitic forms of life. Infectious disease which antedated the emergence of mankind will last as long as humanity itself, and will surely remain, as it has been hitherto, one of the fundamental parameters and determinants of human history.[25]

The emergence of new and widely pervasive diseases will continue, and we cannot foretell their effects. These plagues are ubiquitous, life-threatening, and invisible. With the skills of the biological sciences, they can be understood, contained, often prevented. If and when we decide to save precious lives, offer hope, and be with and for those who suffer and die, we will be living the life we were meant to live. Faith can inform a lively and dedicated response to plague. We can confront the plague and ally ourselves with its victims, or we can leave town. Our religions and our philosophies are clear about the roles that compassion and love play in defining our selves by our responses. It is the self-centered self, separated from the social network we live in and denying the presence of a spirit that animates and upholds, who must face the horrors of inescapable plague alone.

NOTES

1. T. S. Eliot, "The Hollow Men," in *Collected Poems 1909–1962* (New York: Harcourt Brace Jovanovich, 1963), 82.
2. Susan Sontag, *AIDS and Its Metaphors* (New York: Farrar, Straus & Giroux, 1988), 60.
3. Randy Shilts, *And the Band Played On* (New York: St. Martin's Press, 1987), 15.
4. Ibid., 12.
5. Sontag, *AIDS and Its Metaphors*, 72.
6. Shilts, *And the Band Played On*, xxiii.
7. Ronald Bayer and David L. Kirp, "The United States: At the Center of the Storm," in *AIDS in the Industrialized Democracies* (New Brunswick, NJ: Rutgers University Press, 1992), 43.
8. Tony Kushner, *Angels in America*, part 2, *Perestroika* (New York: Theatre Communications Group, 1994), 158.
9. Larry Kramer, *The Normal Heart* (New York: Penguin, 1985), 21.
10. Andrew Holleran, "Introduction," in *The Normal Heart*, 26.
11. Tony Kushner, *Angels in America*, part 1, *Millennium Approaches* (New York: Theatre Communications Group, 1993), 51–2.
12. Sontag, *AIDS and Its Metaphors*, 38.
13. Ibid., 45.
14. Matthew 8:1–3, NRSV.
15. Kushner, *Millennium Approaches*, 38.
16. Joseph Brodsky, *On Grief and Reason: Essays* (New York: Farrar Straus Giroux, 1995), 480.
17. Paul Monette, *Last Watch of the Night* (New York: Harcourt Brace & Company, 1994), 300.
18. John 5:8–9, NRSV.
19. Kushner, *Perestroika*, 148.
20. Mirko Grmek, *History of AIDS*, trans. Russell C. Maulitz and Jacalyn Duffin (Princeton, NJ: Princeton University Press, 1990), xii.
21. Barry R. Bloom, and Christopher J. L. Murray, "Tuberculosis: Commentary on a Reemergent Killer," *Science* 257 (August 21, 1992): 1061.
22. David H. Walker, Alan G. Barbour, James H. Oliver, Robert S. Lane, J. Stephen Dumier, David T. Dennis, David H. Pershing, Abdu F. Azad, and Edward McSweegan, "Emerging Bacterial Zoonotic and Vector-Borne Diseases," *JAMA* 275 (1996): 468.

23. John Bunyan *The Life and Death of Mr. Badman*, ed. James F. Forrest and Roger Sharrock (Oxford: Clarendon Press, 1988), 148.
24. Georgina D. Feldberg, *Disease and Class* (New Brunswick, NJ: Rutgers University Press, 1995), 7, 9.
25. William H. McNeill, *Plagues and Peoples* (New York: Anchor Books, Doubleday, 1977), 257.

T w e l v e

WE ARE THE ULTIMATE PLAGUE

Incidentally, it is not absurd to class the ecological role of humankind in its relationship to other life forms as a disease.

—William H. McNeill, *Plagues and Peoples*

IN THE EARLY 1960s, we awakened to a number of crises in our world. The struggle for civil rights in the South seemed the most pressing one, mobilizing strong emotions, often for opposing reasons. Other issues demanded attention, and two books were central to my awakening to this strident decade. In 1962, Rachel Carson published her landmark book *Silent Spring*, overwhelming us with evidence of the damage we inflict on the environment with poisons used as pesticides and herbicides. Certainly, this book is a milestone in the struggle to reverse the destructive effects of "progress" on the earth. Her gentle yet insistent and unrelenting demand that we look at what we are doing was a major force in creating a strong lobby of people committed to reversing the steady increase of pollution and poison pervading our culture. Her closing paragraph calls us to attend:

> The "control of nature" is a phrase conceived in ignorance, born of the Neanderthal age of biology and philosophy, when it was supposed that nature existed for the convenience of man. The concepts and practices of applied entomology for the most part date from that Stone Age of science.

195

It is our alarming misfortune that so primitive a science has armed itself
with the most modern and terrible weapons, and that in turning them against
the insects it has also turned them against the earth.[1]

Silent Spring put into simple and accurate language a warning that we are
destroying life on our planet. Her illustrations of the impact of the new
technology—notably, toxic chemicals such as DDT—sounded the alarm, and
a new word, *environmentalism*, appeared both as a public concern and commitment and as a new profession.

The second book that awakened me was *Night Comes to the Cumberlands*,
a 1963 study of eastern Kentucky by Harry M. Caudill. His description of
the relentless destruction of the land and its people, the picture of desolation and abandonment he portrays, and the scenes of utter hopelessness un-
settled me and confirmed my fading confidence in government to do its
work for the people, protecting us from industry. The rapacity and detach-
ment of both industry and unions were startling in their forthright abandonment of their workers. Toward the end of the book, Caudill writes:

> Most saddening of all are the myriads of men, women and children who
> sit on the front porches of shacks and houses gazing with listless uncon-
> cern at the world. . . . The cloak of idleness, defeat, dejection and surren-
> der has fallen so heavily as to leave them scarcely more than half alive.
> Their communities are turning into graveyards peopled with the living
> dead and strewn with the impedimenta of a civilization which once needed
> them but does so no longer.[2]

These two books highlight plagues that are caused directly by human beings
and affect all that lives: serious damage to the delicate balance of living
plants and animals that inhabit the earth, and irreversible destruction and
pollution of the land and its waters. If pressed, I probably would have said
that I "knew" what these authors were describing, but I had certainly not
made that information a part of my experience as a physician, as a citizen,
as a created being, as a Christian. The emotional impact of these two books
was considerable. But it would be a few more years before I understood
what these writers saw.

In 1969, I was at the University of Kentucky to give a talk on possible
ways to approach the problem of hungry children in our country. While
there, I was taken on a tour of eastern Kentucky, the site of Caudill's study.
Similar to my direct confrontation with hungry children in Mississippi was
my experience of seeing the men in the small towns on the Cumberland
Plateau. Caudill describes them well:

> The broken and the ill are truly legion. Some suffer from "miner's asthma."
> They wheeze like dying men, their lungs filled with silica, "rock dust" or

fine coal. . . . Others are blind in one or both eyes, display empty sleeves or hobble on artificial legs. Here and there a paralytic sits in a wheel chair . . . a reminder of the sudden slate fall that crushed his spine. . . . These broken men are part of the price America has paid for her industrial pre-eminence. . . . Their pain and poverty are a hidden part of the highly touted "American standard of living."[3]

My face-to-face meeting with amputees, this witness to the human toll of exploitation, was only a small part of what was occurring across the land—across the globe. We have such a long history of using others for our advantage that it had almost slipped away from me what the nature of the human condition is for so many. One of the terrors of these experiences is my realization that I do not know what is going on in the world unless I see it and incorporate it, literally, into my personal knowledge. The opportunity to identify with another person right in front of you is an unforgettable experience. The time for commitment suddenly becomes *now*.

My 1970 visit to southern Florida for the Field Foundation documented widespread exposure to pesticides. I photographed men on spray rigs without protective clothes or masks spraying parathion on a windy day fifty feet from the children's playground. Daily spraying of vegetable fields was common, and the men, women, and children who did stoop labor were exposed regularly. Rashes, burning eyes, nausea, and headache—with rapid recovery in a day or so—were common complaints. Empty cans of pesticides and herbicides lined the edges of the canals and ditches, sources of water for home use and of fish for food. I saw the same exposure to pesticides in the citrus groves. The pickers said that the spray rig would often spray the pair of rows next to the ones they were picking that day. It was accepted that the men would probably be sick that night but better by the following day. This experience, like others of those years, impressed upon me the profoundly personal nature of the environmental and ecological crises we were accepting as normal for an advanced industrial country. Rachel Carson had seen and recorded the obvious.

It is not my purpose to document in detail the ecocrisis that our planet is in, this destructive plague that we have brought to our only home. That work continues to be done admirably by others. There is no doubt that we are depleting our natural resources of fossil fuels, polluting our waters and air, warming the planet, destroying species of animals and plants, leveling the forests, and killing one another. Our reasons are many, and consideration of some of them is the theme of this chapter. Our hopes lies in alternative answers to the question, How shall we live?

DOMINION OVER LAND AND SEA

The core question for understanding the plague we face in the destruction of the environment is, Whose world is this? There has been an unquestioned belief that the world is here for the use of human beings. We are the capstone of the evolutionary pyramid, the undisputed owners of this planet, whose resources are ours for our health, wealth, and enjoyment. We have, since the beginning of history, co-opted this earth and one another for our own uses, with little regard for other inhabitants and their requirements for living. As Thomas Berry points out, most living species are confronted by natural conditions and opponents that limit their places and their numbers. Not so with us.

> The human . . . can, for a period of time, subvert the forces that might normally lead to extinction. What the human cannot do is to avoid the degradation in its own mode of being that occurs with a certain inevitability when it fails in fulfilling its niche in the larger earth community.[4]

Diversity of life is essential to existence, with the comings and goings of species an observed fact of all nature. Our interruptions of these processes of creation, selection, and competition have disastrous effects on the world and are the etiological agents of the ecological plague with which we live, suffer, and die.

Attitudes toward using the earth for the exclusive fulfillment of human needs and desires go back to earliest times. The use of the earth solely for our purposes—cutting and burning forests and draining swamps—has been our custom since we got up on our hind legs. The domination of the total environment is a constant in our short evolutionary history. In Western culture, for several thousand years the justification for our behavior has been tied to the very inception of the world. The story of its creation, found in the first book of the Bible, has been read as bedrock evidence for human dominion over all the earth.

> Then God said, "Let us make humankind in our image, according to our likeness; and let them have dominion over the fish of the sea, and over the birds of the air, and over the cattle, and over all the wild animals of the earth, and over every creeping thing that creeps upon the earth. . . . Be fruitful and multiply, and fill the earth and subdue it; and have dominion over the fish of the sea and over the birds of the air and over every living thing that moves upon the earth."[5]

This biblical authorization was accepted well into our own era, at least among believers, and we know the consequences of that acceptance: widespread devastation as the need for farming and grazing land accelerated. Up through the Middle Ages, there was little quarrel with this position. Francis of Assisi

(1182–1226) was a notable exception. His humility before the created order, his acknowledgment that the spirit of God infused all, and his profound faith in that God combined to offer one model for our behavior. His sense of reverence and his unwillingness to see the created world as something given to us for our exploitation can inform us. Sometimes read as sentimentality, his identification with the created world remains a living challenge for us.

A revered predecessor of Francis by some five centuries, Benedict established his monastery at Monte Cassino and began an order devoted to enhancing the earth by scholarship and labor. Rene Dubos, noting the use of the first chapter of Genesis as authorization for our dominion over nature, writes:

> The Benedictine rule in contrast seems inspired rather from the second chapter, in which the Good Lord placed man in the Garden of Eden not as a master but rather in a spirit of stewardship. Throughout the history of the Benedictine order, its monks have actively intervened in nature—as farmers, builders, and scholars. They have brought about profound transformations of soil, water, fauna, and flora, but in such a wise manner that their management of nature has proved compatible in most cases with the maintenance of environmental quality.[6]

It was the scientific revolution developing steadily in the sixteenth and seventeenth centuries that "sanctified" our domination of the natural world. Max Oelschlaeger writes: "Galileo's new science, Bacon's new logic, Descartes's mechanistic reductionism, and Newton's physics are central to our study. Collectively they represent a *paradigm shift* so radical that the very meaning of the word *nature* was changed. . . . Nature is now believed to be the object of scientific study."[7] The natural world was transformed into matter in motion, a concept that discourages a view of universal interdependence among living objects and their environment. The universe, complex and strange as it is, could be known and understood by our minds through the new sciences. Reason based on knowledge would grant us not only understanding but also mastery and opportunities to realize the human potential by making the world ours.

The culmination of these years of investigation and learning was the Enlightenment of the eighteenth century, that astounding era when political, personal, scientific, and economic theories became functional and explanatory of the human enterprise. Oelschlaeger writes:

> As the eighteenth century gave way to the nineteenth, the forces of history—the scientific, democratic, and industrial revolutions, the Reformation, and the Enlightenment—amalgamated themselves into a cultural paradigm so powerful and pervasive that it yet rules the West. . . . Capitalism

and democracy coalesced with machine technology to effect the conversion of nature into a standing reserve possessing market value only. Modernism thus completes the intellectual divorce of humankind from nature.[8]

The destruction of the land by strip mining and deforestation, so poignantly described by Caudill, caused a dehumanization of people that adds a chilling note to "progress." Our insatiable greed and desire for material wealth stain our work in this world. In my own religious tradition, I look back to those who came to a continent seen as wilderness, a place without a civilization, inhabited by savages who would need conversion to a faith that preached sacrificial love for both God and neighbor. It would take two hundred years before New England would hear a voice that admonishes us to attend to that wilderness because it is our hope for salvation and redemption. Henry David Thoreau's famous pronouncement, "in Wildness is the preservation of the World,"[9] summarizes his experiences, his hopes and despairs for us, and his ultimate conviction that our relations with nature determine us both as a people and as individual persons. The importance of Thoreau's writings for our attempts to preserve and sustain this planet has increased with the years; the perennial popularity of *Walden* and several of his essays attests to his clairvoyant vision of the inner and outer lives we would live.

RELIGION, FAITH, AND OUR WORLD

A 1967 essay by Lynn White accelerated the growing movement of concern for the environment. Writing in *Science*, he presents an argument for considering the Judeo-Christian religious tradition as instrumental in causing the ecological crisis we face. In contrast to ancient mythologies and their animistic beliefs,

> Christianity inherited from Judaism not only a concept of time as nonrepetitive and linear but also a striking story of creation. . . . God had created Adam and, as an afterthought, Eve to keep man from being lonely. Man named all the animals, thus establishing him dominance over them. God planned all of this explicitly for man's benefit and rule: no item in the physical creation had any purpose save to serve man's purposes. And, although man's body is made of clay, he is not simply part of nature: he is made in God's image.[10]

White precipitated thoughtful debate, denominational policy statements, and demands for change: thirty years of focused and vigorous appraisal of the interdependence of environment and human life. But there seems to have been no diminution in the drive to exploit the natural world. Attempts to use public lands for private profit, ongoing—perhaps increasing—pollution of air and water, destruction of tropical forests, pesticide use: all these and more attest to our persistence in using up the world for immediate wants and personal gain. Our insatiable need for immediate satisfaction of wants and desires makes long-term and future-generation considerations difficult to implement. To preserve the planet for those who follow us will require a commitment whose sustaining force must be capable of controlling our self-serving drives. As we know so well, it is easy to speak of these issues but difficult to implement change that is more than surface and cosmetic. A realistic look at the political, racial, ethnic, economic, and social chaos endemic to our times warns against easy solutions to our ecocrisis. The toll in human life in the twentieth century makes hope for concern about the fate of flora and fauna seem absurd. Yet we must make the effort to change; it may even now be too late for more than a delaying action.

One of the obstructions to change in our use and abuse of nature is the sense of separation from the nonhuman world. Insects, snakes, brambles, mud puddles, and poison ivy are identified not as coinhabitors but as nuisances, even threats to our work and our pleasure. In premonotheistic times, the natural world was inhabited by spirits that instilled meaning and significance to all living animals and plants and to the earth itself. This animism granted some protection to forest groves, sacred pools, and certain animals, but deforestation and land erosion existed long before the exodus. The modern age, with its Industrial Revolution and Adam Smith economy, has merely provided more efficient tools and clearer logic for ongoing pillage.

WE ARE IN THIS TOGETHER

Individual voices were heard throughout our long and varied history calling for preservation, conservation, and restoration of the earth as a treasure that could be lost. But it was the Romantic movement in Europe in the nineteenth century that raised questions about our use of our environs, documented compelling evidence of our interrelatedness, and provided support for reconsidering the role of human beings in this massive created and creating universe. The detailed and accurate work of Charles Darwin that appeared in *Origin of Species* provided a scientific basis for viewing the earth as an intricate, fragile, and interdependent organism. No longer could we see the world as a stable and functional clockwork set running for our exclusive use. The unfathomable intricacy of the biological world inspired awe and excitement in many, and a new age of science began. Not only was there wonder at this new view of order in our world; the revelations of archaeology about the ancient—almost ageless—foundations of our world startled and frightened many with the obvious threats to the concept of a creation given to "man" for exploitation and gain. It opened the way for a corrected understanding. There was a new way of looking at the structure of the world—begun with the innovative and imaginative cataloging efforts of Linnaeus—and the place of human beings as lords and rulers would be forever challenged. The Genesis account of creation was no longer valid; objections by inheritors of Judeo-Christian traditions were dismissed as anachronisms. A disturbing finding was the apparent extravagance of numbers in each species needed for the slow but insistent development of life. The sheer number of seeds, eggs and sperm, flowers, and offspring needed to merely preserve a species was astounding. Nature was indeed a cornucopia of extravagance.

Coincident with the newest science of evolution was a voice from Walden Pond telling us that we must attend to this world of nature. The interdependence of all is a critical fact that we ignore only at our final peril. Thoreau opened a door to nature for us. His unrelenting demand that we pay attention to what we are doing is a presence to this day in efforts to preserve our earthly inheritance. Going far beyond the transcendentalism of his onetime friend Emerson, Thoreau presses us to become real and living members of a fabulous created order, recognizing ourselves as functional and cooperative members of an order from which we cannot free ourselves. His developed sense of his place in the natural order of life not only made him aware of the importance of preserving and renewing nature; he also learned and incorporated into his very being what so many of us struggle to even imagine: we are a part of the whole, a segment of reality bound by the most intimate threads to all and to every other. Of course, this information, so heraldic in his announcement of each dawn we should see, produced a new man in him. He was, on the outside, the same man known to saunter in the oddest places, swim at unusual times, converse with animals and plants, and labor little at the chores of living. But on the inside was a man awakened to his own selfhood, an acknowledged member of the created order with a message for us: we, too, can become whole persons living a graced life in full accord with the best hopes and desires we can imagine. We can accept our dreams of a fulfilled life and live them out. Life is a possibility if we will but awaken and accept its gifts and delights. The desperation in which most of us live is our choice, not our sentence.

Thoreau grasped as fully as did Darwin the intricate balance in nature, the interdependence of all. There is nothing outside the web of relationships: each pebble cast into the water initiates ripples that exist, whether we feel them or not. It is this awesome sense of being a part—with all else—of a universe that is beyond our wildest fantasies that can lead us to a renewal of faith in a creator and sustainer. This realization also brings the choice of being a help or a hindrance to that created order. To destroy other members of the creation is to commit a form of suicide, for we are killing a part of our own selves, a segment in the seamless garment that is our world. Although Thoreau directs us to simplify our lives, he does not imply that life is simple. It is a highly complex matrix of relations, and our responses to them will—and should—vary. There is a contrariness to observed nature. Donald Worster, writing of Thoreau's "vacillation between pagan naturalism and a transcendental moral vision," says:

> Any whole, be it an individual life or the entire ecological order, is a system of paired tensions working against each other, none surmounting its opposite, each in its own existence implying the existence of the other. Nothing was more fundamental to the Romantic mind than this oscillating between extremes—the concept of the dialectic.[11]

The perpetual struggle we live out to make sense of our selves and of our world is clearly written in *Walden*. This text of a life, crafted by a man who struggled to know himself in his world, is a text for my own life. It is a scripture that I use to awaken myself to my self, to who I am in this complex, confusing, and beautiful creation I call my home.

WHOSE LAND IS IT?

When the Puritans settled in New England, they brought with them two concepts inimical to the beliefs of the peoples living there: the separateness of humankind from the rest of creation, and the idea that we could possess part of that creation, the earth. Creation, for American Indians, places all living things together in origin. The differences now apparent on the earth are differences in form, not in essence of being. Oelschlaeger writes that "Native Americans, it might be said, are more humble in their conception of the nonhuman world, believing not that they are above and superior to it but rather that they are a part of it."[12] All creation is alive, and the relatedness of every part is obvious. The second English concept—ownership of land— was inconceivable to American Indians: land is for the use of all, animated by a spirit that is central to understanding the natural world as well as the self. The fence has a function that is unacceptable for community life. To this day, fences are not seen in many Indian cultures. This simple example shows the inherent problem facing current conservation and ecological concerns. If land is a commodity to be exploited for profit without regard for the needs—present and future—of society, there is vanishing hope for its preservation, to say nothing of its improvement.

Aldo Leopold, founder of the Wilderness Society and author of the classic *A Sand County Almanac and Sketches Here and There*, published posthumously in 1949, developed a land ethic. He writes:

> All ethics so far evolved rest upon a single premise: that the individual is a member of a community of interdependent parts. His instincts prompt

him to compete for his place in that community, but his ethics prompt him also to co-operate. . . . The land ethic simply enlarges the boundaries of the community to include soils, waters, plants, and animals, or collectively: the land.[13]

Critics have generally seen Leopold's lifework as that of a person who understood our history as a species in the whole, alert to the critical need we have to start thinking in the terms of nature and not limit ourselves to the gains possible for humans. "The Land Ethic" section of his book ends with these words:

By and large, our present problem is one of attitudes and implements. We are remodelling the Alhambra with a steamshovel, and we are proud of our yardage. We shall hardly relinquish the shovel, which after all has many good points, but we are in need of gentler and more objective criteria for its successful use.[14]

The question, of course, is what will be the motivating force for the radical revision of our land ethic necessary for conservative uses of the land: its plants, animals, minerals, and waters? It is all well and good to define the right ways for us to live with one another on this fragile planet so that fulfilled lives, enriched environments, and healthy recreation areas are realities for all. It is altogether a different issue to find a belief system, a conviction about ultimate values, a reasoned and acceptable code of interrelational behavior and sacrifice for the common good that supports a common land ethic. The power sufficient to create a personal or a public ethic must inform our call to work for the common good.

THE ROLE OF FAITH

Roger Gottlieb, in the introduction to his anthology *This Sacred Earth*, observes:

For many people religious beliefs provide primary values concerning our place in the universe, our obligations to other people and other life forms, and what makes up a truly "good" life. . . . [T]he significance of religion is heightened because several of the guiding lights of modernity have become increasingly suspect. Faith in science and materialist/liberal democracies has been undermined by the political violence, technological disasters and cultural bankruptcy of the late 20th century. Purely secular radical politics have been rendered doubtful by the economic failures and totalitarian political excesses of communism. . . . Our response is, in the broadest sense of the term, a *spiritual* one; that is it involves our deepest concerns about what is truly of lasting importance in our lives.[15]

This is the ultimate question, one that few of us attempt to answer: "what is truly of lasting importance in our lives?" For many of us, the answer is the polar opposite of the obvious goals of our lives. It has been observed that the most avid environmentalists keep up with the lecture circuit by airplane, drive cars, and generally live their lives as the rest of us do: consuming scarce resources, furthering global warming, and investing in companies that destroy wilderness areas. A deep spirituality that leads to one's modifying behavior relevant to nature is seen rarely: Thoreau—a model for that behavior— is seldom copied. I have difficulty keeping my focus on the very things that I know to be essential to the future of my world, of my children and grandchilden, even of my own self. I am distracted by the details of daily living and my silly wants and pleasures. Even when I am saddened, even terrified, by the future aspects of our earth and I try to mold my life in a different pattern, I find that I follow the experience of that great seven-teenth-century English poet and divine John Donne, who writes:

> I throw my selfe down in my Chamber, and I call in, and invite God, and his Angels thither, and when they are there, I neglect God and his An-gels, for the noise of a Flie, for the rattling of a Coach, for the whining of a doore; ... A memory of yesterdays pleasures, a feare of tomorrows dangers, a straw under my knee, a noise in mine eare, a light in mine eye, an any thing, a nothing, a fancy, a Chimera in my braine, troubles me in my prayer.[16]

I, too, am easily diverted from those deepest spiritual needs and practices that would keep my commitments and my hopes abreast of the severe needs we know. How do I develop a spiritual life that provides the power to keep the needs of this world right up front in my thoughts and actions? I ac-knowledge the pressing reality of a deteriorating environment, the steady and irretrievable loss of resources, the bleak prospects for the future. How do I muster the courage and the conviction to do more than speak about it?

Religious faith, in its broadest definitions, offers hope for uniting many of us in serious efforts to preserve and conserve our world. Lying at the base of that faith are several convictions: (1) we live in a created world, inhabit-ants for a while of a universe beyond our comprehension; (2) we have brought nothing into this world and will take nothing out of it; (3) we are but one in an unknowable number of species; (4) the future of this earth for those who follow us is dependent on our use of it; (5) the resources of the earth are limited. A serious deterrent to religion becoming the bond that unites and empowers any ecocentric movement for preservation is the lack of confi-dence in organized religions' ability to seriously think through faith's rela-tion to an ethic of ecological survival. John Macquarrie, in a lecture published in 1971, asked:

Is is not perhaps too late for this theological rethinking to take place? I do not mean too late in the sense that the ecological crisis is so pressing that there is no time left for the reshaping of our attitudes before the day of reckoning arrives, though that, unfortunately, may be true. I mean rather that it may be too late for any theological model to have an influence because of the decline of theology and the secularization of our outlook.[17]

We identify our times as the post-Christian age. Albert Schweitzer, writing in the early 1930s, also notes the increasing separation between the real world of oppression, destruction, and killing and the decreasing ethical and spiritual commitments of Christianity. He writes, "the bonds between Christianity and active thought were loosened, and the situation to-day is that Christianity has completely withdrawn into itself. . . . It loses . . . its connection with the spiritual life of the time and the possibility of exercising any real influence upon it."[18]

Our spiritual lives are informed, even defined, by the world of nature in which we have our very being. In our existence from day to day, many of us have minimal contact with nature, none with wilderness. We do not grasp the interconnections among all living and nonliving things; we are isolated from much of this astounding earth. Living with the modernist belief in the separation of mind and nature, we do not sense the links that tie all together. Despite our attitudes, humankind does not occupy center stage; if we persist in believing that all else is here for us to use and abuse, our fate is sealed earlier than predicted. A return to a sacramental understanding and valuation of nature raises some hope. But our history has not been very hopeful here. John Haught writes:

> By understanding the promising God of history to be alone holy, Judaism and Christianity (as well as Islam) seem to have divested any present state of nature of its supposedly sacral character. . . . The biblical desacralization of nature may even have helped open up the natural world to human domination and exploitation. Biblical religion expelled the gods from the forests and streams once and for all, and because of its "disenchantment" of nature, along with its focus on the historical future, it is problematic to some religious ecologists of a more sacramental or cosmological persuasion.[19]

There is a call today to return to an understanding of all of creation as sacred; our relations with all of creation are real, are actual. We are kith and kin with all that is. If this concept of the sacredness of nature can be restored or even generated, there is some hope for survival on a delightful planet. But we need to open ourselves to the sacred and work ourselves away from our intense self-concern and self-worship. Any ethic that directs our relations with the earth must have a transcendent base, or else it will descend to our concerns for ourselves and our goods. Schweitzer warns us:

The great fault of all ethics hitherto has been that they believed themselves to have to deal only with the relations of man to man. . . . A man is ethical only when life, as such, is sacred to him, that of plants and animals as that of his fellow-men, and when he devotes himself to all life that is in need of help.[20]

We are beholden to develop that ethic of responsibility to all that *is*. The foundation for that ethic of responsibility must be, like Thoreau's, a rock that will support the entire creation, below which one cannot go. There must be in us a conviction, a confidence, a faith that is capable of holding up the world.

Martin Buber, in a delightful commentary on his observation of a tree, offers a serious religious reflection for us:

Whatever belongs to the tree is included: its form and its mechanics, its colors and its chemistry, its conversation with the elements and its conversation with the stars—all this in its entirety.

The tree is no impression, no play of my imagination, no aspect of a mood; it confronts me bodily and has to deal with me as I must deal with it—only differently.

One should not try to dilute the meaning of the relation: relation is reciprocity.[21]

This puts a different meaning on our uses of trees.

A faith with these demands will require a textual foundation, a story, a cohesive tale of creation, sustenance, revelation, and hope that will bear the freight of our needs. These sacred stories are known to many peoples and serve to illumine and direct lives in the very ways I have spoken about: preservation of life, conservation of nature, an offering of hope, even enchantment. For many of us in the Western tradition, the Bible is our text for this work. A story of human striving, of divine intervention and revelation, and of moral and ethical debate, the Hebrew Bible and the New Testament offer gifts, choices, directives, and codes that point to ways to live out our time here in concert with the rest of creation. Each of us, through study, prayer, conversation, debate, and experience, can find our way through these texts for our enlightenment and empowerment, for that is what we search for: the power to do what we know must be done. We are to be with and for others—all others—as our way of finding ourselves. In the concluding section of *Caring for Creation*, Oelschlaeger writes:

Our culture is caught between a failed past and a future powerless to be born. Religious discourse has been privatized, pushed by utilitarianism to the edge of our cultural conversation. . . . We live in an era of controlled capitalism where ordinary people, deprived of *effective participation* in a political community, find themselves threatened by statism.

Noting that our culture is not knowable apart from our biblical traditions, he continues:

> The biblical tradition contains within itself the seeds of renewal, the energy to rise up and throw off the monster that envelops us, whether this be Job's eloquent testimony to an irrepressible human dignity and indefatigable sense of responsibility or the parables of Jesus, which subtly yet powerfully undermine the final vocabulary of the state.[22]

Only if I place myself in a continuum with the history of my world—the incomprehensible universe we observe micro- and macroscopically—and acknowledge my absolute dependence on a source of life and love beyond my frail self will I be able to be with and for this world. Certain as I am that, in most of my work and my relationships, I will be found wanting, that biblical faith will nevertheless enlighten my life and lighten my burdens. Only thus will my ethic of living be derived and encoded in my heart. I need a model for my behavior that will not fail, that fully acknowledges my inadequacies while offering a form of forgiveness that encourages reentering the struggle. The need persists to attend to current scholarship on my faith and the social and political accompaniments to its development, and to heed the experiences of believers as we search for courage and insight. William McNeill tells us:

> Time and again, a temporary approach to stabilization of new relationships occurred as natural limits to the ravages of humankind upon other life forms manifested themselves. Yet sooner or later . . . humanity discovered new techniques allowing fresh exploitation of hitherto inaccessible resources, thereby renewing or intensifying damage to other forms of life. Looked at from the point of view of other organisms, humankind therefore resembles an acute epidemic disease, whose occasional lapses into less virulent forms of behavior have never yet sufficed to permit any really stable, chronic relationship to establish itself.[23]

Perhaps a renewal of our faiths in a creative and sustaining God, shared by many of us in this modern world of technology and industry devoted to material gain, will offer an ethic for our behavior that will save our precious earth.

NOTES

1. Rachel Carson, *Silent Spring* (Boston: Houghton Mifflin, 1962), 297.
2. Harry M. Caudill, *Night Comes to the Cumberlands* (Boston: Little, Brown, 1963), 346.
3. Ibid., 351.
4. Thomas Berry, "Ecological Geography," in *Worldviews and Ecology* (Lewisburg, PA: Bucknell University Press, 1993), 232.

5. Genesis 1:26, 28, NRSV.
6. Rene Dubos, *A God Within* (New York: Charles Scribner's Sons, 1972), 169.
7. Max Oelschlaeger, *The Idea of Wilderness* (New Haven, CT: Yale University Press, 1991), 76–7.
8. Ibid., 95–6.
9. Henry David Thoreau, "Walking," in *Excursions* (Gloucester, MA: Peter Smith, 1975), 185.
10. Lynn White, "The Historical Roots of Our Ecological Crisis," *Science* 155 (March 10, 1967), 1205.
11. Donald Worster, *Nature's Economy*, 2d ed. (Cambridge: Cambridge University Press, 1994), 107–8.
12. Max Oelschlaeger, *Caring for Creation* (New Haven, CT: Yale University Press, 1994), 177.
13. Aldo Leopold, *A Sand County Almanac and Sketches Here and There* (New York: Oxford University Press, 1987), 203–4.
14. Ibid., 226.
15. Roger S. Gottlieb, *This Sacred Earth* (New York: Routledge, 1996), 11.
16. John Donne, *The Sermons of John Donne*, vol. 7, ed. Evelyn M. Simpson and George R. Potter (Berkeley: University of California Press, 1954), 204–5.
17. John Macquarrie, "Creation and Environment," in *Ecology and Religion in History*, ed. David Spring and Eileen Spring (New York: Harper & Row, 1974), 46.
18. Albert Schweitzer, *Out of My Life and Thought*, trans. C. T. Campion (New York: Henry Holt, 1933), 274.
19. John F. Haught, *The Promise of Nature* (New York and Mahwah, NJ: Paulist Press, 1993), 105–6.
20. Schweitzer, *Out of My Life and Thought*, 188.
21. Martin Buber, *I and Thou*, trans. Walter Kaufmann (New York: Charles Scribner's Sons, 1970), 58.
22. Oelschlaeger, *Caring for Creation*, 236, 238.
23. William H. McNeill, *Plagues and Peoples* (New York: Anchor Books, Doubleday, 1977), 20.

EPILOGUE

God himself culminates in the present moment, and will never be more divine in the lapse of all the ages. And we are enabled to apprehend at all what is sublime and noble only by the perpetual instilling and drenching of the reality which surrounds us.

—Henry David Thoreau, *Walden*

I HAVE USED PLAGUE and pestilence both as actual occurrences and as metaphors to describe events in our histories and in our personal lives that place demands—often extreme—on us. Our responses to the plagues I have described define us as they reveal our ultimate—our final—basis for our behavior. Some plagues are overwhelming in their destruction of life: the Holocaust and the bubonic plague of the fourteenth century are examples. Other plagues are insidious and hidden from many of us by circumstances: racism, a conviction of the meaninglessness of life, and AIDS can be acknowledged as existing but may not be immediately relevant for a particular individual.

What are the sources of strength and courage for those who choose to stay in the time of plague? They are many, of course, and we each are charged with the task of securing our own. As I have noted many times, the metaphor of a foundation is central to my thought and my faith. I have to work my way down through the many layers of human experience and culture, through the words and actions of others, through my obvious desires for pleasure and accomplishment, and through the reality of my sinfulness and separation from the good, until I find the basement, the final stone of foundation that will support the house I am building—my self. As I search for the support that will not fail me, I turn to the stories and the accounts I have discussed: novels, biographies, poetry, and histories that show me the paths that others have followed, the gods that others have chosen as underpinnings of their faith.

We all have a god. Some of us maintain a pantheon of gods, but there is one that is our last resource. Among the known gods are oneself, nature, science, the mind, wealth in its many forms, adoration, sensuality, and affection of others. I am fully aware of the appeal of all of them for my allegiance, and I live in full knowledge of those appeals. Life is a recurring struggle to

211

return to God, our creator and sustainer. Martin Buber assures me that "Whoever is dominated by the idol whom he wants to acquire, have, and hold, possessed by his desire to possess, can find a way to God only by returning, which involves a change not only of the goal but also of the kind of movement."[1] It is the examined self, the studied and dissected mental and spiritual experiences and knowledge of my self, that instigates that movement and brings me to the search for God, for that certainty—granted, often tinged with gnawing doubt—of the very center of my being. I seek the heart of creation, so that I will know myself as a creature. This knowing is a reflection, literally a mirroring, of the experiences of others that I take to my heart and mind so that I may know my self more honestly. Informed by the poetry of Emily Dickinson, I search for God; I do this by accepting my anima, the other part of me that Dickinson represents in her work. The writings of Elie Wiesel pull me back, again and again, to the power of a faith that praises God in the most hopeless of places and times—a faith that must be remembered if it is to be lived. A hand is placed on us to call us to the work to be done. Whether we are alert to the touch will be determined, in large part, by our preparation for it. The awesome and inspiring fact of nature, made so poignant by our destruction of it, demands my attention and my promises.

The two texts to which I return, again and again, are the Bible and *Walden*. The first, the gift of a teacher over sixty years ago, is the text of my religious faith; one of many faiths in human history and experience, it is the one I have been raised in through years of instruction and observation, a diverse record of encounters with the divine as a people and as persons. Poetry, narrative, fantasy, prayer, and revelation—all are part of the story of a covenant I choose and cherish as instructive for me. The sorrows of prophecy, the tragedy of human encounters with evil, the victories over death and degradation—these stories are mine for the preserving of my peace, the fortifying of my will. As with any reading, it must constantly be informed by scholarly research, by observed experience, and by community response. This makes each reading a new one, a reopening of the book, a retelling of the old story.

I find myself blessed in having the gift of faith, graced, as faithful language would put it, by God with that assurance. The voice from the whirlwind that spoke to Job is sometimes heard by my spirit if I am alert to it. The search for God is a quest for the means by which I engage the world. How I am to be, in and for the created order, pushes me to seek God. Again, Martin Buber writes:

The encounter with God does not come to man in order that he may henceforth attend to God but in order that he may prove its meaning in action in the world. All revelation is a calling and a mission. . . . When you are sent forth, God remains presence for you; whoever walks in his mission always has God before him: the more faithful the fulfillment, the stronger and more constant the nearness.[2]

Walden, the gift of another teacher fifty years ago, is the second scripture for my life. Thoreau accepted none of the New England Congregationalism or Boston Unitarianism of his day. He would be amazed that I refer to his work as "scripture." But he demands that I search my life, that I find that foundation, that I take, with many grains of salt, what I am told, what I read. It is essential that I subject my life—its goals, means, and grounding—to constant scrutiny so that I will not be waylaid and mistake the shadow for the real thing. He calls me, by metaphor and simile, to awaken to the dawn that is now, the very beginning of a new day for me and for creation. Thoreau is chanticleer crowing to awaken me; he persistently warns me not to accept all that I see; he points me within to explore that undiscovered continent that is me, knowing that there is a priceless treasure within, were I but to search it out.

What is the source of the faith that will make me choose to stay in the hour of pestilence? What will empower me to resist the destruction of the environment, and to do so with persistence? How do I find the courage to stay in the city that is being swept by the plague—this time of violence, hopelessness, and a withering loss of meaning for life? How will I resist the ubiquitous and noiseless discrimination based on biological and religious factors endemic in our cultures? An example of staying with the sufferers and the dispossessed is the brief comment of Jesus to his disciples as he speaks of the love of God for him translated into his love for them. A new directive is offered. "This is my commandment, that you love one another as I have loved you. No one has greater love than this, to lay down one's life for one's friends. You are my friends if you do what I command you."[3]

This ultimate example of love—the giving of one's life for others—undergirds, I believe, the ability of some to stay with the afflicted. There is a sense in which the final definition of the self is determined by that action. If I believe in the foundational quality of love for others and for nature as our gifts from God, then the gift of my life for them is a seal on that commitment to that God. Experiences of others detail the freedom recognized when this life is taken for what it is—a gift without price, a brief borrowing of a bit of creation for our use and our service. With a host of others I stand humbly before those who opened my heart and my mind in the search for my God, thankful for their gifts.

NOTES

1. Martin Buber, *I and Thou*, trans. Walter Kaufmann (New York: Charles Scribner's Sons, 1970), 154.
2. Ibid., 164.
3. John 15:12–4, NRSV.

INDEX

Abrahamson, Irving, 64
absurdity, and suffering, 29
"Address Unknown," 60
After Auschwitz, 62
AIDS, 179–93; as epidemic, 180–84,
186; as judgment, 179, 181–83, 185,
188; care of patients, 185–88;
demographic shifts, 184–85; drug use
and, 181, 184–85; gay responses to,
186–88; history of, 180–93;
homosexuality and, 179–86; moral
and ethical questions, 182–85;
privacy and, 182; response of love,
186–87; sexual transmission of,
181–85
Alphabet of Grace, The, 85
Alzheimer, Alois, 167
Alzheimer and the Dementias, 166
Alzheimer's Dementia, 167–68; as
plague, 174; characteristics of cases,
168; number of cases, 168;
symptoms, 167; test of how we die,
171–72
ambivalence: faith and truth, 138; in
life, 139
*An American Dictionary of the English
Language*, 155
Anderson, Charles R., 155–57
Angels in America, 185, 187–88, 190
anima. *See* Jung, C. G., psychology of
Answer to Job, 62
Arabian Nights, 138; and Bible, 138
art, role of, 132; as mediator, 133; as
transmitter of Other, 140
As You Like It, 166
Augustine, Saint, 152
Aurelius, Marcus, 176
awaken, 149–50; see and, 50; to dawn,
48, 63; to each day, 141
awakening, as realization of self, 94; to
call by God, 88; humility and, 88;
Thoreau, H. D., and, 92, 202;
through faith, 88; to racism, 80; to

civil rights movement, 94; to events,
88, 94–95; to humility, 99; to lives
of people, 97; to revelations, 135; to
social order, 92
awareness, consciousness is, 71; of
four choices, 71; of God, 88–89; of
self, 147–50; of self-righteousness,
99

Barclay, William, 91
Barker, Wendy, 145
Bayer, Ronald, 184–85
Benedict, rule of, 199
Bernanos, Georges, 51–52, 57
Berrios, G. E., 166
Berry, Thomas, 198
Bible, The: as scripture, 47, Dickens
and, 107
Black Death, 4, 16
Bleak House, 107
Bloom, Barry R., 191
Boccaccio, Giovanni, 16, 25
Book of God and Man, The, 69
Bosley, Harold A., 79, 135–36
Brenner, Joseph, 50
Bridges, Ruby, 94
Brodsky, Joseph, 189
Brothers Karamazov, The, 36, 66
Brown, Robert McAfee, 9, 72
Brown v. Board of Education, 54, 80,
92
Browne, Sir Thomas, 148, 150
Bruno, Giordano, 152
Buber, Martin, 207, 212–13
Buechner, Frederick, 84–85
Bunyan, John, 108, 191
bureaucracy, as plague, 115–16
Bush, William, 52
Byrd, Max, 20–22

Cain and Abel, 22
calling, 41–57; and books, 42;
and prayer, 42, 45; by faith, 88;